# THIS I RECALL

# THIS
# I RECALL

Revised Edition

BY JOHN W. BEHNKEN

CONCORDIA PUBLISHING HOUSE • SAINT LOUIS

This edition copyright © 2014 Concordia Publishing House
3558 S. Jefferson Ave., St. Louis, MO 63118-3968
1-800-325-3040 • www.cph.org

All rights reserved. No part of this publication may be reproduced, stored in a retrieval system, or transmitted, in any form or by any means, electronic, mechanical, photocopying, recording, or otherwise, without the prior written permission of Concordia Publishing House.

First edition © 1964 Concordia Publishing House.

Unless otherwise indicated, Scripture quotations are from The ESV® Bible (The Holy Bible, English Standard Version®), copyright © 2001 by Crossway, a publishing ministry of Good News Publishers. Used by permission. All rights reserved.

Quotations marked KJV are from the King James or Authorized Version of the Bible.

Manufactured in the United States of America

1 2 3 4 5 6 7 8 9 10        23 22 21 20 19 18 17 16 15 14

*To my family and my Synod*

## CONTENTS

| | |
|---|---|
| FOREWORD | ix |
| PREFACE | xi |
| *1 Cypress, Fedor, Winfield* | *3* |
| *2 St. Louis to Houston* | *15* |
| *3 Widening Horizons* | *33* |
| *4 Houston to St. Louis* | *43* |
| *5 Lengthening Our Educational Cords* | *51* |
| *6 Strengthening Stewardship Stakes* | *67* |
| *7 Mercy Mission—Europe 1945* | *77* |
| *8 Theological Mission—Europe 1947–57* | *95* |
| *9 Experience of a Lifetime* | *103* |
| *10 Cementing Australian Ties* | *109* |
| *11 Fraternal Visit to the Far East* | *117* |
| *12 Missouri with a Latino Accent* | *131* |
| *13 In Pursuit of Unity* | *139* |
| *14 Roses and Thorns* | *161* |
| EPILOGUE | 179 |
| POSTSCRIPT TO *THIS I RECALL* | 181 |
| *Introduction* | *183* |
| *Lacunae* | *185* |
| *The Growing Doctrinal Controversy in the Synod* | *195* |
| *Behnken As Preacher* | *207* |
| *Behnken—Person and Family* | *213* |
| *Lord, Let at Last Thine Angels Come* | *225* |

# FOREWORD

*Remember your leaders, those who spoke to you the word of God. Consider the outcome of their way of life, and imitate their faith. Jesus Christ is the same yesterday and today and forever. Do not be led away by diverse and strange teachings.*
(Hebrews 13:7–9a)

John W. Behnken was one of the most extraordinary personalities in the history of American Lutheranism. In his day people quipped, "Rome has John XXIII. The Missouri Synod has John the Everlasting." Behnken was elected at the 1935 Synod Convention, defeating sitting president Friedrich Pfotenhauer—76 years old at the time—a former student of C. F. W. Walther, and the last German-born president of the Synod. One of Pfotenhauer's grandsons once told me that he remembers his grandfather, father, and uncles feeling rather stung by the defeat. Without the details of history, one tends to forget that these great men were all too human.

I believe I was a student in Adelaide, Australia (1987–88), when I first read *This I Recall.* As I spent time studying the writings of Hermann Sasse (1895–1976), I discovered that Sasse and Behnken had shared a great deal of correspondence after the Second World War. Upon Behnken's death in February 1968, Sasse wrote to a friend and confided that he had collected Behnken's letters and burned them, for they were filled with his disappointment with men in his church body. Perhaps it was from Sasse, as much as anyone, that the rumor spread that Behnken was morose over the Missouri Synod (particularly the liberal bent of the St. Louis Seminary) during his final years. Perhaps Sasse, one not given to understatement, painted a picture too one-sided.

For the record, we asked Behnken's son-in-law, Professor William Schmelder, to write for this edition a history of his father-in-law's last years. Professor Schmelder gladly complied and tells of his dear father-in-law's enduring confidence and cheerfulness, even in the face of the very trying times in the Synod that emerged amid the *Zeitgeist* of the postwar era.

Sasse was struck by Behnken's deeply orthodox Lutheran convictions and his warm pastoral countenance and demeanor. (See pp. 90–91.) Behnken's unique leadership just after World War II, which resulted in so much aid being sent to Europe from the Missouri Synod and the other Lutheran churches in America, was deeply appreciated by state church Germans like Sasse. This story and many others are found in this delightful memoir of faith in Christ.

We are honored to be able to present Behnken's autobiography in this new form.

MATTHEW C. HARRISON
*Lent 2014*

# PREFACE

When Synod's Commission on Church Literature requested me to write my memoirs, a stream of reasons at once coursed through my mind urging me to decline.

No one realizes better than I do that I can lay no claim to the "pen of a ready writer." What literary skill and training I possess chiefly have been applied in the sermonic field. Some preachers, it is true, write sermons that are beautiful literary gems. Mine do not belong in that category. And if they did, this volume would have little relationship to a book of sermons. In revising and polishing the manuscript for publication I gratefully acknowledge the editorial assistance of Rev. Albert W. Galen, assistant editor of the *Lutheran Witness*.

Nor can I claim descent from a distinguished family. My father was a preacher whose very brief career was spent among the cotton patches of rural Texas. His father, I am told, was a teamster who drove the tow horses pulling barges up the Weser River in Germany. Mother's father was an immigrant farmer in Harris County, Texas. That is about as far as anyone has traced the family tree. Please understand me, however. I am both proud and grateful because of my family line. I can pay all my known forebears the very choicest tribute a child and heir can give—all were humble, God-fearing, and truly Christian people.

I am aware, furthermore, that ordinarily memoirs are penned by people of true stature. In that respect I do not qualify. I realize that the good people of our Synod have bestowed high honors on me. I acknowledge them most gratefully. But I know full well that I have not deserved them. If time should record any exceptional accomplishments to my name, it was not I, but the grace of God that was with me.

What reason, then, could I have had to accede to the commission request to write about myself? The answer lies in one word: "history."

## This I Recall

The span of years during which God permitted me to live and work was flooded with events of vast and far-reaching significance to our world, our nation, our church.

These were the years of catastrophic droughts, dust storms, and a nearly disastrous depression. The years of cataclysmic wars consumed the flower of two generations of men and revolutionized the world's maps, manners, and morals. These were years that men came to measure as "ages"—the automotive age, the air age, the electronics age, the nuclear age, the space age, the age of power ideologies, that of nationalism, that of urbanization, that of breakthroughs heralding swift and sudden change.

These and the other developments that news people often refer to as [space or technological] "races" and as "explosions" have had telling effects on The Lutheran Church—Missouri Synod and will continue to do so.

Though in a book of this nature my own person and experiences and activities will necessarily be given greater prominence than they deserve, *This I Recall* is intended to reflect this historical context. One thing, above all, is important: that the reader should recall and realize with a grateful heart how graciously and bountifully God has blessed our church during this period. To that end may He bestow His gracious blessing on these memoirs.

JOHN W. BEHNKEN
*Reminiscere Sunday 1964*

# THIS I RECALL

*{Chapter One}*

# CYPRESS, FEDOR, WINFIELD

From birth I was a privileged child. Many today, I know, would think otherwise; yet as I look back, I have never thought it other than a privilege that the good Lord permitted me to be born in a lowly home—yes, doubly privileged, because that home was a parsonage.

It had but two rooms and stood on the prairie about two miles northwest of the village of Cypress, in Harris County, Texas. Born March 19, 1884, I was the first child of Pastor and Mrs. George W. Behnken. Father was then serving St. John's, Cypress and Trinity, Neudorf, two small congregations planted by emigrants from Germany some eight years before.

My recollections of Father are all too few. He died when I was not quite four. A graduate of Northwestern College, the preparatory school of the Wisconsin Synod at Watertown, Wisconsin, he contracted tuberculosis while continuing his theological studies at the synod's seminary in Wauwatosa (since relocated to Mequon).[1] Following the usual medical advice of those days, he sought the warmer, sunnier climate of southeast Texas, where he could lead a year-round outdoor life, ride, fish, hunt, and the like. A kind family at Rose Hill, Texas, opened their home to him.

As his health returned he took a position teaching school and also preached occasionally. By continuing his studies privately he was able to pass his ministerial colloquy in the Missouri Synod's Southern District, of which Texas then formed a part. Shortly afterward he was called by the Cypress and Neudorf congregations.

Father chose this time to ask Helene Wunderlich to share his humble parsonage. Mother was a native Texan. Her mother, my

---

[1] Wisconsin Lutheran Seminary is still located in Mequon, Wisconsin.

wonderful Grandmother Wunderlich, had come to the Lone Star State as a youngster of 12 and after her marriage settled on a farm with Grandfather near Klein, a German community in Harris County. A brave pioneer soul, she was left widowed with six small children when Grandfather lost his life in a powder-mill explosion during the Civil War.

## Texas Homestead

After only four years in the ministry Father's dreadful malady again flared up and forced him to resign. Our little family of four (Sister Meta was also born at Cypress) thereupon moved to Klein, where Grandmother Wunderlich had provided us with a parcel of land from the family homestead. She also assisted us to build a small home. One of my vivid early recollections is how one day Father was helping to shingle the roof of this home and how he came down the ladder with the carpenter to enjoy the lunch I had laboriously trudged over from Grandmother's, about a quarter mile away. I had gotten terribly thirsty on the way but simply couldn't uncork the water bottle I carried to take a drink.

I remember Father as one who "placed the apple beside the rod." He was strict but also kind and loving. I remember his hearty laugh and how he loved to sing. I remember, too, how kind he was to Mother, and she to him. Memories are few, but to me they are very precious.

For five years the little farmhouse at Klein was home for my widowed mother and her brood of three. Brother Will had followed Sister Meta into the family a month after Father's death. Both brother and sister are still living.—Will is in Houston and Meta, who married J. G. Steglich (now deceased) resides in Austin.

Such things as a synodical Board of Support and Pensions were unknown in those days.[2] But God provided. Mother raised vegetables, chickens, and eggs for the market. A few cows supplied our milk and butter. Mother did her own sewing and also sewed some things for

---

[2] The Board of Support and Pensions developed into the present Concordia Plan Services. Additional aid for church workers is handled by the Soldiers of the Cross and Veterans of the Cross programs.

others. She helped Grandmother around the home and my uncles in the field, and they in turn helped us. Very early in life I learned to hoe corn, to "chop" cotton, and to keep up with the others in filling our long shoulder sacks at cotton-picking time. That we all should pitch in and help one another was simply taken for granted. All in all it was a wonderful relationship and proved to be a genuine blessing.

Like most young Texans I learned to ride horseback quite early. For my fourth birthday Jacob Zahn, my sponsor, gave me a little tame bronco with saddle to match. I would ride out to the open prairie each evening with Uncle Will to drive home and "pen up" the cattle. At six, when I started to go to school, Cousin Clara Wunderlich and I would ride horseback tandem style to and from the little one-room school of Trinity Congregation in Klein, about three miles from our home.

My teacher, John P. Daenzer, was a wonderful Christian gentleman. It so happened that with the exception of some two months he was my teacher throughout my elementary school years. For shortly after our family moved from Klein to Fedor, Teacher Daenzer followed a call to this Lee County parish, where I lived for the remainder of my youth.

## *Fedorensis*

After five years of widowhood Mother was married to the Rev. Gotthilf Birkmann, pastor of Trinity Church, Fedor. Pastor Birkmann was a widower with three children. Overnight our family had doubled in size. In the course of time God blessed our household with seven more children, one of whom died in infancy. Thus we were a family of brothers and sisters, stepbrothers and stepsisters, half brothers and half sisters. A story sometimes related in Texas pastoral conference circles told how a fellow pastor, while visiting Father Birkmann one day, saw him jump up, run to the window, and call: "Mother, come quick! Your children and my children are beating up our children." The story is quite apocryphal, I can assure you; just a little joke to badger Father a bit. We were normal children, of course, and had our little tiffs and spats. But thanks especially to Mother's kind nature and her remarkable homemaking abilities, we became a closely-welded family and seldom even thought of ourselves in any other way. Truthfully, the only time we spoke of one another as stepbrother or half-brother was when we had to explain to someone why we had different names.

Father Birkmann was a man of prodigious learning, largely self-taught. He could handle a half-dozen languages amazingly well and was especially well versed in the original Bible tongues. His brethren in the ministry often remarked of his prowess as an exegete, dogmatician, Church historian, and homiletician. Yet he was always quiet and retiring. With the exception of two years in Dallas, he spent all his active ministry of more than 40 years in his beloved rural parish at Fedor. Concordia Seminary, St. Louis, awarded him the honorary Doctor of Divinity degree in 1936.

Father was also a recognized naturalist. Evidence of his accomplishments in this area may be seen from an item appearing in the May 20, 1944, Houston *Chronicle,* written by O. E. Connor, which states: "Two groups of insects are known as the *Birkmanii* and the *fedorensis*. . . . Harvard University's entomology department years ago obtained from Pastor Birkmann some of his bee and wasp collections, containing some 20 varieties unknown to American entomologists until described by the Fedor pastor."[3]

For us youngsters bug hunting for Papa was a favorite pastime. We chased down hundreds of butterflies, beetles, bees, and wasps, and soon were able to distinguish the more common varieties from the rarer specimens Father was interested in.

## *Parsonage Sorcery*

Life in a country parsonage in a large family circle was always interesting and enjoyable. Certainly it brought us advantages and blessings that could not be had elsewhere. Time and again, as my brothers and sisters and I reviewed the "life in Fedor" chapter of our lives, we agreed that we would not want to trade it for any other and voiced thankfulness to God for leading us as He did. We may not have had all the cultural advantages that many city children enjoyed

---

[3] The bee *Centris birkmanii* usually appears as *Centris lanosa. Nomia fedorensis* is a species of sweat bee.

in the 1890s, but Father did try to provide some of them. We, for instance, had an Edison phonograph, the model that used the cylindrical records and had a large trumpet-like amplifier perched over the sound box—one of the true marvels of the day.

One day I remember Mrs. M., one of the good old ladies of the congregation, happened to call when we had the phonograph going full blast. She rigidly refused to go near the contraption but stood off in the doorway muttering darkly: *"Das geht nicht mit rechten Dingen zu."* (Something mighty suspicious is going on here.) She thought it was some kind of sorcery.

My thoughts returned to good Sister M. and the old Edison when I returned to Fedor a few years ago to preach in the old church for the first time in 50 years. We had whizzed the 13 miles from Giddings to Fedor—once a three-hour trip by horse and buggy—in just 15 minutes. Part of the overflow congregation could not get into the church. Nevertheless it participated in the entire service while seated in the schoolhouse—by means of a loudspeaker system. Dropping in later to visit a daughter of the country storekeeper from my childhood days, I saw the men in the living room watch the New York Giants play the Baltimore Colts in the world championship football game direct from Yankee Stadium, 1,800 miles away in New York City. If our raucous, crank-handled Edison aroused dire suspicions of black magic, what good Mrs. M. would have called such goings on in Fedor was simply beyond my imagination.

Our parents also saw to it that we were plentifully supplied with good reading material. We loved Margareta Lenk's stories and the ever-fascinating volumes of *Blätter und Blüten*, issued by the Louis Lange Publishing Co. in St. Louis. We also looked forward eagerly to the arrival of such a family magazine as *Die Abendschule* and such a paper as *Die Rundschau*.

Though practically all our reading material was in the German language and stories and accounts of the old fatherland predominated in it, we were proud to be Americans. I recall how incensed I became when, as a lad of ten, I heard one of the older men, who had been a drill sergeant during his compulsory service in the German army, brag to a group down at the store about the German soldier and poking fun at the American soldier. Only the fact that I had been repeatedly warned that children must not be disrespectful to old people kept me from stepping up and saying: "If you think it's so much better in your old Germany, why don't you go back there?"

I do not remember exactly when I first entertained the desire to enter the holy ministry. God apparently implanted that desire into my heart very early. As I look back, it seems that both my parents and I simply took for granted that I would become a pastor. Evidently my younger brothers and sisters felt likewise, for whenever we played church, I was the one who had to take the part of the preacher.

## *"Johnnies"*

In September 1897, when I was 13, I started out for St. John's College, Winfield, Kansas with Oscar Ernst, the son of a neighboring pastor. The Missouri Synod was 50 years old that year. During the previous decade it had experienced its sharpest rate of growth, from 350,000 to nearly 700,000 members. By today's standards the trek of a day and a night to Winfield would, I am sure, be called a terrible trip. Somehow, we didn't seem to mind it too much. To make the trip we had to ride the old San Antonio–Aransas Pass Line to Cameron, where we made connection with the Santa Fe.

St. John's had been built just four years previously by a Lutheran businessman, John P. Baden, and presented to the English Synod of Missouri and Other States. In 1908 the English Synod transferred the property to the Missouri Synod. In 1911 the English Synod joined Missouri as the English District.

Just why my parents decided that I should attend this school, where the English language was the medium of instruction, I have never learned. I have always been grateful, however, that this was their choice. It brought me the advantage of being fully at home in both English and German. With the Concordia college in Conover, N. C., which Synod decided to close after the main building was destroyed in a disastrous fire in 1934, St. John's pioneered not only in English-language instruction for Synod's future pastors but also in coeducation, a feature that in recent years has been added to all of Synod's pre-professional schools except the one at Milwaukee.[4]

The small student body at the Winfield school permitted us to enjoy another wonderful blessing: an almost ideal relationship between faculty and students. We were, in a very real sense, a campus family. The professors often invited us to their homes for meals and social occasions and in many ways showed a personal and individual interest in us, just like "one of the family."

The Winfield faculty of those early years—President Adolphus W. Meyer, Professors Henry Stoeppelwerth, Charles Scaer, and Louis Steiner—were true men of vision. Serving on the academic staff for many years, they left a lasting impression. More than any others they helped to give the school a unique character, which alumni and alumnae have long called the Johnnie spirit. Former "Johnnies" have given these professors of their school's formative years the affectionate title of the Old Guard. Often in later years, when recalling the profound influence they had on us, as well as the love, kindness, and patience they ever showed in their dealings with us, I could not help giving them another name—the Four Grand Old Men.

## *Thistle Sifter*

Another Winfield instructor whom I have reason to remember with lasting gratitude is Miss Kate Henderson. She was our high school teacher in English and elocution and drew the assignment of training some of us "backwoods Dutchmen" in English reading. The book we used was McGuffey's *High School Reader*. What a job she must have had—and what patience!

Like so many of German extraction we had our troubles pronouncing the English *v* and *th*. *V* somehow always liked to come out as *w* and *w* as *v*. We would pronounce "very well" as "wery vell." Also, our *th* often lost the soft *h* and sounded like hard *d*.

To get the correct pronunciation of the English *v* Miss Henderson kept reminding, "Say it like the German *w*, as in *wir wollen wissen!*"

---

[4] Concordia College in Milwaukee became the present Concordia University Wisconsin, headquartered in Mequon. St. John's in Winfield closed in 1986. All schools in the Concordia University System are now coeducational.

She would add, "Save your 'wery's' and 'werses' when you come to a *w.*" She would make us pause when we came to a word beginning with *v* and shape our mouth correctly before pronouncing it. We soon got to the point where we could spot a villainous *v* lurking several lines ahead.

To master the *th* sound, which does not occur in German, she had us trip our tongues from the edge of our upper front teeth, then drilled us endlessly on the following twister:

> Theophilus Thistle, a successful thistle sifter, sifted a sieve full of unsifted thistles and thrust three thousand thistles through the thick of his thumb. Now if Theophilus Thistle, a successful thistle sifter, in sifting a sieve full of unsifted thistles thrust three thousand thistles through the thick of his thumb, see thou that thou in sifting a sieve full of unsifted thistles thrust not three thousand through the thick of thy thumb.

Most of us could finally sail through it without a halt or a slip. I can still rattle it off at the drop of a hat. I would certainly advise anyone unfortunate enough to have to break in a new set of dentures to use this drill. I can assure you, it will do the job.

How often in my career in pulpit and on platform I have blessed the memory of good Kate Henderson and her insistence on proper enunciation, emphasis, accent, and inflection! Throughout the years her quiet but adamant "Be natural" helped alert us against slipping into such preacher pitfalls as speaking or reading affectedly or trying to imitate the style and mannerisms of others. If God gave me any speaking talents, it was this faithful high school teacher who taught me to use them effectively in His service.

Because of my experience with this course at St. John's I have always wondered why speech training is not stressed more in the high school courses of our Synod's professional training schools. To be sure, some remarkable advances have been made at the terminal schools and the senior college with their speech laboratories, clinics, trained specialists, and the latest in mechanical devices—I wish we could have had some of them—but why not also use the earlier years when good (or bad) speech habits are first formed and due corrective measures can best be taken?

## *Brush with Death*

One night at Winfield stands out unforgettably. Near the close of my high school sophomore year I came down with the mumps in a particularly virulent form. On commencement night I lingered near death in my room, which happened to be located next to the upper part of the chapel where the graduation exercises were in progress. Never did music and singing and echoing applause affect me so adversely as that night. I committed myself into God's gracious hands and was ready to die. In the early morning, as the students were happily leaving for home, I was taken to the Winfield hospital. Some of my friends later told me that when they saw me taken out on the stretcher they waved goodbye, thinking they would never see me again.

But God willed otherwise. After ten days I was released from the hospital—weak and shaky. A shortage of funds in the family exchequer at the time did not permit me to go home even then. I stayed that summer at my good friends, the Henry Vespers, in Topeka. I regained my strength sufficiently after a few weeks. Then I could do some work, helping the Vespers in their modest bakery.

I shall ever be grateful to these good people. They treated me most wonderfully. Later I spent another summer vacation with them. Still another summer when the long trip home to Texas was out of the question I spent working at the Dietrich Baden farm near Independence.

As a matter of fact, during my later years at Winfield and the earlier years at St. Louis, there was a stretch when I hadn't been home for three years. Then, just before Christmas came a letter from Father: "We sent you to school these many years to become a preacher, and we still haven't heard you preach. Come home and bring two good sermons."

Needless to say, that was a memorable vacation—saddling up and riding the countryside to look up old friends and visit schoolmates. They plied me so generously with meat and sausage from the holiday butchering and with other country "vittles" that it prompted Mother to wonder whether perhaps I shouldn't have come home more often.

## *Handball Mishap*

Somehow I cannot escape a twinge or two of envy over the student of today when I see how in recent decades the coach, the directed physical education program, and the well-equipped gym have become a campus fixture at our synodical schools. In our day such things lay far beyond our fondest dreams. Whatever we learned in the way of athletics, we learned by observing the upperclassmen and exercising personal initiative. We students planned, prompted, promoted, and paid for our own sports and "phys ed" activities.

Though I can't claim (as some of my contemporaries did) having reached anything like professional finesse, I did learn to play a fair game of baseball, football, and tennis. Whatever I played, I played hard. When the Milwaukee Concordia grads introduced basketball at the St. Louis seminary in the fall of 1904, I plunged right in "up to my ears." It was then that we organized the now storied "Rough-House League." The name was a natural for the kind of game we had to play in the old (Jefferson Avenue) seminary gym with its floor the size of a postage stamp, hemmed by bone-cracking pillars and skin-scraping walls. To top it off, we almost always played at the most unwholesome time possible—at noon right after lunch. But we survived.

Though I had no prep school experience in this sport, I was kept on as a member of the sem squad and had the opportunity to play on what was called the second team in intercollegiate games. Participation in athletics, I am convinced, was a factor that contributed a great deal in making me physically strong and fit.

However, it was not an unmixed blessing. During a game of handball one day in the spring of 1905 a teammate missed with a desperate swing at the ball and struck my right eye with his fingertip. It resulted in a detached retina. Under the care of an excellent specialist I spent eight weeks—practically my whole summer vacation—flat on my back in the Lutheran Hospital in the hope that the retina might again become attached. But the best that could be done through the skills and treatment known at the time was to save the eyeball. The sight was gone.

God, however, was exceptionally gracious in granting me superior vision in the left eye. One eye has served me better than the two eyes of many with impaired vision. By 1932 a tumor—fortunately nonmalignant—developed in the blinded eye, which necessitated its removal and replacement with an artificial eye.

## *Pedagog and Theolog*

Shortly after Easter during my freshman college year at Winfield an SOS arrived from Father Birkmann: Would I come home and teach the Fedor school? His teacher had accepted a call to another parish. It sounded like a welcome change from Latin, Greek, and Hebrew, but what a job I had!

In the light of later events I must say the experience was quite invaluable. But whether the 75 children in that one-room school were equally benefited by my efforts is another question. All I'd had to go on was a one-semester course called pedagogy. I can only say it was a good thing that teaching certificates were not required. One benefit I certainly gained was a new appreciation of the value of the Christian day school and of the valiant task being done by that oft-forgotten man or woman—the Lutheran school teacher.

Although my two months of absence from the classroom did not help to improve my class grades, the faculty of St. John's nevertheless issued me a diploma declaring me qualified for the study of theology. Of the dozen or so in the class of 1903 two others, George C. Jacobsen and Charles H. Kenreich, were candidates for the St. Louis seminary. Our commencement exercises at the time were quite formal affairs, and we three "theologs" were required to prepare and deliver 12-minute orations.[5] Since I was the proud Southerner of the class, I chose "Robert E. Lee" as my topic.

---

[5] The title of this section and its references in the body are plays on words. Older German *Theolog* and *Pedagog* rhyme their endings with "vogue" but are spelled like English "log."

*{Chapter Two}*

# ST. LOUIS TO HOUSTON

WITH MY ARRIVAL in St. Louis in September 1903 to take up the study of theology, a whole new realm of experience opened to me. It was the first time I lived in a big city. The metropolis on the Mississippi, then in the heyday of its World's Fair years, throbbed with activity and excitement to our unaccustomed eyes. Here I had my first ride on an electric trolley and was introduced to other marvels of the up-and-coming electrical age.

Since we students enjoyed the advantage of reduced rates, I was able to go out to the fair on three or four occasions to take in the sights and wonders of the Louisiana Purchase Exposition grounds. Particularly fascinating to me were the unbelievable lighting effects and ingenious fountains and falls of the Cascades.

A half century later I had occasion to recall very vividly my visit to the fair's Filipino Village, located very near the place where our Concordia Seminary now stands. Here Igorot tribesmen depicted the life and customs of their native islands, which a few years before had become a US protectorate. In 1956 on a visit to the Philippines I had the privilege of officiating at the baptism of the first Igorot child won for the Lutheran faith by our missionaries in the hinterland of Luzon.

*Nothing But Jesus Christ*

New and exciting to us was also our introduction to the theological branches: exegesis, homiletics, hermeneutics, propaedeutics, isagogics, liturgics, patristics, etc.[1] When I entered the seminary

---

[1] Propaedeutics includes basic skills foundational to theological study. Biblical theology includes exegetics that establishes the best witness to the biblical text; hermeneutics, that is, biblical interpretation; and isagogics, the study of the biblical books in their literary and historical context. Homiletics is the theology and art of

all instruction was by medium of the German language. There were but six on the faculty—but what a faculty!—Dr. Francis Pieper, president, George Stoeckhardt, Frederick Bente, George Mezger, Ludwig Fuerbringer, and A. L. Graebner. After teaching us for only a matter of weeks, the last-named professor became seriously ill and died a year later. During my seminary years Dr. E. A. W. Krauss was called to the chair of Church history, and Dr. W. H. T. Dau was added as English professor in the field of dogmatics.

The very names of this second-generation faculty in Concordia's history are still spoken with deepest respect and reverence. Every one of them was a scholarly theologian, yet how implicitly they bowed before the Word of God! The Savior's "It is written" was the watchword that dictated all their instruction. Guided by Christ's statement "And the Scriptures cannot be broken," they were ever ready to defend every part of the Bible as the inspired Word of God. Whether they taught systematic or exegetical, practical or historical theology, when the Word of God had spoken, that settled the matter with utmost finality.

These men made a profound impression on us. Their influence touched every part of our later ministry. Particularly deep and lasting was the impact of the emphasis they placed on the centrality of Jesus Christ and His work of redemption.

In one of the last lessons in our pastoral theology courses Dr. Pieper reminded us in his candid and earnest way: "When you now begin your work in your congregations, never fail to point out the way to salvation clearly in every sermon. Should anyone happen to attend your service who has never heard the Word before and who may never hear another sermon, he should hear from your lips how to be saved." His words left an indelible impression. I, for one, always tried to carry out that advice, which after all is nothing else than a direct application of the apostle's own inspired motto: "I am determined to know nothing among you save Jesus Christ and Him crucified."

One evening years later Dr. Pieper's classroom words were brought home to me with new force. My Houston congregation at the

---

preaching. Liturgics is the theology and practice of worship. Patristics is the study of the Church Fathers and their writings.

time was conducting a week-long series of what we called Soul-saving Services, quite similar to the services popularized in recent years in our preaching-teaching-reaching missions. Pastor Karl Kretzschmar of Fort Smith, Arkansas (later one of Synod's vice-presidents) was our guest speaker that week. One evening as he came into the sacristy from the pulpit, I saw he was quite upset. "Behnken," he blurted out, "such a thing has never happened to me before, but suddenly I realized I did not preach Christ to those people as the only Way to salvation. Please, won't you let me take your place in closing the service?" Naturally I agreed. He then proceeded to lead us in a fervent *ex corde* prayer in which he took all of us to the Cross, pleading for faith in Christ and His redemptive sacrifice as our only but certain hope of salvation.

## *Six Dollar Refund*

College meals posed a problem that reached an acute stage during my seminary days. Such meals have been sources of student complaint ever since there have been colleges. The students met it head on. John Molstad, a Norwegian student who had come from his synod's college at Decorah, Iowa, felt that the Norsemen could teach us obtuse Dutchmen a thing or two along the eating line. "Why not have the student body take over the management of meal service?" he asked.

With more enthusiasm than knowledge the student body adopted the suggestion, and so the seminary Boarding Club came into existence. As organized by vote of the student body, six students were named to manage the club business: Alfred Doerffler, secretary; Fred Leimbrock, treasurer; Carl Demetrio, buyer; Gerhardt Schmidt and Henry Weinert, auditors; and John Behnken, manager.

My year at the managerial helm turned out to be a valuable experience—doubly so for us club "officials," since we were given free meals in return for our work. The students too were more satisfied—perhaps I should say less dissatisfied. The real success story, however, came at the end of the school year. We gained real status when we refunded to each student six dollars of the $72 charged for the year's board.

# This I Recall

The Boarding Club, I am told, lasted 21 years. I cherished the secret hope that somehow this grand old institution might survive the transfer of the seminary to its new Tudor Gothic quarters out on the city limits in 1926. But it evidently became a casualty of the age of the streamline and the efficiency engineer. Perhaps we should have chosen a more imaginative name for it.

## *Preacher Pinions*

As loyal sons of the college at Winfield, George Jacobsen and I attended Grace Church, the mother church of the English Synod in St. Louis. Going to Grace, well over on the North Side, meant a long, crosstown streetcar ride. But it resulted in some definite advantages.

For one thing, we regularly heard a true pulpit master, Pastor Martin S. Sommer, a most impressive speaker. He later became an editor of the *Lutheran Witness* and a seminary professor. Then, too, we were enrolled quickly on Grace's Sunday school staff and attended the weekly teachers meetings conducted by Pastor Sommer. For this experience I have ever been most grateful. It gave me an insight into the organization and administration of a Sunday school, which was somewhat of a rarity in our early 20th-century synodical picture. Later on, not only was I able to apply my experience in my own congregation, but I also had many an opportunity to give the benefit of my know-how to brother pastors who sought my advice on how to organize and conduct a Sunday school.

During my seminary "middler" year I recall an unforgettable demonstration—wholly extracurricular—of what can be done through the power of the spoken word. Some of us attended a political rally to hear the Honorable William Jennings Bryan. For well over an hour the "silver-tongued orator of the Platte" held an immense crowd at the old St. Louis Armory literally spellbound. To us fledgling pulpiteers, eager to develop our preaching pinions, the masterful way this prominent political figure had of swaying his audience made quite an impression. Here surely was a gift to be earnestly desired and cultivated by every minister for the proclamation of the greatest message on earth.

## St. Louis to Houston

The first sermon I was privileged to preach was for Pastor F. W. Herzberger at the City Infirmary, one of the institutions he served as "city missionary" in St. Louis. He began what was to be his lifework in 1899—a true trailblazer in the work that is today usually called the institutional chaplaincy. Many years later it was my privilege to visit "Daddy" Herzberger, as he was known to thousands, shortly before his death in the St. Louis Lutheran Hospital. He certainly was a grand gentleman and a faithful servant of the Lord.

While at the seminary we had far less opportunity to know our ever-busy professors than at prep school, yet there were occasions when we learned something of their "human side" outside the classroom. One such occasion, to cite an example, was when a group of about a dozen of us were invited to the home of Dr. and Mrs. Stoeckhardt to help Karl, one of their adopted sons, celebrate his birthday.

Mrs. Stoeckhardt was a wonderful hostess, and we were having a good time. Hearing footsteps announcing Dr. Stoeckhardt's arrival, my friend and fellow Texan William ("Taffy" to us) Klindworth nudged me and groused: "Well, here goes for a stale evening."

But the good doctor really surprised us. He began regaling us with stories of his student days at the university in Germany, interlacing them with so much good humor that he had us all laughing uproariously. Suddenly—in the impulsive way he always had—he scurried into the kitchen and just as suddenly popped back into the room, darted a finger at Taffy and asked: "Are you over 21?"

Taffy's surprised nod drew an invitation to come into the kitchen for a conference. Handing him a half dollar and a good-sized *Kübel* (bucket), he asked him whether he would be so kind as to get some beer.

"Where shall I go for it?" Taffy wanted to know.

"Oh, go where you always get it!" was the quick retort.

Klindworth soon was back with the *Kübel,* full to the brim, and handed it to Dr. Stoeckhardt.

"Say," he said after hefting it with a weighing motion, "you must know that bartender pretty well!"

This man was a sterling exegete and topnotch theologian. Yet how thoroughly human! And what a startling sense of humor!

## *Call-less Candidate*

When the Board for Call Assignments met at the seminary in May 1906, we were all but consumed with eagerness and curiosity to know where we would be assigned.[2] We were quite sure there were more than enough calls to go around. Our class of 43 was the smallest to graduate for many a year and the smallest, I believe, of all classes graduated since then. Besides, two of the members were from the Norwegian Synod and one from the Slovak Synod, who were certain to be called into their respective church bodies.[3]

It was a solemn group that filed into one of the classrooms at the announced time and with racing thoughts contemplated the all-important documents Dr. Fuerbringer had brought with him. He announced that he would read the assignments in alphabetical order. My heart skipped a beat or two, for I would be second on the list. He began to read: "Walter Albrecht—Olds, Alberta, Canada." Then it came: "J. W. Behnken—Birmingham, Alabama." As I hurriedly pored over my first solemn call, devouring every word, I recall the feeling of deep gratitude that surged through me. God and my Synod had bestowed on me the undeserved honor of assigning to me the pastorate of an established congregation.

Naturally I wasn't prepared for the anticlimax that cropped up the very next morning. President G. J. Wegener of the Southern District sent word that he wanted to see me in the seminary office. The Birmingham congregation, he informed me, had requested him to secure a seminary candidate, but in the meantime it extended a call for the second time to Rev. F. W. Weidmann. Accordingly, I was to bide my time for the present, pending Pastor Weidmann's decision. In

---

[2] This task currently falls to the Placement Subcommittee of the Council of Presidents.

[3] Behnken offers more on the Norwegian Synod later in this volume. The Slovak Synod merged into the LCMS as the SELC District, a non-geographical district like the English District.

the event he accepted, President Wegener told me I could be assured of receiving another call.

Within a week I received notice that Pastor Weidmann had accepted. I waited, patiently at first, but with mounting impatience as weeks crept by. My parents were deeply disappointed. Dr. Fuerbringer was also concerned. Graduation day came in mid-June. Still no call. As I bade friends and classmates farewell, I was, to say the least, a sorely perturbed candidate. To leave the seminary call-less when there had been more than twice as many calls as candidates simply baffled all explanation.

From St. Louis I went to Wisconsin to pay a long-hoped-for visit to my relatives on my father's side, whom I had never seen. There, finally in early July, a call came to me from the congregation at Manheim, Texas, a rural church only seven miles from my home. A few days later another call arrived from the Texas District Mission Board to start a mission in Houston. Within a week still another call followed from Decatur, Alabama. Three calls in ten days! What to do now?

On my way home I stopped at St. Louis to seek the advice of Dr. Fuerbringer. At home I discussed the matter at length with Father Birkmann. But as always in the consideration of calls, the final decision rested with me. After prayerful deliberation and weighing of advice received, I was led to the conviction that I should accept the Mission Board call to open a mission in Houston.

Before starting on my new venture, however, another task confronted me. Father had scheduled one of his very few vacations that year, a long-dreamed-of trip to Nebraska and Colorado, where he could indulge in his fond naturalistic pursuits. He had arranged with the Mission Board that I take charge of the Fedor congregation for three months. This meant that I must be ordained before he left. Accordingly, on Sunday, August 12, I was ordained to the noblest office on earth—to be Christ's own ambassador. Pastor G. Buchschacher of Warda preached for the occasion, and my father officiated.

This I Recall

*Fifth Ward Missionary*

Shortly before Father's return I started out for Houston with a heart that held many a tremor, yet at the same time brimmed with hope and confidence in God's gracious help. My sister Meta went along to keep house for me. We rented a small place at 2008 Fulton Street and furnished it with the most essential items bought on the installment plan. To get by on my princely salary of $40 a month—and no rent allowance—required management techniques of a high order. The raise of $5 a month that I received after a year took on true life-saving proportions.

I set to work immediately in Houston's Fifth Ward, north of the Southern Pacific Railroad shops. In those days we knew next to nothing about neighborhood canvasses or systematic mission surveys. I simply worked with a follow-up method. The two names I had to start with led to others, and in the course of a few weeks we began services in a German Methodist church. We had to have services in the afternoon, an arrangement that proved most unsatisfactory. So we rented a lodge hall where we could conduct services and also a Sunday school on Sunday mornings.

When attendances had grown to some 35 or 40 per service and the Sunday school enrollment to about 50, we organized as Evangelical Lutheran Redeemer Church with seven voting members. We also purchased lots as the site for a future church.

However, progress at the mission soon slowed down. Malaria fever, then quite common in the area because of poor drainage, had invaded the family of Rev. C. A. Waech, then pastor of Trinity Congregation, and, with consent of the Mission Board, I was asked to help him out by taking over Trinity's evening services. Then in spring Trinity's lone teacher resigned, and I was called on to fill in till the end of the term. (Largely because of malaria, Trinity during that period had trouble holding its pastors and teachers for any length of time.)

As a result, much of the work at Redeemer began to suffer. Nevertheless, in September 1907 I opened a Christian day school at my mission and continued teaching it the next six months. We had only nine children—certainly nothing spectacular—but, convinced as

I was of the value of a school for building a solid congregation, I felt the only way to begin is to begin.

## *Double-Duty Parish*

In November that year Pastor Waech received a call to the congregation at Klein. Because this promised relief for his malaria-prone family, he felt constrained to accept. Trinity asked me to be vacancy pastor. Despite my objections the congregation insisted on placing my name on the list of candidates for Pastor Waech's successor. The congregation promptly sent me the call, and I just as promptly declined it.

After months of fruitless calling, Trinity again placed my name on its "Diploma of Vocation." This gave me pause: Was the Lord making known His will for me more earnestly? Again I consulted the Mission Board and again the board voted to advise me to decline. Yet strangely, and to me very significantly, two of the three board members shortly after the meeting wrote to tell me that, though officially they had voted as they did, personally they felt I had no other course than to accept. This decided the question for me. I was installed as pastor of Trinity, Houston, on Judica Sunday, April 5, 1908.[4]

Here I was, just turned 24, unmarried, an unseasoned ministerial rookie if there ever was one, now charged with all the responsibilities of a full-blown parish. Trinity, it is true, was not a very large congregation—about 240 communicants at the time—yet I felt my inexperience keenly. Services had to be held both in German and in English every Sunday, the former in the morning, the latter in the evening. Other phases of church activity, as Sunday school, the ladies' societies, etc., were also bilingual and required double duty.

Of deeper concern to me, however, was the fact that ours was the only Missouri Synod congregation in Houston and for a radius of 20 miles. (Most of the families of Redeemer decided to attend Trinity after I became pastor there.) Furthermore, we had strong competition, even outright opposition, from an Evangelical (Reformed) church that had a more strategic location near the heart of town and had a most

---

[4] Judica is the fifth Sunday in Lent in the historic one-year lectionary.

disconcerting habit of palming itself off as "Lutheran" upon unwary Lutherans.[5]

But in deep water one soon learns to swim! We plunged in, and though we lacked the fancier swimmers' strokes, we did more than just float. Looking back, I can see how God supplied the needed wisdom and courage. At times it seemed to me that we were not moving fast enough. Like many young pastors I was often quite impatient. Often after preaching once or twice on some phase of Christian sanctification, of faith going into action, I expected quick results. Again and again I had to learn the difficult but ever essential lesson that people must await God's time. He alone, not we, converts people; He alone can motivate them to a life of godliness and consecration. We can only be His faithful witnesses, instruments used by Him to accomplish His purposes.

## *Pastoral Discoveries*

In my work as *Seelsorger* (I still haven't found an English term quite as good to describe the minister's task of shepherding individual souls) I am afraid my inexperience showed even more glaringly than in preaching. I shall never forget my first call on one who was critically ill. How I quaked at the thought that I might not say the right thing! And how clumsily I stumbled through the whole painful affair! I had had none of the supervised fieldwork that enables seminarians nowadays to build up practical experience. Nor did I have the advantage of a vicarage year, which was then not required at the St. Louis seminary in view of the ever-pressing need for pastors and missionaries. All I actually had to go on in my sick visitations was the advice of Dr. Pieper in his pastoral theology course. He cautioned: "In dealing with the sick and dying, see to it that the patient does not trust in his own righteousness but wholly in the righteousness of Christ." Wonderful advice, to be sure, but how elusively hard to put to practice!

During my first few years in the ministry I dreaded making sick calls. In later years there was nothing I loved more. I came to realize

---

[5] The Evangelical Synod was the equivalent of the Prussian Union. It is now part of the United Church of Christ.

that no other phase of the ministry forms closer bonds between pastor and parishioner. Every pastor, I am sure, has often had experiences such as the one I had when a hospitalized lady, long a faithful member, confided to me the "discovery" she had made while sick: "Pastor, I never realized that you meant so much to me."

In the many other thorny spots that beset the path of the young pastor—the duty of reprimanding and admonishing the delinquent, the indifferent and straying, of counseling in marital troubles and family spats, of comforting the grief-stricken and despondent—I had my full share of difficulties and have often been moved to fervent thanks to God that He graciously blessed my work despite many sorry mistakes.

An inestimable blessing to me in those early years was the ever-ready help and cooperation of our faithful parish school teacher, Louis Kasper. We were both young and teamed up to do our work whenever possible. I still think back with real joy to the summer days when we would hitch up my horse and buggy and sally forth to persuade skeptical parents that they ought to send their children to our day school.

Every so often, stories have come to my ears of pastors and teachers "just not able to get along together." At such stories—perhaps many were largely rumor—my mind flashes an almost automatic reaction: "And why not?" Shouldn't pastors and teachers both remember that both are God's called workers, called to the highest service this side of heaven? Should they not realize that both are human, given to faults, foibles, and imperfections of every variety, but that both are Christians, "sanctified and meet for the Master's use and prepared unto every good work," as the apostle expresses it? Teamed together by God's call, harnessed by His great commission to common tasks, why should they not work together? In my 27 years at Trinity it was a real joy and privilege to work hand in hand with the consecrated teachers the Lord gave us.[6]

By pushing steadily ahead to raise classroom standards Teacher Kasper soon was able to have Trinity School fully accredited. One

---

[6] In Behnken's time only male teachers were called. He is not arguing for the ordination of women.

result of this success literally came pouring in—through the school doors. Our enrollment doubled.

Eighty children, however, were more than even the redoubtable Mr. Kasper could very well handle. The congregation had to deal promptly and decisively with a prickly question: Must a second schoolroom be added and another teacher called? As often when a congregation faces a project requiring a sizable financial outlay, this proposal touched off a heavy shower of complaints that it would cost more than we could afford. As debate on the issue ebbed and flowed, William Dube, a pastor who had temporarily retired and taken up membership in Trinity, got up to say: "If we are convinced that a larger school and a second teacher are really necessary—and we surely must admit this—then even though we were poorer than church mice, we should trust God and go ahead with calling and building." That did it. We voted for school expansion.

## *Language Skirmish*

I suppose there were few pastors of my generation who did not at one time or another find themselves with a "bilingual battle" on their hands when the stubborn streak, characteristic in many of German extraction, clashed with the over-eagerness of those who wanted nothing but English. At Trinity our little skirmish began after eight or ten who understood no German whatever joined the voters' assembly. We then had to take time in our all-German meetings to translate all resolutions and pertinent remarks into English. This made meetings much too long and unwieldy.

To solve the difficulty it was decided that a vote be taken at the beginning of each meeting to determine which language was to be used. The voting soon ran consistently in favor of English-language meetings. By and by a disgruntled group organized a propaganda campaign, stacked the meeting with pro-Germans, and won the day for a good, old-fashioned meeting in German. This led to some verbal sniping and an intemperate blast or two. Some walked out. This bit of fireworks, however, turned the trick. After this all meetings were in English.

Other touchy spots on the "language question" front still remained: the two-language Sunday school, a *Frauenverein* and a ladies' circle, a German pre-confirmation instruction class and another in English. We didn't poke at these spots very much. After it could be shown that there wasn't a child attending Sunday school who could not very well understand English, the two Sunday schools merged with scarcely a ripple. The ladies' societies soon followed suit. In fact, the suggestion to merge came from the good ladies of the *Frauenverein*.

The dual confirmation class problem, however, was not that easy to hurdle. There were some who insisted: "I was confirmed German, and Mamma was confirmed German, and the children have to be confirmed German." The solution, it finally turned out, was the children's own abysmal lack of appreciation for the beauties of the German language. I recall, for instance, good old Mr. S., who had a fine large family. All the rest had been confirmed in German, and now nothing else would do but that the youngest be instructed and confirmed in German too. After struggling several weeks with the lad, I told Father S. that I would like to carry out his wishes, but to do so I would need his cooperation. Would he kindly help the boy in preparing his catechism lessons at home? Two weeks later he was back at my door. "Pastor," he said, "I decided to have the boy instructed in English."

## *Bible Class Dividends*

What should be said about a church that calls itself the Bible-teaching church and yet does not have a Bible class? When I was working down there in what is often called the Bible Belt, it irked me to see people carrying their Bibles walk past our church and turn into other churches, and we at Trinity with not the semblance of a Bible class. Eager as I was to introduce the idea, the spirit of "It just isn't done" seemed a bit too formidable for my inexperience to cope with.

The merger of the Sunday schools provided an opening. We started a junior Bible class, and the congregation passed a "rule" that all newly confirmed were expected to attend this class for two years following confirmation. These young teenagers, however, had an uncanny ability of knowing just when their two years were up and unceremoniously simply "graduated" themselves.

Then one Sunday a faithful lady—I had confirmed her as an adult—and her husband visited our class. When they returned for the third Sunday in a row, I had my ammunition ready. Why not go out and get more young people into our group, I suggested to the class. What's to keep us from having more young married people attend? The class reacted with real enthusiasm. "Pastor, give me some names," said our lady visitor. "I'll get busy on the telephone." She must have been a persuasive talker. Enrollment jumped sharply. Others joined the recruitment venture. Before very long the class had to be divided into junior, senior, and adult sections.

I am convinced that nothing we did at Trinity paid richer spiritual dividends than launching into Bible class work. And it was work, to be sure. To conduct the class, I found, took as much and as thorough preparation as my sermons. To keep it a class and not a mere lecture takes skillful work and imaginative planning. But surely the rewards are more than enough to make it all very worthwhile.

I still chuckle when recalling the unsolicited testimonial from a class member of the early days. "Pastor," she said before the entire class, "I get more out of your Bible class than I do out of your sermons." We understood what she meant, of course; she wasn't taking a sly dig at my sermonic efforts. As a matter of fact, she attended morning and evening services with unfailing regularity. It was her way of saying that at Bible class she could get her particular questions answered.

## *Above Rubies*

No doubt there were those in Trinity who, concerned about the empty look of their parsonage, were measuring this or that young lady in terms of a fine wife for the young minister. I soon put their worries to rest. A year after I came to Trinity I was married to Gertrude Geisler in her home church at Riesel, Texas.

It has been said—and my own intimate association with hundreds of clergymen over long years bears out this observation—that the parson's wife either makes or breaks him. The inspired writer of

Proverbs 18:22 says, that "He who finds a wife finds a good thing and obtains favor from the LORD." This truth holds a hundredfold more so of the pastor. Favored indeed is the pastor who is blest with a "help meet for him" in his demanding office, one who as "mistress of the manse" knows when to speak and when to keep silent, when to take the lead and when to follow; who knows how to set a good example and yet how to be humble, how to give her husband constructive criticism when needed and yet how to keep his morale at high level. Truly, "her price is far above rubies" (Proverbs 31:10, KJV).[7]

Here, too, God was surely very good to me with His blessings. In Gertrude He gave me a wonderful helpmeet. However, He did not permit me to keep her long. In His perfect wisdom He took her to our eternal home a few days after our son Victor was born. Four years later, in 1914, He returned to replenish my blessings in overflowing measure when He granted me another faithful and conscientious helpmeet in Hilda Grassmuck.

To add to our blessings God gave us seven more children—Ruth, John W. Jr., Donald, Lloyd, Lois, Kenneth, and Helen—and continued to watch over and keep us a united, lively, happy family. There was always "something doing" around the house and a good deal of coming and going, especially after the five boys, one after another, began going off to college and seminary, and the girls began making friends, both male and female.

All are now married, and all are in the service of the Church—the boys as pastors (except for our "nonconformist" Donald, who is a parish school teacher) and the girls as pastors' wives. In September 1961 word came from the West Coast announcing that I had been promoted to the select circle of great-grandfathers. Nothing, I assure you, since the first time a young pastor addressed me as "venerable father" has so contributed to giving me that "dated" feeling. And nothing has so deepened my sense of gratitude for the "undated," ever new, and perpetually overflowing mercies God has so long and so undeservedly shown me.

---

[7] A "helpmeet" comes from the phrase "help meet," a "suitable helper." "Manse" is a term for clergy house mainly from Presbyterian and Methodist usage.

Demands multiplied on my time and energy in my growing parish. Added official duties and frequent preaching engagements made it necessary for me to be "on the road" more and more often. Due to this workload, an increasingly disproportionate share of the family duties fell to my now sainted wife. To her, next to God, must go all credit for bringing up the children in the nurture and admonition of the Lord. For nigh 40 years she was a staunch, ever dependable, more-than-better half. Ten years have now gone by since the Savior fulfilled His promise to her: "I will come again and take you to Myself" (John 14:3). Though my spirit rejoices that she is with Him, I have missed her very much.

## Mission Mothering

Of all the lessons Trinity as a congregation and I as her pastor learned, none were more important than those that developed and corrected our mission vision. The 32 Missouri Synod congregations now spotted throughout Greater Houston speak eloquently of an alert, dynamic mission spirit. I can remember when it was otherwise. A few years after our little Redeemer Mission folded up (though most members joined Trinity) the Mission Board called Candidate George Beiderwieden to make another mission start. This too proved abortive. Today I understand why. We were too Trinity-minded and not sufficiently Kingdom-minded. We just stood by and watched.

Then in 1919 we were virtually dared by another Lutheran body to open a mission in Houston Heights. Again a young missionary was put to work there. Trinity had a number of families living in that section. But did we release them as a nucleus around which to build a new congregation? Out of question! Instead, we made a deal with the Mission Board—I still shake my head in disbelief at the very thought of it—that it would be quite proper for Trinity people to attend services out in the Heights as long as their contributions continued to flow into Trinity's treasury! Well, it worked out reasonably well for a while. Then the Heights mission decided to organize as Immanuel Congregation, and the people attending there began to ask for transfers. These requests, of course, we could not refuse—and naturally we had to transfer their offering envelopes along with them.

## ST. LOUIS TO HOUSTON

Almost immediately our interest in Immanuel perked up. And why not? She was our daughter. And my, how she grew and flourished! The effect on Trinity was the reverse of that predicted. We now had to exert ourselves more to show ourselves a worthy mother. Within a year we found we had even more members than when we began the "fatal" releases.

Trinity—I, too—got the message. During the remaining years of my pastorate Trinity mothered five more congregations, each time releasing a sizable group and each time coming back stronger than before. We learned that Christ's "Give, and it will be given to you" (Luke 6:38) applies no less to congregations than to individuals. When I left Houston in 1935, Trinity still had nearly 1,000 communicants, and it has since then doubled this number. Her daughters in turn continued the "mothering" pattern—one that I fervently hope other hesitant or dubious congregations will be encouraged to follow.

Somewhat unique, for its time at least, was that four of our Houston missions were started through tent services. We held these informal services every night except Saturday for two weeks. Folks who perhaps could never have been persuaded to enter a church building were less reluctant about drifting into the tent or standing outside to listen. In that way we got acquainted with them to help "break the ice." In one case a missionary, Rev. A. O. Rast, was ordained in a tent service and continued for several weeks to have regular services there. He is now Executive Secretary of Missions for the Texas District.

During the early decades of the twentieth century, as our church has experienced in recent years, a continuing acute shortage of pastors and teachers in Synod resulted in many calls. A goodly number found their way to my desk. I might have lived in the New York area, in New Orleans, Chicago, Los Angeles, and various places in between. Calls also arrived asking me to become executive secretary of the Walther League and president of my Winfield alma mater.

In each instance I consulted with Trinity, and in each instance the decision reached was the same: I stayed in Houston. Though calls bring a certain disturbing element, I found that they also have decided spiritual advantages. Their prayerful consideration by the pastor and thorough discussion by the congregation help both to evaluate themselves and to appreciate each other more. Above all, pastor and flock will regard more highly the holy, God-given office of the ministry. Both come to realize that a change in pastorate is not to be measured by the yardstick of "improving oneself," as some like to express it, but rather by service. For the pastor or teacher who has received a call one question alone must carry the decisive weight: Where does God want me to use the gifts He has granted me to the greatest advantage in His kingdom?

*{Chapter Three}*

# WIDENING HORIZONS

M<small>Y</small> S<small>YNOD-CONSCIOUSNESS</small>, which remained somewhat hazy and remote during my seminary and early ministerial days, was sharpened considerably after I had attended a number of circuit and district pastoral conferences and two or three district conventions. Our Texas District—organized the year of my graduation—was new and untested and bravely optimistic. Among the constitution signers at its second convention you will find the signature that made me a member of Synod. It was a solemn moment (I have often recalled it when observing our young pastors and teachers in the constitution-signing ceremony at district and synodical conventions). It brought home to me as never before the meaning of synodical membership—the many blessings of fellowship to which it entitled me and the obligations that wonderful privilege brought with it: wholehearted loyalty to the Scripture-based doctrine and practice of my church and readiness to cooperate fully in attaining her objectives.

I have never ceased to marvel at God's grace in preserving purity of doctrine in our Synod. Nor have I ceased to urge our church's members with all the earnestness at my command to heart-and-soul, word-and-deed thankfulness for this great blessing. Because the Holy Spirit keeps us in the one true faith through the Word of God, the value of the precedent set by our fathers of having regular pastoral conferences and discussing doctrinal essays at district and synodical conventions is beyond calculation. Recalling the deep impression those conference essays and discussions made on me in my earlier experience—an impression that attendance at hundreds of conferences and conventions has certainly deepened—I am fully convinced that, under God's blessing, they have been the most powerful factor in solidifying our Synod and preserving its doctrinal soundness.

## *Eye on the Umpire*

The Texas District convention that stands out most unforgettably in my mind was that at Giddings in 1913. It was the first Texas convention visited by Dr. Frederick Pfotenhauer, my predecessor in the president's office. The way he presented the work of Synod held all of us delegates enthralled. He was one of the thin line of stalwarts who had opened up the Northwestern plains to the spread of Lutheranism, and he spoke from the depths of a great missionary heart. Synod and its work took on new and nearer dimensions for all of us.

At that time, mainly because delegates needed time to travel Texas' magnificent distances, our conventions opened on Wednesday and continued till the following Tuesday noon. At Giddings that year the visiting pastors and teachers had a challenge to take on the town team in a baseball game on Saturday afternoon. As a homegrown Texan I was a mutually agreeable umpire. In announcing the batteries and ground rules I added, by request, that no profanity would be allowed. Dr. Pfotenhauer, flanked by my father and Pastor Buchschacher, were seated in the stands. A year later, when I was the Southeast Texas Circuit delegate to the synodical convention at St. Luke's Church, Chicago, I happened to be near President Pfotenhauer after leaving the sessions one day. To be polite, I extended my hand to him and began: "You can't be expected to remember me, of course." "Oh, yes," he quickly interrupted. "You are the young man who forbade us to use profane language at our Texas baseball game."

That 1914 convention in Chicago was a real "eye opener" for me. As I have heard others say repeatedly, it is no doubt true that "Synod awareness" does not burst into full flower until one has the privilege of serving as delegate to the "big" triennial convention. I remember how I marveled at the parliamentary skill of Dr. Pfotenhauer. The ease and dispatch, yet complete thoroughness, with which he handled so much convention business! And what important business! If I knew and loved my Synod before, the impressions I gained at my first convention stirred me to new heights of appreciation for Synod and the throbbing vitality of its tasks. My enthusiasm, as some told me later, was at once reflected in the vigorous way I spoke to my congregation and my conference brethren about the work of Synod and the support we should be giving it.

A few years later, in October 1917, an event arrived that instilled in me—as I am sure it did in many others—an even greater enthusiasm for the cause to which Synod was dedicated. The event was the quadricentennial celebration of Luther's Reformation. At that time every congregation in Synod held special services, and wherever possible churches joined for large mass services in a ringing demonstration of loyalty to "Luther's doctrine pure," especially that great central truth of Holy Writ which Luther proclaimed anew, that man is justified before God not by his works but by grace, for Christ's sake, through faith. Soul-thrilling and spirit-lifting, to say the least, was the realization that hundreds of thousands throughout Synod were at the same time joining hearts and hands and voices with yours in giving praise and glory to God. As a rather remarkable coincidence, during the Reformation jubilee year Synod by God's grace reached a membership of one million souls.

### *"The Last Time"*

The year 1917 also precipitated our country into World War I. As hundreds of our church's young men were being rushed into camps and training bases through successive draft calls, President Pfotenhauer appointed an Army and Navy Board to do whatever could be done for the spiritual welfare of our men in military service. Our church at that time had very few military chaplains, as was true also of other bodies. Most Protestant churches during the war made arrangements to have YMCA workers look after the spiritual interests of their servicemen. Our church, however, was given permission to serve our men through camp pastors. It was my privilege to be named camp pastor to serve the men at three nearby military bases—Camp Logan and Ellington Field, both near Houston, and Fort Crockett, down at Galveston.

Though camp pastors were not attached to any branch of the service, they also wore uniforms, but of a darker color than regular Army khaki. Nor were they permitted to go overseas with the "boys." I shall always remember the night that the 33d Division (Illinois National Guard), which had been training at Camp Logan, received orders to "pull out," bound for a port of embarkation and the trenches of France. It was on a Sunday, and that evening I was having my usual service at Trinity. After the service a young man in khaki asked whether he and a few of his buddies might have Holy Communion. "It may be the last time we shall have," he remarked. When the people leaving church became aware of what was happening, many quietly filed back into church. All seemed to feel the full solemnity of that hour. Never have I conducted a more touching Communion service.

The young man who had made the request was a Lutheran day school teacher. Called up early in the draft, he had filed for exemption, but in being transferred from camp to camp his exemption papers always arrived too late. Nor did they catch up with him before he embarked for "over there." On the front line in France with his regiment in November 1918, he was ordered "over the top" and was killed in action only hours before the armistice went into effect. When the news reached me, I could not but relive that evening Communion service and remember: "It may be the last time...."

## *Not March Alone*

This and other war day experiences, sad to say, were to be revived for me all too often less than a generation later. Fortunately when our nation was so suddenly plunged into World War II, our church was in a far better state of readiness to minister to our men in service. Already at the time of the prewar draft under the National Defense Act our church was in a position to provide its share of military chaplains and to set up Lutheran service centers near the larger training bases.

It can only be viewed as the Lord's guidance that the Cleveland synodical convention in 1935 passed a seemingly minor resolution asking that a committee investigate whether our pastors might be extended calls into the military chaplaincy without compromising our church's confessional principles. This committee—Dr. George A. Romoser, Dr. J. Frederic Wenchel, Rev. H. D. Mensing, Rev. A. G. Dick, and Rev. Frederick C. Proehl (all except the last now deceased)—reported favorably. As a result an Army and Navy Commission (now known as the Armed Services Commission) was appointed in 1936. Working closely with government and military authorities, the commission began processing and calling qualified pastors for the chaplaincy. By its capable work the commission was able not only to fill the quotas allotted to our church and to secure a fair distribution for them among the various services but also to build up a chaplain's reserve corps.

Thus when war burst upon us and increasing numbers of our young men and women were scattered to fighting fronts the world over, our church's resolve "They Shall Not March Alone" was more than a pretty slogan. I must mention that one of our Navy chaplains was preparing for his regular morning service aboard the ill-fated *Arizona* the morning of the sneak attack on Pearl Harbor. I am convinced that our church did as much as, if not more than, any church body to hold the war's spiritual casualties to a minimum. This was done through our chaplains, of whom we had as many as 236 on active duty at one time; through our service centers, established in cooperation with the National Lutheran Council on a "you serve your men, we serve ours" basis; and through a remarkably efficient system of following up our military personnel with Christian literature.

Another cause for gratitude during the war was the draft status of our parish school teachers. Under the Selective Service System male teachers of our Lutheran schools were given the same 1-A classification as public school teachers. Our plea to authorities that they be granted a lower rating was first declined. Thereupon Dr. Arthur W. Klinck, then president of our teachers college in River Forest, Illinois, and I drew up documentary evidence showing that, doctrinally and historically, the position of parish teacher in our church has always been that of a minister of religion. Together with Congressman John W. Boehne Jr., we presented this evidence to the Director of Selective Service, General Lewis B. Hershey, and members of his staff at a conference in Washington. At this hearing we were shown every consideration, and in a few weeks we received a favorable ruling. Some time later a similar ruling was handed down granting a lowered draft classification to all bona fide theological and teacher-training students at Synod's schools. In this way God directed matters so that the work of the Church suffered no undue stringencies because of the war.

## *Precarious Spot*

The first office to which my Texas brethren elected me was chairman of the District Church Extension Board. Then at the 1919 convention, someone pointed out that the district lacked a second vice-president. Evidently enough delegates felt that I might be able to handle that too, and I found myself holding two offices. A district vice-president, particularly the number-two man, had very few responsibilities in those years. My most difficult job, I used to say, was to uphold the dignity of the office.

In 1921, however, the convention voted to raise me a notch to the first vice-presidency. Though my duties were only slightly more demanding, I realized it put me in a precarious spot: I was next in line of succession if something should happen to the president, a post then held by my good friend Dr. Henry P. Studtmann.

All too soon something did happen. In 1926, before his three-year term expired, Dr. Studtmann accepted the presidency of our newly opened Concordia College in Austin. This meant I had slipped into the Presidency "through the back door," as it were. It also placed my friend and seminary classmate, Rev. C. M. Beyer, in the "precarious" first vice-president spot. The next time we met he told me in all seriousness: "Jack, if you ever leave Texas, I'll resign."

Three years later Synod at River Forest elected me second vice-president, thus catapulting Pastor Beyer into the top district office. Recalling how he had worded his threat, I at once wired him: "Congratulations! I do not leave Texas. You do not resign."

To break me in on my vice-presidential duties Dr. Pfotenhauer asked me to represent him at the Southern District convention in February 1930 at New Orleans. Fortunately both for myself and for the convention, in presenting the cause of Synod I could lean on the example of such men as Dr. Pfotenhauer and Dr. F. J. Lankenau, both of whom I had seen in action. I was also able to pluck encouragement from some very kind words of Dr. W. H. T. Dau, one of my former professors, who happened to be essayist at the New Orleans convention. It's remarkable how a few commendatory words can spur one on to do one's work more effectively.

## *"Gone Again?"*

Congregations usually feel quite proud when their pastor is elected to high office in district or Synod. Trinity was no exception. That feeling of elation, however, doesn't last very long as a rule. Again, Trinity ran true to form. Happy smiles soon gave way to annoyed frowns and tart questions: "Is the pastor gone? Is he gone *again?* Pastor seems to be out of town quite a bit, doesn't he?" Disenchantment apparently reached a kind of climax one time when official visits to the Minnesota and the three West Coast districts took me away from my parish almost a full month. When I got back, the president of the congregation greeted me by blandly extending his hand and announcing, "My name is Swetland." He spoke jokingly, of course, but I understood.

In such double-duty situations a pastor soon learns to rearrange his work and delegate some of it to teachers, elders, and other members. By enlarging our board of elders from six to twelve, having more effective meetings, planning work assignments, and the like, we managed quite well. Trinity also applied regularly for a vicar assistant. To her credit let me add that Trinity also paid the vicar's salary. Today, as is only proper, Synod pays the salary of vicars engaged to assist the congregations of its vice-presidents, as do districts in the case of vicars who assist their presidents. (To tell the full story I should perhaps add that Trinity's vicars were expected also to teach school, a little chore that today's seminary vicar is very seldom called on to do.)[1]

---

[1] District presidents originally were part-time, being also parish pastors, until around the early 1970s. The LCMS presidency had been full-time since 1881, but it had no permanent location until 1952.

However, congregations whose pastors serve in synodical and district posts need not feel too badly "imposed on." They will find their pastor growing in leadership qualities, in Kingdom vision and inspiration, which in turn will soon be communicated to the congregation. To cite an example from my experience—for 18 consecutive years the Lutheran Publicity Organization of St. Louis invited me to preach for a week of noonday Lenten services that they conducted at a downtown theater during the entire Lenten season. Each year at this time I had to miss a Sunday at my church. One year for some reason the invitation was quite late in coming. Asked at a church council meeting whether I was planning on my usual spring trip to St. Louis, I of course answered no. When some were curious about the reason, I countered, "Why do you ask?" To my surprise they explained that each time I got back I seemed to mean more to the congregation because I always brought them so much good, live information from St. Louis sources and somehow always showed fresh vigor and enthusiasm in my work.

## *"Let God Decide"*

I have a strong suspicion that my good friends since seminary days, Pastor Alfred Doerffler and Louis Sieck, both prominent in the St. Louis publicity organization, had something to do with these repeated invitations as noonday Lenten speaker.[2] Wittingly or unwittingly, with each new appearance in St. Louis, they helped publicize my name. Otherwise it would have been difficult to explain why Synod in 1929 should think of electing a man from the far-off fringes of Texas, one who neither was a "name personality" nor had "prominent connections," to be its second vice-president. My fellow vice-presidents that term were Dr. F. J. Lankenau (first), Dr. Frederick Randt (third), and Dr. William Dallmann (fourth). Dr. Lankenau and Dr. Dallmann had both served one term, while Dr. Randt and I were new in office.

Three years later at the 1932 Milwaukee convention, balloting revealed that once again I had been placed on that precarious spot—

---

[2] Louis Sieck followed Ludwig Fuerbringer as president of Concordia Seminary.

the first vice-presidency. Dr. Pfotenhauer, elected to his eighth term as president, had reached the age of 73.

As the 1935 convention approached, the members of my church council wanted to know whether there was anything to the rumor that I would be elected president. I assured them that it wouldn't happen, since I had been reliably informed on my visit to St. Louis that spring for the noonday services that synodical leaders had persuaded Dr. Pfotenhauer not to refuse reelection. With Dr. Pfotenhauer available, I informed the church council, the matter was settled as far as I was concerned, since in all elections in my memory he had won decisive majorities on the first ballot.

How wrong I had been in my judgment was shown when the primary ballot at the 1935 convention indicated a closer than usual election. After a number of ballots and still no majority, I asked President Pfotenhauer whether I might make a statement. "Not now," he told me. "Just wait." When finally the balloting was narrowed down to a vote between Dr. Pfotenhauer and me, I again asked him to permit me an opportunity to speak. His answer was: "You must not say anything. Let God decide the matter by the vote of the convention."

The high, noble view taken by my predecessor in this very important matter in which he was directly concerned is something I have never forgotten. How could I help but honor and respect him all the more? His was the attitude and advice I strove to pursue whenever zealous or impatient souls chafed to press for a decision in matters of vital moment to the Church: "Let God decide by the vote of the convention."

*{Chapter Four}*

# HOUSTON TO ST. LOUIS

By the vote of the 1935 convention delegates my church laid upon my shoulders the heavy obligations and responsibilities of its highest office. No one realized the gravity of that truth more fully than I did. Why, I asked myself, had God permitted me to be the one? With our country now gripped for five years in the strangling clutch of the Great Depression, frustrating problems and dark uncertainty hung over our church. Even darker clouds hovered on the horizon. Well aware of my own weakness and shortcomings, I could only pray with Solomon that God might give me an understanding heart to lead His people wisely. In announcing my acceptance I asked the delegates and all members of Synod to join me in asking that God would grant me a double portion of the spirit with which God had endowed my predecessor. I was mightily encouraged when the district presidents held a special recess-period meeting to tender me the assurance of their prayers and full cooperation. Similar assurances were accorded by my co-workers on the Board of Directors.

### *533 South Kenilworth*

One of the first decisions I had to face as president was where to live. Houston was too far out on Synod's rim for consideration. St. Louis seemed most logical, but Synod, as yet without its own headquarters building, had most departments operating under already overcrowded conditions in Concordia Publishing House. My predecessor, a resident of Minnesota previous to his election, found Chicago to his liking. We were willing to follow his lead—but not quite. We chose one of the city's western suburbs, Oak Park, which likes to call itself "the biggest village in the land." It offered all the advantages of the big city and few of the disadvantages—a wonderful place to live. Synod purchased 533 South Kenilworth Avenue as our home, an address that for some 16 years was quite familiar throughout Synod as "the Office of the President."

The first winter we spent "up North" is still a live conversation piece among us Behnkens. It was the severest the Windy City had experienced in many years. As I recall it, the thermometer plunged below the zero mark for some 30 successive days. To us Gulf Coast Texans the sight of a minus-25-degree reading on the thermometer was a bloodcurdling experience. We often remarked about the "cold reception" the North gave us—only weather-wise, however. Otherwise, our welcome to Chicago could not have been any warmer. The grand reception the Chicago-area pastors, teachers, and laymen arranged for us at a "Loop" hotel helped to dispel any last lingering regrets over leaving the only hometown our family had known.

For our family, and certainly for me, the change from parish life to that of synodical executive involved huge adjustments. It was not like when a pastor accepts a call to another parish. Then the family is still the pastor's family, and life continues in much the usual pattern. Now, however, our situation was both new and different.

Happily, the ladies of St. John's Church, Forest Park, which we had joined, were not long in inviting my wife to join in some of their activities, and she soon felt at home. The children, too, soon formed a new circle of acquaintances at school and church. As for me, I missed the touch of the shepherd's staff. To this day I have never entirely escaped a tinge of homesickness for the parish ministry—the regular preaching of the Word to one's own flock, the instruction of young and old, the bedside ministry to the sick and dying, teaching the adult Bible class, and working with teachers and Sunday school teachers. Now I was caught up in the swirl of executive and administrative tasks—a continuous succession of meetings, conferences, consultations, appointments, innumerable trips, and an endless flow of correspondence. The whole course of my life was changed. I do not intend this as a complaint. I realize that if the church is to function, someone must hold executive office. God evidently wanted me to serve Him in that way.

## Initiation

As I settled down to learning the routine of the president's office, I quickly realized that I needed to become better acquainted with Synod itself. After all, my life and ministry had been confined largely to the South, and I knew all too little about most of the districts, stretching from Synod's heartland to the four corners of the continent. True, I had visited some 20 District conventions during my six years as vice-president, which helped considerably. But in most sections I was a comparative stranger. So I was more than happy to concur in the suggestion of the Board of Directors that I visit all the various areas of the church. I met with pastoral conferences and addressed larger gatherings, emphasizing the assignment we faced together as a Synod and pleading for wholehearted cooperation. Dr. Lawrence Meyer, who at that time was serving as Synod's publicity director, arranged the entire itinerary and, in fact, accompanied me to most of the meetings.

This get-acquainted tour was a real initiation for me, filled with interesting experiences. One evening up in Ontario, I remember that a Canadian lumberjack came in and introduced himself as we were in the pastor's study at the parsonage before the service. He inspected me thoroughly and remarked several times that I certainly looked hale and hearty—yes, indeed, a fine specimen of physical fitness. By way of acknowledgment I waved aside his remarks, but some said later that I braced up rather proudly. As he left a bit later our caller repeated his remarks. Feeling my biceps and shoulder, he observed: "Why, you don't appear to be a year older than 65 or 67." It was a somewhat deflated president who admitted meekly: "I'm 51."

During my early years in office it was evident that Synod was passing through the same painful transition from German to English as we had in my congregation. In my seminary days it was about as difficult to get a student to preach English as it is nowadays to get one to preach German. Synod's official name included the word "German" until the revised constitution was adopted in 1917, and German was considered the "official" language at conventions. Use of some English on the convention floor began during the constitution revision period. Then for two decades practically everything in the line of convention transactions was bilingual. There were two opening sermons, one in each language. Resolutions and minutes were read in both languages. This was still the case at the 1935 convention, when I came into office. In opening the 1938 convention, since we had no synodical ruling to the contrary, we began in the usual bilingual way. When the time arrived for the president to make his report in German, a delegate made the motion that Synod dispense with the report. It carried without a murmur. That ended the use of German as Synod's "official" language.

To some it may seem incredible that Synod should have continued so long to give official standing to the German language. However, it should be remembered that this was the case also in many congregations as well as in some districts. Whether we may lay this reluctance to change to a basic conservatism, to a lack of vision, or to plain "Dutch stubbornness," as has been variously claimed, it does seem rather strange in view of prophetic voices and events that pointed to the handwriting on the wall.

Already when Synod observed its Golden Jubilee (1897), in a series of articles in Synod's official organ (*Lutheraner*, Vol. 53, Nos. 11–13), Dr. A. L. Graebner called attention to the fact that while the use of German by our church had been a great blessing, especially to the great flood of immigrants, our church must now realize that "the years of the great immigration of Germans are past." If our church hopes to continue to grow, he emphasized, we must think in terms of a type of mission work different from gathering scattered German Lutherans into congregations. Pointing to the many losses in membership due to "mixed" (German-English) marriages, he trumpeted the urgent need for congregations to introduce English services and to concentrate their efforts on America's vast numbers of unchurched people. He quoted the words of a leader of another Lutheran body: "You Missourians ought to let your light shine among the English-speaking people of this country; you would find among them a field equally as large as you find among the Germans."

Sound advice indeed from this forward-looking theologian! However, his call went largely unheeded. Except where congregations, usually in the cities, bowed to a demand for English services—and these were usually held in the afternoon or evening—emphasis on the German continued. As early as 1887 the English Evangelical Lutheran Conference of Missouri wanted to join Synod as a district but was advised to form an English Synod of its own.

In 1911, however, this Synod, which had organized in 1888 in St. Louis as "The English Evangelical Lutheran Synod of Missouri and Other States," was received into synodical membership as the English District. In the course of time, it was felt by many, the English District congregations would become members of the geographical district in which they were located. Except for isolated instances, however, this early dream has not materialized. A notable exception came in 1939 when English District churches in Virginia, the Carolinas, Maryland, and the District of Columbia joined Eastern District congregations in forming Synod's Southeastern District.

## *Lesson in Liberty*

No doubt certain advantages can be found in the language insularity we cultivated—greater homogeneity, close fellowship bonds, peaceful development. But the unpleasant fact cannot be shrugged aside that many members either drifted away from the Church altogether or joined other churches simply because they could not understand German. Scandinavian Lutherans experienced similar losses. Mr. Henry Dahlen of New Jersey, a man who had given this matter close study, once told me that according to his estimate, if all Lutherans from Germany and the Scandinavian countries and their descendants had remained with their church, Lutherans in North America would number about 25 million instead of the 9 million we have today.

Like nothing else, America's entry into World War I gave jarring impetus to the language transition. In this respect at least, as some expressed it, the war was "a blessing in disguise," though it proved a painfully difficult period for our church. A wave of ultrapatriotic feeling bordering on hysteria seemed to sweep the country, which took the strange twist of labeling everything German as anti-American. In some places anyone heard speaking German on the street was under suspicion of being "pro-Kaiser." Volunteer Councils of Defense that made it their task to enforce "100 percent Americanism" were organized. Sometimes they resorted to violence to punish those whom they regarded as "enemy propagandists." A number of pastors and their families were mistreated, churches and parsonages daubed with paint, and services invaded by self-appointed "vigilantes." Congregations that had only German services were forced to add English sermons. In some states legislative measures were introduced to ban parochial schools.

All in all, as we look back, it was a rather sad chapter in the glorious history of our "sweet land of liberty." Swayed by fanaticism, some actually fought a language. As if a person's patriotism or loyalty can be determined by the language he speaks! Not long after the war newspapers and national magazines reexamined the facts of these incidents. They not only established that few groups were as thoroughly loyal as the so-called German-Americans but also severely condemned those who in the name of Americanism used such un-American measures to repress fellow citizens.

When our country was plunged into World War II, it was soon evident that this lesson on the meaning of freedom had not been forgotten. There was little anti-Germanism in evidence. While some Japanese-Americans were made to suffer indignities and many on the West Coast were placed under detention as a war measure, the strange phenomenon of "help win the war" by denouncing the enemy's language and culture did not reappear. Shortly after that dreadful December Sunday in 1941 I had the opportunity to speak with Mayor Best of Evansville, Indiana, who was about to leave for the US Conference of Mayors in New York City. Recalling the ugly situation that had developed in 1917, I asked him to seek the advice of New York's Mayor La Guardia, who was president of the conference and also director of the Office of Civilian Defense, on whether I should recommend to our congregations that services in German be discontinued. After the council discussed the matter I was advised that no recommendation would be necessary, since the government wanted all to have the opportunity to worship in the language they best understood.

## View of Five-Star Generals

We Lutherans of North America, spared in both world conflicts from the indescribable horrors of direct enemy onslaught, do not always realize that world Lutheranism has been one of the greatest casualties of these wars. Particularly in those lands that, time and again, became "war theaters"—Russia, Poland, Germany, Hungary, Slovakia, and the Baltic countries—the Lutheran Church suffered well-nigh irreparable havoc, both from the wars themselves and from the surge of communism that followed in their wake. That we were spared while the worst of all divine scourges was permitted to fall so heavily on fellow members of our faith must certainly come as a sobering thought to each one of us.[1]

Twice within my lifetime I have watched a hopeful, war-weary generation succumb to bitter disillusionment. What was to have been a brave, new world—a world made "safe for democracy," a world secure in the "four freedoms," has each time become a world of terrible tensions and fears and crises. For a decade now it has precariously poised on the thin line of what has come to be called a balance of terror.

When I met General Dwight D. Eisenhower at the Allied Supreme Headquarters in Europe shortly after the close of hostilities, he told me personally that wars do not settle issues. General Douglas MacArthur expressed the same conviction in an exchange of letters I had with him a year later. Both of these great American leaders stated that the hearts of men must be changed if we are to win the peace. We Christians know that only the Gospel of Christ can effect such a change in heart. Only in the measure that we bring the Spirit of Christ into men's lives can we expect a better world.

---

[1] Behnken frequently refers to "Red communism" and "Reds" in the original text. Mindful of his historical context and understanding of today, we use "communist," "Soviet," and other terms for Russian and Chinese contexts.

*{Chapter Five}*

# LENGTHENING OUR EDUCATIONAL CORDS

A PRESIDENTIAL DUTY that I learned to relish was one that Synod's bylaws required—at regular intervals to "visit officially all the educational institutions of Synod." Another regulation requires the president or his representative to be present at Board of Control meetings when professors and associate professors for the school faculties are elected. During my 27 years as president I found it possible to attend personally all but very few of these election meetings.

At such official visits we are of course aware that the campus has been put on "inspection alert" and we do not get to see things quite as they are ordinarily. The students take precautions to have their rooms, as well as their classroom work, all nicely shipshape.

Once when visiting one of the junior colleges that had introduced coeducation but as yet had no on-campus housing for women, I ate my noon meal at the home of a professor who had opened his home to some of the young lady students. One freckle-faced girl, who had taken a lively part in the conversation, suddenly turned to me and confided: "Dr. Behnken, I wish you were here all the time." I asked her why. "Well," she replied, "when you are here our professors all seem so different."

I also recall hearing an "old grad" reminisce about a former professor who gave his class standing orders. "Remember," he said, "any time the president drops in here our lesson will start back on page 75."

These and other instances of "visitation jitters" come to mind, I realize, only because they are the exception. Anyone who visits the classrooms of our training schools, officially or unofficially, cannot but carry away the impression that our church has been remarkably blessed with highly dedicated and competent teaching personnel. I was careful to note the thorough teaching, the admirable patience, and the high Christian discipline our professors brought to their classroom tasks. Throughout the years I have also observed how instruction has been focused more and more on the students' future calling.

Some have called our professional school system unique. At least, no other church body in our land has had any quite like it. However, it has remarkably served the purpose for which it was designed and developed—that of placing into Kingdom service as many and as fully equipped ministers and teachers of the Word as the church was capable of. For this reason Synod has been loath to tamper much with its basic structure, rather, it has centered its efforts on making the good we knew we had into something ever better.

## *Providential Plantings*

Perhaps this is the place to mention that when I began my studies at Winfield in Synod's 50th anniversary year, Synod had but two junior colleges—Concordia at Fort Wayne, Indiana, and Concordia at Milwaukee. The schools at Winfield and Conover, North Carolina, were also junior colleges, but at that time both still belonged to the English Synod. The three other synodical "prep" schools then in existence—Concordia Collegiate Institute, Hawthorne, New York (now located at Bronxville); St. Paul's, Concordia, Missouri; and Concordia, St. Paul, Minnesota—were all high schools, or academies, as they were usually called.

The story of the expansion of Synod's training school system, largely during my lifetime, to its present 16 colleges and seminaries, with a 1962 property value of some $60 million, is told most simply in a table.

### HOW OUR TRAINING SCHOOLS DEVELOPED

| *Theological Seminaries* | *Founded* |
|---|---|
| St. Louis, Missouri | 1839 |
| Springfield, Illinois | 1846 |

## LENGTHENING OUR EDUCATIONAL CORDS

| Teachers Colleges | | Full College |
|---|---|---|
| River Forest, Illinois | 1864 | 1939 |
| Seward, Nebraska | 1894 | 1939 |

| Junior Colleges | | Full Junior College |
|---|---|---|
| Fort Wayne, Indiana | 1839 | 1839 (Relocated and opened as Senior College, 1954) |
| Milwaukee, Wisconsin | 1881 | 1881 |
| Bronxville, New York | 1881 | 1907 |
| Concordia, Missouri | 1883 | 1905 |
| Conover, NC[1] | | |
| Winfield, Kansas | 1893 | 1893 |
| St. Paul, Minnesota | 1893 | 1905 |
| Portland, Oregon | 1905 | 1950 |
| Oakland, California | 1906 | 1918 |
| Edmonton, Alberta | 1921 | 1926 |
| Selma, Alabama[2] | 1922 | 1922 |
| Austin, Texas | 1926 | 1951 |
| Ann Arbor, Michigan | 1963 | 1963 |

As an interesting historical footnote, one that is often overlooked today, let me recall that only the schools at Edmonton, Austin, and Ann Arbor were established by Synod as such. All the others, including the seminaries, were started as local projects by Lutherans who were convinced that their area needed such an institution. This of course does not apply to those colleges and seminaries that Synod found it advisable to relocate.[3]

---

[1] The Conover school, founded by Rev. Paul C. Henkel of the Tennessee Synod, was offered to and accepted by the English Evangelical Lutheran Synod of Missouri in 1892. It became part of Synod's college system when the English Synod amalgamated with the Missouri Synod in 1911 and was closed by Synod in 1935 after fire destroyed the main building.

[2] Alabama Lutheran Academy and College was opened in September 1922 by the Synodical Conference as a teacher training school for African-Americans. It was transferred to Missouri Synod ownership in 1961 and is being expanded through a building and recruitment program. Today it is Concordia College Alabama.

[3] Presently the college in Edmonton belongs to the Lutheran Church Canada, the former Canada District of the LCMS. St. Paul in Concordia, Missouri again became a high school. The Senior College was dissolved and its campus became the home of Concordia Theological Seminary in 1977, relocated from Springfield, Illinois. The

It is also interesting to note the locations of these schools. Though started largely through local initiative, they are well distributed. In view of modern developments in transportation, today we might be minded in a few instances to choose a different location. Nevertheless it must be viewed as nothing short of providential that many of our training schools were located in areas where larger concentrations of Synod's membership are found and that others were founded in areas where heavier population thrusts later were to develop. Though all the early schools had humble beginnings, we have good reason to bless the vision that prompted these Lutherans to open them. Because college was "not too far from home," many parents were persuaded to enroll their youngsters to study for the preaching and teaching ministry. Quite a number of pastors and teachers have indicated to me that they probably would not be in the ministerial or teaching office had there not been a synodical school "handy."

## *Alpine Years*

A big year for our teacher training program was 1911. That year the convention at St. Louis decided to move the so-called teachers seminary from its 47-year-old location at Addison, Illinois, to a site in River Forest, a suburb of Chicago. The chief reasons advanced for relocation were greater accessibility and enlarged cultural advantages. Construction was still under way on the new campus when a disastrous fire broke out and destroyed the administration building. Voices soon were raised that interpreted the conflagration as an act of God visited on the church to punish the haughty pride, which would no longer be satisfied with the less pretentious facilities at Addison. An emergency appeal, however, brought a quick and willing response throughout Synod for the necessary funds to rebuild.

Dedication of the River Forest college was held in connection with the 1914 convention in Chicago, the first convention I attended. The thousands who were present for the occasion, not only convention delegates and Chicago-area Lutherans but also hundreds from more distant points, long remembered this signal event.

---

colleges in Winfield and Oakland were dissolved. In 1972 Christ College was founded in Irvine, California and is now Concordia University Irvine.

Particularly inspiring to me was the singing of this vast throng. I had never heard anything like it. As this was in the days before the public address system, three festival speakers gave addresses at the same time—at different locations, of course. It was certainly a great day and an auspicious beginning for our Concordia Teachers College, River Forest, whose beautiful campus in recent years has accommodated student bodies of well over a thousand.

Another year of towering importance for our training schools was 1923. By this time swelling enrollments had brought a decided space pinch to most campuses, and pent-up demands for expanded facilities burst upon the Fort Wayne convention like a flood.

The St. Louis seminary in particular had long found its facilities at the South Jefferson Avenue location wholly inadequate, making relocation almost mandatory. Delegates at the Fort Wayne convention that year were shown preliminary sketches for a future seminary, prepared by Day and Klauder, a prominent Philadelphia architectural firm, for a previously approved 72-acre site just west of the St. Louis city limits. The project bore a $2,500,000 price tag, an almost astronomical figure in that day. Though it was debated warmly and at some length, the delegates evinced keen interest in the big project. The motion to accept the committee recommendation, as I recall, was made by a delegate from rural Oklahoma. It carried overwhelmingly. Some said it was unanimous. However, we later heard that one delegate in reporting back to his circuit insisted (perhaps to disavow personal responsibility for such wild spending): "I 'nayed' everything."

## *Texas Flapjack*

I came to the Fort Wayne convention under instructions from my district to plead the cause of opening a synodical training school in the great state of Texas. Our request had to be presented to Floor Committee 1, which handled all college and seminary matters. Because of the St. Louis relocation proposal and a large number of urgent requests from other colleges, it took me a long time to gain a committee hearing. Even after my appearance before the committee, prospects still were rather bleak. Though admitting that our Texas cause had much merit, several members frankly told me: "But not right now." The committee, however, was good enough to grant me an opportunity to present the matter on the convention floor.

I had carefully marshaled all my arguments and must have spoken a good 15 or 20 minutes. I don't recall all that I said, but one point I wanted to get across to every delegate was the vast distances our Texas students had to travel to attend any of our colleges. To dramatize the point I said: "If you will think of Texas as a big pancake and would turn it over eastward from the Louisiana line, then El Paso would be in the Atlantic Ocean; turn it over westward from El Paso, and Beaumont and Texarkana would be in the Pacific Ocean. Flip the state over northward from the Panhandle, and Brownsville would land near the Canadian border. Flip it southeastward from the Gulf Coast, and Texas would cover practically the whole Gulf of Mexico."

"Quite a geography lesson!" a rather loud voice remarked from the floor. Whether it was my little Texas flapjack lesson or whether the delegates were just in a granting mood, the result was a resounding vote for a college in Texas, and there was rejoicing among my Lone Star brethren from the Gulf to the Panhandle and from Texarkana to the Rio Grande.

The total amount voted by the 1923 convention for colleges and seminaries, including the 19-building St. Louis campus, came to $3,850,000—by far the largest figure a convention ever had authorized. Some expressed themselves as extremely dubious as to whether our church's constituency could be persuaded to raise that kind of money. However, a very alert and efficient committee—Dr. John H. C. Fritz, Dr. John C. Baur, and Mr. Theodore W. Eckhart—was named to head the effort. They organized a very thorough and systematic campaign. Soon a stream of information and inspiration flowed through the length and breadth of Synod, accompanied by much fervent prayer and consecrated work. The result was an amazing $4,600,000. A flurry of building activity followed, which enabled Synod to meet its expanding educational and manpower needs for some decades to come.

## Rank-and-File Speaker

Dedication day for the new seminary was set for Sunday, June 13, during the time when the 1926 synodical convention met in St. Louis at Holy Cross Church—the last time, incidentally, that convention sessions in a church were found feasible. It turned out to be a tremendous occasion. From far and near people converged on the sparkling new campus. For Missourians it was "Meet me in St. Louis" all over again. By this time the onrushing auto age had put the nation "on wheels," and thousands came by car for the event. Other thousands came by special train or chartered coach from Chicago, Fort Wayne, Detroit, Indianapolis, and other metropolitan centers. Official estimates of the crowd ranged from 70,000 to as high as 90,000.

This time, happily, a public-address system could be used. Loudspeakers placed in many of the buildings enabled people to hear the complete ceremonies from many vantage points. This was certainly fortunate, because under a blazing sun the crowded area about the speakers' platform became stiflingly hot.

President Pfotenhauer gave the main address. In his masterful German he stressed that the cause of our rejoicing was not to be sought merely in the beautiful buildings but in the grace of God that had preserved His truth to us pure and untarnished, particularly the cardinal truth of salvation solely by faith in Christ. "Let us rejoice with trembling," he said, urging us to prayer and watchfulness that God's Spirit and grace may continue to abide with our church and its institutions.

I was honored with the invitation to give the English address for the dedication. In inviting me the committee on arrangements stated that since Dr. Pfotenhauer would speak as an official of Synod, they would like to have someone who was not a synodical official to speak for the rank and file of Synod's clergy. However, shortly after I accepted, it so happened that Dr. Henry Studtmann, president of the Texas District, accepted the presidency of the new college at Austin, and as his successor I had now slipped into the ranks of higher officialdom. The committee nevertheless felt that this "accident" should not disqualify me as a "rank-and-file" dedication speaker. It was one of the great privileges of my life. I spoke on the text: "Not unto us, O Lord, not unto us, but unto Thy name give glory, for Thy mercy and for Thy truth's sake" (Psalm 115:1, KJV), which, as I sought to convey, rang out the "God-pleasing Notes in Our Song of Dedication": deep humility, heartfelt gratitude, and earnest consecration.

Later that same year I had the privilege of preaching for the dedication of our Austin Concordia. Our Texas Lutherans had pledged a gift of $30,000 toward the new college, and they turned out for the service in large numbers. The building dedicated that day, the first on the campus, was appropriately named Kilian Hall, a memorial to Pastor John T. Kilian, who in the early 1850s led a colony of Wends to southern Texas. The coming of this group of Lutherans to our shores was in many ways a Texas counterpart of the Saxon Immigration to Perry County, Missouri, in 1839.

Pastor Kilian had struck up a friendship with Dr. C. F. W. Walther, Synod's first president, during their student days at the University of Leipzig, a factor that no doubt helped to draw the two groups together. The Wendish Lutherans played a prominent role in the work of our Synod in Texas, and one may still see traces of their influence in the Wendish names (Symmank, Mutschink, Synatschk, Hobratschk, Tschatschula) appearing on the roster of Synod's pastors and teachers. Father's congregation at Fedor was composed largely of these stalwart people.[4]

## Educational "Unding"

Perhaps because we have so often referred to Synod's Fort Wayne school as "the *new* senior college," we tend to forget that behind the development of this school lies a long and interesting history. Already before the World War I period the call was raised that Synod provide four years of college training for its clergy. A memorial directed to the 1920 convention at Detroit brought the question of expanding several junior colleges to four-year colleges on the convention floor in a committee report. An ardent advocate of this

---

[4] The Sorbian or Wendish people are a distinct West Slavic minority group from Germany and Poland.

proposal was Dr. William Dallmann, a dynamic Milwaukee pastor who later became a synodical vice-president. I can still see him standing before the convention declaiming his convictions. Then realizing that his spirited oratory was going for a lost cause, he closed by saying: *"Aber es bleibt wieder beim Alten*—good night!" (The German means "Everything will remain as is," and the "good night" was a then popular slang expression of undisguised disgust.)

And "good night" it was. The proposal was turned down. But "good night" time is also the time for dreams, and the dreams of some continued to hold visions of a senior college. The issue was merely postponed. By 1935 it was back on the convention floor. However, by this time the Depression had clamped a tight grip on our country. The number of candidates without calls was growing from year to year. Retrenchment was the order of the day. Building or expansion of any kind was simply out of the question. In fact, many during these years came to the definite conclusion that some of our colleges would have to be closed.

As a matter of fact, delegates to the 1935 convention will recall that the Springfield seminary actually was closed—but only for a single night. After a rather heated floor discussion a resolution to close the seminary carried by a single vote. However, the next day the convention voted to reconsider the motion, and this time the resolution was defeated, but again by a narrow margin, 283 to 256. What a remarkable blessing in disguise that reconsideration motion has turned out to be!

Pondering solutions, the convention after lengthy debate decided that the answer lay in adding one year to the pre-theological course and—rather than add it to the colleges—making it a fourth seminary year. The added pre-theological year would include some subjects ordinarily taught at college, such as Hebrew, logic, philosophy, etc., and students who then completed the first two seminary years would be eligible for the Bachelor of Arts degree.

Vigorous objections were voiced to this plan, particularly by members of the St. Louis faculty. Spokesmen at the convention labeled it *ein Unding* (a monstrosity). Whoever heard of a theological seminary granting an AB degree, they asked. Some made dire predictions that we would be making ourselves "the laughingstock in educational circles."[5]

The plan nevertheless was adopted. For the next 22 years—until the Senior College was opened in the fall of 1957—the seminary had four classes on campus and one class in the vicarage, which since 1935 has been a course requirement. It meant that students entering as high school freshmen had to look forward to 11 years of preparation before entering the ministry.

Few apparently were satisfied with the arrangement at Saint Louis. Complaints piled up, and clamor for four years of college at the pre-seminary level increased rather than subsided. Meanwhile, as ordered by the 1941 convention, our harried Board for Higher Education engaged Professor Theodore W. Hausmann of the Bronxville Concordia to make a full-scale survey of the entire educational system as a prelude to future planning. Meanwhile the Depression was also becoming a fading ghost of the past as a more fearful specter stole on the world scene. War had been unleashed by the Axis powers, and before the close of 1941 a now prospering America had shifted from being "the arsenal of democracy" to all-out belligerency.

It thus happened that the Hausmann survey report was a major item at Synod's wartime convention (1944) at Saginaw. (With victory in sight, restrictions had been lifted just in time for this convention to be held as scheduled.) While the report unquestionably contributed much valuable material, one who peruses it today will find that some sections make strange reading. Many findings in the report were naturally colored by Synod's experiences of the 30s and early 40s, when at times we had a surplus of more than 400 ministerial candidates and some 300 unassigned teacher graduates. Unbelievable as it may sound, debated at Saginaw were such questions as whether some of the schools should be closed, whether the colleges at Concordia, Missouri, Winfield, Kansas, and Seward, Nebraska, might be combined into one school, and whether the Springfield seminary should be discontinued in progressive stages as a training school for pastors.

---

[5] An AB degree (*Artium Baccalaureus*) is the Latin name for a Bachelor of Arts.

## Another "Unding"

Despite all this, clamor for an expanded pre-theological course continued and proposals were made to the convention as to how it should be done. Because of the divergent opinion, the convention finally passed a resolution requesting the Board for Higher Education "to make further studies regarding the advisability of changing over to a four-year college course in preparation for entrance upon a three-year course in theology in St. Louis and to submit a report with recommendations to Synod in 1947."

Thus the moment of decision for the long-belabored "senior college question" came at Synod's Centennial Convention, held at the Palmer House in Chicago. After a thorough study of no less than 18 different specific plans that had been suggested, the Board for Higher Education recommended that Synod establish a two-year senior college (junior and senior college years) as an additional unit in the professional training of ministerial students.

The recommendation met with a storm of objections, this time from faculty members of the junior colleges. Such a school, they argued would throw our church completely "out of step" with the generally accepted policies of education in this country. We were hatching another *Unding,* they declared. Whoever heard of a two-year senior college? The objectors advanced a variety of counterproposals, chiefly the addition of two years to one or more of the junior colleges—anything but this monstrosity of a separate two-year senior college. But the convention seemed to know what it wanted. Persuaded that the "additional unit" in the training system was in full harmony with the "fundamental objectives of ministerial training" that the board had included in its report, the Chicago convention voted to establish a completely new college.

But now another big question moved into the foreground: Where should the new school be located? A number of communities plainly considered themselves to be the only logical choice. Others too began promoting their "ideal locations." Having struggled through to one major decision, however, the convention was content to leave the "sticky" location question to a committee. Perhaps to ensure that no area and no interests would be slighted, the convention decreed that the site committee should consist of the president and vice-presidents of Synod, the Board of Directors, the Board for Higher Education, the College of District Presidents, a lay representative from each district, with the presidents of the colleges and seminaries included as advisory members.

Someone called this committee the Ninety and Nine, and the name stuck. It was so large that the meetings were almost a small convention. It turned out that the committee was unable to decide on an actual site; however, by January 1952, through a process of elimination, it agreed that the location should be in the Chicago or Milwaukee suburban area and that the final choice should be made by the Board of Directors and the Board for Higher Education.

## *Two Birds—One Stone*

When the Ninety and Nine began deliberations, minutes of an early meeting show, the cost of the new college, excluding the land, was reliably estimated at $2,750,000. Evidence of skyrocketing construction costs during the next few years can be seen in much higher estimates quoted in reports given at subsequent fiscal conferences. Space needs too were revised upward when the synodical growth curve showed that we would have to be ready to train many more clergymen. After a thorough review of the entire picture the 1956 convention at St. Paul finally set the cost ceiling for the new institution at $7,200,000.

The Board of Directors and the Board for Higher Education, as a result of extensive studies, decided that the choice of a site be narrowed to the suburban area northwest of Chicago. Before a final choice could be made, however, a new development came to the fore. Indiana Technical College in Fort Wayne made an offer to purchase Concordia Junior College in that city for one million dollars. The Board for Higher Education felt that this proposition merited consideration, particularly since board plans already included sizable expenditures for improving and expanding the Fort Wayne campus. Some viewed the offer as "providential," since it opened up a two-birds-with-one-stone possibility: disposing of a campus with a cost problem and solving the senior college site question by locating the proposed campus in the Fort Wayne area. This, however, meant that the whole question would have to be recommitted to Synod for consideration at the upcoming convention.

After a long second look, and after giving the Fort Wayne alumni an opportunity to express their views in an open hearing, the 1953 convention at Houston finally settled the matter. It ordered the historic Fort Wayne school sold and awarded the senior college to Fort Wayne on a new campus. By fall that year the Board of Directors had inspected a number of sites and purchased a 186-acre tract five miles north of the heart of the city. The site, nicely wooded with a clearing that sloped gently to the St. Joseph River, offered an ideal setting for the architectural genius of the renowned Eero Saarinen, who was engaged to submit a design expressive of the school's unique character and high ideals.

By September 1957 construction had sufficiently advanced to permit enrollment of the 192 who had graduated from the junior colleges that spring. Building operations continued through the school year so that by the following fall everything would be in readiness for both junior and senior classes. Thus, most fittingly, the first student body could share in the dedication ceremonies, held May 30, 1958, at the close of the first school year. The Board of Control honored me with an invitation to preach the dedication sermon. On the basis of 2 Timothy 3:14–17 I stressed that the new school, designed specifically to be a vital bridge to a spiritually and intellectually mature ministry, would truly serve its purpose only when it manifested deep concern for the personal faith of its students and when it strengthened their conviction that Scripture is the inspired Word of God.

## *Trailblazer?*

The passing of the Fort Wayne junior college did not go unlamented, as was to be expected. To many the historic old campus on the Maumee River was indeed hallowed ground. The hundreds of alumni who had often rehearsed her fame in song and story did not take kindly to the loss of their 118-year-old alma mater. Fort Wayne Lutherans, whose sentimental attachments to Concordia reached back several generations, could not easily reconcile themselves to the thought that their Concordia should pass into other hands. However, now that I myself have become a resident of Fort Wayne, I have noticed that most of my fellow citizens are becoming nicely adjusted to the change and increasingly are transferring their affection and traditional loyalty to the new senior college, which, as even the reluctant had to agree, has become one of the city's showplaces.

Also those who had held a decidedly dim view of opening such an educational oddity as a two-year senior college are having second thoughts on the matter in the light of recent trends in American higher education. Already in 1957 the *Newsletter* published by the American Association of Junior Colleges pointed out that the University of Michigan had opened community colleges at Flint and Dearborn, both beginning with the junior college year; also that the New York Board of Regents had indicated the need for a senior college "as a capstone to an integrated educational system" for that state. The *Newsletter* also noted Synod's venture into a senior college and added: "Cue—watch this trend. It's in the making." States now striving desperately to keep abreast of the rising tide of college enrollees by building junior colleges will undoubtedly be forced to consider starting senior colleges to absorb the tide when it issues from the junior colleges. It may well be that the two-year or perhaps three-year senior college will become a fixture in our educational system, and the Missouri Synod will be among those who helped blaze the trail.[6]

## *Holy Imponderable*

For well over a decade now our church has been faced with a decided shortage of pastors and synodically-trained teachers. Each year at graduation time the number of vacant pulpits and classrooms is reduced somewhat, only to rise again, it seems, to higher proportions each year. Vacant parishes have risen beyond the 400 mark, and requests for teachers, especially women teachers, for Lutheran schools in recent years have run as high as 1,100 and 1,200.

---

[6] The junior colleges have become colleges or universities offering baccalaureate and graduate programs.

The reasons are not hard to find. Since the late 1940s our North American districts have been opening new missions at an average rate of over 100 a year. At the same time the manpower demands have risen sharply along the entire perimeter of our overseas mission fields, particularly those opened since World War II. Over the last 20 years enrollments in Lutheran elementary schools have risen by 100,000, and high school enrollments have grown by 10,000. Along with the increase in the number of clergymen and teachers there has also come a corresponding increase in replacements necessary to fill the ranks of those who retire or who die in office.

Due to the chronic shortage problem new and ever more thoroughgoing surveys and projections have been made to chart the future course of Synod's pre-professional training efforts. It is certainly right and proper that the church plan well and that the church, no less than the business world, use all available technical and professional assistance to measure past performance and project future needs. With all our surveying and projecting, however, we need to remember that "the best-laid schemes o' mice an' men / Gang aft agley."[7] The future rests with God. In all our church planning we may not for a moment overlook the work of the Holy Spirit. After all, it is He who builds the Church. He alone converts people, and He alone can lead Christians to carry on the Lord's work with eagerness and energy. It is the Holy Spirit, too, who equips young men and women with the necessary talents and moves them to dedicate their lives to full-time service in the Church.

In all its planning and projecting I pray our Synod may ever remain sensitively aware of this mighty imponderable of all Church work—the activity and blessing of the Holy Spirit.

---

[7] Behnken quotes Robert Burns's 1785 Scots poem: "To a Mouse, on Turning Her Up in Her Nest with the Plough."

*{Chapter Six}*

# STRENGTHENING STEWARDSHIP STAKES

I CANNOT RECALL a time when Synod was wholly without financial problems. In the earlier years, of course, the method of raising the funds needed for Synod's work was quite simple. Notices calling attention to needs and appeals for gifts were placed in the columns of our church publications. Pastors would follow up with announcements from their pulpits, or they would have the congregation remain for a brief meeting after the service, and the people would generally respond. I remember how members would sometimes come to the Fedor parsonage, hand Father some money, and say, "Pastor, here is something for Synod." I also recall Father asking me to hitch up the buggy and drive him around to several homes to gather gifts for Synod.

At that time, of course, Synod's financial requirements were quite modest. Our overseas mission work, for one thing, was only beginning. In 1895 we had made a small start in India with two missionaries, Pastors Theodore Naether and F. J. Mohn, and our work in South America began a few years later (1901).

### *Laymen Show the Way*

By the early teens of the twentieth century, however, Synod's work had expanded in all areas, and the synodical treasury was beset by mounting deficits. By the time of the 1917 convention in Milwaukee the debt had soared to about $100,000, quite a formidable figure for the modest economy of those days. The debt was all the more worrisome because Synod was rather at a loss as to how to remedy the situation.

It was the laymen who showed the way. During the convention a dozen faithful and consecrated laymen met at the Milwaukee home of Fred C. Pritzlaff to talk over the church's financial troubles. They decided to organize a Lutheran Laymen's League with the stated objective: "To aid Synod by word and deed in business and financial matters." To demonstrate that their slogan meant what it said, they at once subscribed and solicited sufficient funds to liquidate Synod's debt.

Meeting at Chicago later that year, the LLL set itself the task of raising a $3 million endowment fund, the proceeds of which were to be used to support the "Veterans of the Cross," the aged and incapacitated pastors and teachers and their widows and orphans. Many members gave one or more of their "Liberty Bonds," purchased during the war, to this cause. Although the full fund goal was not quite reached, the Synod-wide campaign proved remarkably successful. This fund-raising effort—by far the largest attempted up to that time—was in many respects a real eye-opener. We learned, for one thing, that the membership of our church had the financial capability to raise large sums of money. We learned also that for a successful collection systematic efforts and modern techniques are necessary.

The LLL formally presented the Endowment Fund to Synod at the 1920 convention in Detroit. The stipulation that the fund remain intact and only the earnings be used for the Support Fund has been held inviolable ever since. Efficiently administered, along with other trust funds, by the capable men who comprise the Board of Trustees of Synodical Trust Funds, the LLL Endowment Fund throughout the years has yielded substantial help for the cause administered by the Board of Support.

The thorough and careful attention our faithful trustees have applied to investment matters so as to ensure the highest possible yield with the lowest possible risk has often been a source of amazement to me. During the Depression, when many fortunes were wiped out and countless investments evaporated, the Endowment Fund and other synodical trust funds remained soundly intact.

Synod did not remain debt-free very long after the laymen pulled it out of the red in 1917. During the early 20s the budget system and the fiscal conference were called into being, both designed to improve the financial situation. Despite these measures and the tremendous rise in the economy of those boom years, Synod was faced with annual deficits. I do not recall who conceived the idea, but a plan was adopted to operate with an A budget and a B budget, the former to include all operating expenses, the latter all capital investments. The idea may have sounded good, but it proved wholly unworkable. The B budget existed merely in name. We had great difficulty even in attaining the A budget, while the B budget, as someone has said, was a "let it be" budget.

Of course, the special collection for colleges and seminaries during the 1923–26 triennium was an over-the-top success and enabled Synod to pay not only for the new St. Louis seminary and new campuses at Austin and Edmonton but also for capital improvements on other campuses as well. Offerings for Synod's operational budget, however, continued to run short, and the indebtedness continued.

When the crash hit in 1929, Synod felt the pinch quickly and sharply. With the nosedive in business and farm prices many of our members sustained severe losses. During the early 30s unemployment mounted steadily, soaring at times as high as 12 and 14 million. Upwards of 20 million people were on relief, others worked for a mere pittance. Congregations, especially those with building debts, found it difficult to cover their current expenses. Pastors' and teachers' salaries had to be slashed and sometimes even fell in arrears.

### "Spare That Tree"

The convention at Milwaukee in 1932 was a real Depression convention. The atmosphere was charged with deep pessimism. I recall that when President Pfotenhauer gave me the assignment of preaching the English opening sermon, I chose as my text the words of Esther 4:14 (KJV): "Who knoweth whether thou art come to the kingdom for such a time as this?" It was indeed "such a time," worse in many respects than the 1917–18 war days and a dark judgment of God upon a land and a Church that had certainly grown heedless and spiritually careless in the gleeful days of the "roaring twenties."

The Milwaukee delegates simply turned problems that defied solution over to the Board of Directors. The convention, however, charged the board to take whatever steps were necessary to keep the debt from exceeding one million dollars—and it was already dangerously close to that figure. I know what a struggle the board members had in trying to conduct Synod's business and still hold the line drawn by the Milwaukee resolution. It meant that the salaries of professors and all others dependent on Synod's treasury, which had already been cut ten percent, would have to undergo a further and even more drastic reduction.

I remember that at the Milwaukee convention an Oklahoma pastor, a good cartoonist, drew a picture of a forest with large limbs cut off the trees. The missing limbs, marked 20 percent, 25 per cent, 30 percent, represented the salary cuts given parish pastors and teachers. In the foreground was a fine, large tree with only a few small branches missing, marked 10 percent. This was the synodical tree. Beneath it stood a scholarly-looking professor gazing up at the tree with the words "Woodman, spare that tree!"

## *Slow Crawl*

During the next year or two a "Pay Synod's Debt" effort was launched. It turned out to be almost an exercise in futility. The deficit was lowered slightly only to inch up again to the same depressing figure. Other efforts to free Synod from the shackling deficit, such as the Open Bible Thankoffering in 1934, had little better results.

It was a discouraging period. Requests for urgently needed repairs on college and seminary buildings had to be declined or postponed by the Board of Directors again and again, even though it was evident that further deterioration would result and run up repair costs even higher. But the board had little choice. It got so that the boards of control of the colleges came to expect nothing but negative answers from Rev. William Hagen, the grand old man who at that time served as corresponding secretary for the board.

At one of the conventions during that time a man came up to me and said he knew a good way for Synod to save a lot of money. Naturally I was interested. "Have the board use penny postcards," he explained. (Yes, there really were such things as penny postcards!) "Simply print up a stack of them with a big NO and a dotted line for the signature," he said.

"In that way you will save both postage and the salary of a secretary."

To add to the general discouragement, mission expansion soon slacked off to a slow crawl, with the result that seminary and teacher college graduates were not receiving calls. The districts were urged to find ways and means to keep the candidates active in Church work. Many accepted work at mere subsistence pay, some as low as $25 a month.

This whole situation had a very demoralizing effect. Some congregations began to think that they were doing the graduates a favor by offering them temporary positions; others scouted around to get workers as cheaply as possible. Overeager candidates, on the other hand, actually began "fishing" for calls when they heard of a vacancy. In one instance, I was told, a congregation had 27 applicants. Others, after waiting in vain for a call, entered secular callings. I know that quite a number of Church-trained young men with excellent talents and great promise never reached their coveted goal in the pastoral or teaching ministry. To my knowledge, exactly how many there were has never been determined.

## *Thanks in Millions*

A trend to better times had appeared about the time the 1938 convention met in St. Louis. At this convention, which festively observed the centennial of the Saxon immigration, plans were formulated to gather a million-dollar Centennial Thankoffering in a concerted effort to wipe out Synod's debt. By the end of 1939 we were able to announce with deep gratitude to God that at last the "old" debt was gone, although a small "new" debt of some $38,000 still showed on the books at the close of the fiscal year.

By 1940 the "war boom" began to boom in earnest, and for a number of years the Board of Directors had little trouble in balancing the budget. Employment soon reached an all-time high. As incomes skyrocketed, the per capita contributions of Synod's members, which had fallen as low as $12.73 in 1933, had more than doubled ten years later.

Early in 1945, amid mounting signs that God would soon grant victory of our arms in Europe, the Board of Directors gave the "go" sign to carry out a Fiscal Conference resolution of the previous fall calling for a $5 million Peace Thankoffering. The purpose of this offering was to supply Synod with the huge sums that would be needed to relieve human suffering in war-ravaged lands, to rehabilitate missions at home and abroad, and to carry out a building program at various colleges as soon as wartime restrictions were lifted. Our grateful people certainly responded nobly. During that and the following years $4,680,884 poured in for postwar reconstruction and mission expansion and close to $4 million more for relief in Europe and Asia. What tremendous blessings this thankoffering made possible perhaps only those realize who personally saw the agony and despair these gifts helped to change into joy and hope.

### *History-Making "Conquest"*

Synod's centennial, celebrated with all due solemnity in 1947, was also the occasion for a special thankoffering. It was to be "of major proportions," according to a 1944 convention resolution, and every member of Synod was encouraged to express his gratitude to God with cheerful offerings, which would reflect the abounding blessings He had lavished on our church throughout a century of grace. The Centennial Thankoffering reached a total of $1,243,439. Some were disappointed that it did not go much higher. The Fiscal Conference had suggested $3,500,000. However, considering the large amount our members had contributed to the Peace Thankoffering just two years previously, one is inclined to view the results in a more favorable light.

Time had been taking its toll in wear and tear at many of our colleges and seminaries. Meanwhile costs were rising, and it became evident that inflation was here to stay awhile. It also became increasingly plain that our training schools would have to be expanded considerably if we were to have enough workers to meet future demands. Accordingly, in 1949, another special offering was launched under the slogan "Building for Tomorrow" to provide the needed expansion funds. Whether it was because the "specials" were following too closely on the heels of one another or because they lacked proper planning and execution, this effort also was not as successful as many had hoped. It came to $1,676,800, about $500,000 less than the minimum requested.

By the time of the Milwaukee convention in 1950 it had become very clear that if our church was to meet the vast Kingdom-building opportunities the Lord was literally pushing her into, a large and vigorous financial effort would be needed. (Delegates will recall that we met just as the Korean incident flared into a shooting war that was to involve thousands of American troops in months of bloody conflict.) Resolutely the delegates went on record to raise a $10 million offering over and above the regular budget "to promote the expansion of all branches of synodical work throughout the world."

After intensive planning and organization this "Conquest for Christ" collection was carried out in 1953. In practically every congregation through the length and breadth of Synod, trained "ambassadors" made house-to-house visits to inform all members of the challenges and needs. It was perhaps the most successful effort in Synod's history. Our people responded with almost $4 million more than the proposed $10 million goal. Needless to say, Conquest for Christ was a mighty blessing for Synod's work and a source of genuine joy to our people.

Meanwhile a number of auxiliary agencies, which are not included in Synod's budget, had been pleading for permission from the Board of Directors to have Synod-wide collections to meet their pressing expansion needs. The board, however, urged these agencies—Bethesda Lutheran Home, Watertown, Wisconsin; Valparaiso University; the Mill Neck (Long Island) School for the Deaf; the Lutheran Deaconess Association; and Synod's Board for World Relief—to postpone their appeals until Synod had completed its own Conquest for Christ effort. The board also advised these groups to pool their efforts in a single campaign rather than have a series of individual fund drives within a year or two. To insure maximum success, the board even offered official sponsorship for the campaign. Thus the "Building for Christ" offering came into being. Completed in 1955, it totaled some $4,700,000.

## New Plateaus

By this time complaints had begun to build up that special collections were coming too fast and too big, that they were meeting increasing resistance, and that "all-out drives" were a deterring factor in the ongoing stewardship training programs of congregations. Accordingly, all circuit counselors were asked to attend Synod's fiscal conference in July 1955 at St. Paul, Minnesota, for a thoroughgoing review of the entire financial picture. Grass-roots opinion, the counselors agreed, was that special collections should be discontinued.

The conference thereupon decided that beginning in 1956 all capital investment items should be included in the annual budget along with current operations. This, we all knew, meant a sharp increase in the annual budget. In 1956, for example, the jump was from $9.1 to $12.9 million. Progressively higher plateaus beckoned for the years ahead.

The new budget plan, known as "Our Venture of Faith," received a generally favorable response. Many congregations picked up the challenge and turned their "venture" into success. To handle the dual burden of operational costs and capital investments in one budget, however, has posed real difficulties. For the years 1956 and 1957 budget receipts fell $1.5 million short, and in 1958 the budget could be balanced only after the Board of Directors ordered a 12 percent cutback "all along the line" in expenditures.

As the 1962 convention approached, Synod faced an accumulated deficit of several million dollars and a steadily widening gap between budget allocations and income. Many leaders in Synod were of the opinion that the only answer to a sustained advance in the work program for the "soaring sixties" was another special offering of major proportions. Quite a number of delegates at Cleveland felt, on the other hand, that a better answer lay in developing "Venture of Faith" to its fullest potential.

Debate on the issue led to the decision to intensify "Venture of Faith" through a "Faith Forward" effort that would have a double thrust: (1) an educational program designed to raise the church to higher levels of spiritual rededication; (2) to add $10 million to the annual synodical budget for the years 1963, 1964, and 1965.

These are high goals, and indeed they must be high—both the spiritual life goal and the dollar goal. One is as necessary as the other.

In recalling the ups and downs of the various major and minor financial "crises" we hold one experience, above others, in grateful remembrance—the remarkable way God's people, impelled by the love of Christ, have responded whenever they were reminded that "the Lord hath need" of their consecrated dollars. In His name and in the Synod's name I again want to thank them sincerely and voice my prayer that God will continue to bless our church with members who "abound in this grace also."

*{Chapter Seven}*

# MERCY MISSION—EUROPE 1945

With the Nazi surrender, May 7, 1945, a tremendous weight was lifted from a war-weary world. Mindful that it is God who "makes wars cease to the end of the earth" (Psalm 46:9), most of our congregations held special services on VE-Day [May 8, 1945] to pour out their hearts to God in humble thankfulness and to implore Him mercifully to shorten the conflict still being waged with suicidal fanaticism by our foe across the Pacific.

A war burden that was long to weigh heavily on the hearts of American Christians was the staggering task of bringing material and spiritual relief to prostrate Europe.

Lutherans of America were naturally deeply concerned over the fate of the Lutheran churches of Europe, particularly those in the land that had cradled the Reformation. We knew that the Evangelical (Lutheran) Church of Germany had already suffered severe reverses under the Nazi regime. At first, to be sure, many church leaders believed that Hitler would permit the churches to have a free hand. Bishop Hans Meiser of the Lutheran Church in Bavaria later told me that Hitler's early promises "sounded as though a new day was dawning for the church." All too soon, however, *der Führer* removed his mask, and it became apparent that he wanted a church that would conform to his own twisted ideals. He appointed a typical Nazi to the church consistory and with customary police-state tactics tried to make the church a tool of the Reich. Those who dared to oppose the nazification of the church landed in a concentration camp or were placed under house arrest.

This I Recall

## *Complete Chaos*

While the war was still in progress (though the downfall of the Reich seemed imminent) Dr. Lawrence Meyer, representing our Synod, Dr. P. O. Bersell, president of the Augustana Lutheran Church, and Dr. Ralph Long, executive secretary of the National Lutheran Council, were granted permission to visit England, Sweden, France, and Switzerland to explore the church situation at first hand. Their reports gave the Lutherans of North America some idea of the size of the rehabilitation task that would have to be faced with the coming of peace. They confirmed what we had already guessed or heard from other sources—that vast numbers of churches suffered untold havoc in the saturation bombings, that thousands of homes had been broken up and families and congregations scattered to the four winds, and that hundreds of German pastors, who were not exempt from military service as in our country, had become casualties or languished in prisoner of war camps.

Immediately after the German surrender we began to make plans for a Lutheran mission to Europe to establish contact with Lutheran church leaders, especially in occupied Germany, and to determine what needed to be done. Our delegation was to include three men from the National Lutheran Council—Dr. Long, Dr. Bersell, and Dr. Franklin Clark Fry—and two representatives of our Synod—Dr. Meyer and myself.

Because conditions in Germany were in a state of complete chaos, we naturally had a difficult time getting passports and visas. Through the kind aid of Herbert Waltke, a St. Louis businessman and a personal friend of President Truman, we were able to secure the necessary documents and to book passage for the Atlantic crossing on October 8.

The NLC group informed us that because of important commitments they could not leave on that date. Dr. Meyer and I decided, however, that we should not delay our departure if we intended to carry out one of the important objectives of our visit. Information had reached us that a movement was under way in Germany, influenced by the Swiss Reformed theologian Dr. Karl Barth and a number of theologians in Germany, to join Lutheran,

Reformed, and *Unierte* (United) church bodies into a single Evangelical Church in Germany. We hoped to reach Germany in time to caution the Lutheran bodies against forming such a union, which in its very essence would involve compromising Lutheran confessional principles.

We learned, however, that the organization of the *Evangelische Kirche in Deutschland* (EKiD) had been effected before we arrived. Some may be inclined to question whether our testimony would have done much good, but we felt constrained at least to try. We learned, too, that a number of German theologians had raised the very warning we intended to give, among them Dr. Hermann Sasse of the University of Erlangen. So vigorously did this scholarly professor protest the dilution of Lutheranism through this hybrid union that it eventually led to a rift between him and former close friends and associates. Yet he remained true to his convictions.

## *Shock and Surprise*

Thus exactly seven weeks after World War II officially ended with the Japanese signing of surrender terms [September 2, 1945], we left New York for Plymouth, England, aboard the *SS Argentina*, one of the many passenger liners that had been converted into a troop transport. The stateroom assigned to us, we were told, had been occupied on the ship's westward run by the Duke and Duchess of Windsor. The duke, you will recall, had once worn the British crown as King Edward VIII but had abdicated the throne because he insisted on marrying a twice-married American divorcee, Mrs. Wallis Simpson (née Bessie Wallis Warfield). I cannot say that it was a particular thrill to me to sleep in a bed once occupied by an ex-king. In fact, we would much have preferred to sleep elsewhere, for it seemed that the men who occupied the cabin next to ours had left ashore whatever moral standards they had. They turned each night hideous with their drinking, cursing, and obscenity. We were glad, after an eight-day run, to step ashore at Plymouth harbor.

Though dusk had started to fall, we got our first shocking glimpse of the fearful destruction inflicted by the German *Luftwaffe*. We were in for a greater shock after the overnight train ride to London. Rev. F.

Samuel Janzow, pastor of Luther-Tyndale and Holy Trinity, the London churches in fellowship with our Synod, showed us some of the blitzed sections of the city. Particularly pathetic was the sight of a completely gutted and leveled apartment section along the Thames River, two miles long and a mile wide, where many of the city's dock-workers had lived.

London just then was blanketed by one of its famous fogs, which grounded all flights to Frankfurt. The delay gave us an opportunity to attend services at Luther-Tyndale Church, known to so many of our servicemen who were stationed in the London area. Members of this flock always accorded our "boys" a very warm welcome and frequently invited them to their homes. One of the members, Immanuel Lutz, whose son Martin was then missionary to India and is now pastor at Adell, Wisconsin, kept a register in his home for his guests to sign. When I saw it, the register had more than 1,500 names of Americans in military service.

Pastor Janzow had asked me to say a few words to the congregation after the service. This I was more than glad to do, since I wanted to thank these good people for all the kindness they had shown our military personnel. Imagine my surprise, as I was being introduced, to spot among a group of men in uniform the familiar face of my nephew Alvin Geisler of Riesel, Texas. He was as surprised as I was. I had the opportunity for a fine visit with Alvin since Mr. Lutz invited us pastors and about ten of the military men to his home after the service, which, incidentally, was held at six o'clock in the evening.

I learned from Alvin that he and two others had been assigned the task of classifying important Nazi military documents that the occupation troops had found hidden in a salt mine, dumped into a lake, and otherwise secreted. They were working through literally bales of these papers, waterproofing and readying them for shipment to the US.

A break in the fog on October 22 allowed us to take off for Frankfurt via Paris. A few minutes out from Paris our plane was ordered back; the fog had closed in on Frankfurt and made a landing there too hazardous. After a brief wait at Paris our plane was again given clearance, and we were able to make the Frankfurt landing without incident, though the fog was still quite dense. We found out later that ours was the last plane to land there for several days.

## *Interview with Ike*

At the Frankfurt landing field there was no one to meet us. Having awaited us for days, Chaplain (Major) Alvin A. Katt had been informed that no more planes were expected. Being completely on our own, two civilians late on a foggy night in a strange land under military occupation, gave us a rather eerie feeling. Fortunately we found a bus that took us to the heart of the city. Along the way the headlights showed grisly heaps of rubble and jagged walls of once beautiful buildings looming like specters out of the misty darkness. I shall never forget those first ghastly impressions of the overwhelming desolation brought by all-out war.

Arriving at the badly blasted *Bahnhof* area, we were directed to sleeping quarters by the billeting office. It meant a walk of some six or eight blocks through pitch-black rubble-strewn streets, but we were glad to have a room assigned to us in one of the hotels requisitioned by the military. Chaplain Katt located us there early the next morning. He saw to it that we were transferred to a better hotel and were provided with the credentials needed to move about in a country controlled by the Allied armies of occupation.

Our first appointment, arranged by Chaplain Katt, was a courtesy call on General Dwight D. Eisenhower at the Supreme Allied Headquarters Command, set up in the I. G. Farben Industrie building, which had not been bombed. What we had anticipated to be a somewhat formal three-minute call turned out to be a very pleasant chat of some 20 minutes. The general showed a keen interest in the purpose of our mission. He asked some very frank and penetrating questions, particularly concerning the attitude of the German church toward Nazi principles and what we felt we could accomplish in our dealings with German church leaders.

We gave him equally frank answers, and he commented freely on the role he felt the Church should play in the restoration of postwar Germany. We naturally felt highly honored to be given the privilege of meeting and conferring with this great military leader, who was soon slated to become an outstanding American president. We can well understand why to millions of Americans—and indeed to people the world over—"I Like Ike" was not a mere campaign slogan but a mark of genuine respect and admiration.

Before leaving, General Eisenhower told Chaplain Katt to be sure to take good care of us. And he surely did. With him we twice crisscrossed Germany, covering the American, British, and French occupation zones, twice taking the *Autobahn* to Berlin, deep in the Russian Zone, and once dipping down through the Alps to Geneva, Switzerland. In all we covered some 6,000 miles.

## Massed Misery

One of the first meetings we attended was at Gross-Oesingen, near Hannover in the British Zone. Here 19 pastors of the Lutheran Free Church—all except those in the Russian Zone—were having their first conference since the war. I know I have never attended a more touching pastoral conference. What stories we heard as they reported how the church had fared during the horrors of war! Some had only recently gotten home from military service. They spoke of the destruction and damage sustained by their churches and parsonages, of the heavy losses incurred by members, of the many who had fled before the Russian advance or were being dispossessed by communist authorities, of the difficulties they were having in finding and serving their scattered members.

Fortunately we had the privilege of making purchases at the army PX canteens, and the food and American "smokes" we had brought to the meeting served to inject a note of cheer into what otherwise would have been a most depressing occasion. While I was not a smoker myself, it was a real pleasure to see how these men enjoyed the cigars we had brought along from the States, how they puffed them down to a finger-scorching nub, and how quickly the box was down to its last Havana.

I shall never forget how heartened they were, and how profusely they thanked us when we assured them that our church would stand by them in their distress. Nor can I forget the remarks made by the now sainted Pastor Hermann Eikmeier when he stood before his fellow pastors and exhorted them to new heights of courage and faithfulness in serving their flocks and especially also the many refugees streaming in from the east. Though already a grizzled veteran of more than 70, he said: "I am determined to work harder now than I have ever worked in all my years in the ministry."[1]

A scene that was to haunt us everywhere we went in Germany was the vast number of refugees shuffling along roads and highways, some carrying babes in arms or leading small children, others pushing or pulling little carts or carrying bundles with whatever they had been able to save from the Soviets. In the cities we saw them in long queues waiting to receive a bowl of potato soup. Some would come from bunkers and rubble-filled basements with buckets and tin cans to scrounge through the cans of leavings near military kitchens. One cold evening, while passing through the roofless railroad station at Frankfurt, we saw several hundred of them in a corner huddled closely together in a solid mass trying to keep each other warm.

Obviously something had to be done—and very quickly—for the relief of these homeless, wandering, suffering thousands. But what to do and how to do it staggered the imagination. Not only was the entire economy disrupted, but the whole transportation and communication system was a shambles. Bombed and blown-up bridges lay crumpled in the rivers. Railroads, especially stations and junctions, were blasted into uselessness. Nothing even approaching a postal system existed.

## *Walking Miracle*

However, the *Hilfswerk* (Relief Operation), which had been initiated by the evangelical churches late in summer, was by this time beginning to function in many places. We saw *Hilfswerk* posters on poles and ruined buildings pleading for donations of potatoes and clothing.

In Stuttgart we looked up the *Hilfswerk* office and found it in a partially bombed building. The man in charge was a Lutheran

---

[1] Eikmeier's father Karl was a student of C. F. W. Walther in St. Louis.

clergyman, Dr. Eugen Gerstenmaier. This man, who more than any other was responsible for getting the miracle of the *Hilfswerk* in motion, was himself a walking miracle. He had been sentenced to die, but somehow was spared at the last moment. Later when American troops liberated the starving inmates of the concentration camp at Bayreuth, they found him at death's door. After two months in a hospital he recovered and at once threw all his energies into the task of reviving the spiritual and political life of his country.

His *Hilfswerk* headquarters, when we saw it, was indeed a sorry-looking place. Windows were out and walls scarred. While we were talking with him and the two or three others who then formed his "staff," a gust of wind blew down the door that had been placed against the opening to keep out the cold. The least we could do, we felt, was to offer him funds to make the place somewhat safer and more presentable.

Early in November we drove down to Geneva to meet with Dr. S. C. Michelfelder, executive secretary of the Lutheran World Federation, and also with Dr. W. A. Visser 't Hooft, general secretary of the World Council of Churches, in order to learn what their organizations were planning in the way of physical and spiritual relief. As we sat down to breakfast at our hotel the morning following our arrival, you can imagine our surprise when we saw Dr. Gerstenmaier at a nearby table. "What are you doing here?" we naturally asked, perhaps a bit too peremptorily. With a respectful glance at the officer's insignia of our military escort, Major Katt, he was careful to explain that he had full permission of the military authorities to cross the border and that he had come to Geneva to buy milk and medicines for war-orphaned and refugee children.

Over our breakfast Dr. Meyer and I discussed what we might do to help Dr. Gerstenmaier in his mercy mission. Surely, we agreed, it was for just such a cause as this that our church members had brought in their spontaneous gifts in the Peace Thankoffering. Rejoining him at his table, we informed him that in the name of the Missouri Synod we were giving his cause the sum of $100,000—one million marks according to the established rate of exchange. Never in all my days have I seen such a look of uncontrollable emotion as that which came over the face of Dr. Gerstenmaier. He was utterly overwhelmed. With tears flowing down his cheeks he gasped: "Why, that will save thousands of lives!"

In later years when we met Dr. Gerstenmaier in Germany or on official visits to our country, he told us repeatedly that it was this gift that really put the *Hilfswerk* on its feet. He also divulged that he had not used the money for food and medicine as he had originally planned, but had rather purchased raw materials so that people could be put to work manufacturing relief articles for themselves. By doing this he had been able to triple or even quadruple the value of the gift and at the same time provide help of a more permanent nature. Such purposeful planning was characteristic of this dedicated man. Small wonder that when the Adenauer government came into power in West Germany, Dr. Gerstenmaier was named president of the Bundestag, a post in which he has served ever since.

## *Wonder in Hannover*

From Geneva we headed northeast through the heart of the great Alps, which gave us opportunity to see such famed peaks as the *Jungfrau* and *Mönch*. Truly a land of breathtaking beauty! However, I recall a remark once made by Dr. Pfotenhauer in recommending that the next time I got to western Canada I should by all means see the Canadian Rockies. "They surpass the Alps," he told me. On one of my trips to the Alberta-British Columbia District some of the brethren took the opportunity to show me "God's country," as they called it, and drove me from Jasper to Lake Louise and on to Emerald Lake. From what I saw I must say that I concur in the opinion of my predecessor. To be honest, as I recall the stunning grandeur of Glacier National Park, or Yellowstone, or the Tetons, or the Mount Hood-Mount Shasta-Mount Rainier area of the Northwest, I don't have the slightest hesitancy about personally endorsing the slogan "See America First!"

Driving north to pick up the *Autobahn* to Berlin again took us into the British Zone, where we stopped at Hannover. Here we saw one of the minor miracles of the war—a church that had escaped damage in one of the most heavily bombed parts of the city. It belonged to one of our Free Church congregations. Coming to the section where it was located, we found the streets almost impassable. "Verboten" signs were posted on the corners. Pushing ahead through bomb craters and rubble, we saw at the next intersection a big sign reading in German "Dangerous to Life." No explanation was needed. Cracked and jagged walls loomed precariously along the street, ready to come tumbling down at any disturbance. But there stood the church almost untouched. Someone told us it had been hit by an incendiary bomb, but several men happened to be there at the time and were able quickly to extinguish it.

At Helmstedt we entered the Russian Zone. Driving eastward, it seemed to us that each city we came to had been hit harder than the last and that Berlin was worst of all. In the divided German capital we first went to see Dr. P. H. Petersen, president of the Evangelical Lutheran Free Church. His beautiful church in Berlin-Steglitz had been almost totally destroyed, and the congregation worshiped in a hall owned by a congregation of the Lutheran *Landeskirche*.

Dr. Petersen invited me to preach to his flock on the next Sunday. It was early November, just past Reformation Day (October 31) and near Luther's birthday (November 10), so I decided to preach a Reformation sermon. Seldom have I had a more attentive audience. Small wonder! For we were the first fellow believers from the United States to worship with them in many a long year. Before the war Lutheran tourists and visitors from America had attended services there quite often.

In Berlin I also wanted to visit Dr. Heinrich Willkomm, the president of the Free Church seminary at suburban Zehlendorf. But the seminary, which had also sustained heavy bomb damage, happened to be in the Russian sector. Lacking the proper entrance visa, I hesitated to cross into the Soviet Zone, lest I be placed under detention. So our escorting chaplain drove over in an Army jeep and brought Dr. Willkomm out.

We had a wonderful two-hour visit sitting there in the jeep. We spoke mainly of the situation of the Free Church in the East Zone and its future welfare. We also discussed the future of the seminary and how best to safeguard its excellent library, which had been spared in the bombing. Dr. Willkomm naturally inquired about his sister in America, the wife of Pastor George Naumann, and her family, and asked me to convey to them his warmest greetings.

## *Hitler on a Bicycle*

While driving us to and around Berlin, Mike, Chaplain Katt's aid, liked to bring up a favorite GI topic: whether Adolf Hitler was still alive. Mike had pretty well convinced himself that the Nazi dictator had given the Soviet army the slip and several times made the joking remark that any day he expected to see old Adolf come riding along the street on a bicycle.

While we were parked on a main street in Berlin one day and waiting for Chaplain Katt to pick up some films, along came a man with a flapping coat, a furtive air, and a toothbrush mustache, pedaling away on a bicycle. "Mike," I said, "here comes your Hitler!" Mike stared hard and long before deciding against becoming the war's No. 1 hero by tackling the hapless Berliner and marching him, bike and all, down to headquarters.

While visiting Dr. Petersen one day I inquired whether any pastors of the Breslau Synod, another of the German Free Churches, happened to live in Berlin. He mentioned several of them and agreed to invite them over so that I could meet them. Arriving for our little gathering in Dr. Willkomm's apartment, we found four of the Breslau Synod men on hand, including Dr. Friedrich Grube and Dr. Matthias Schulz. Both held official positions in their body.

It was a pleasure to be able to tell them that our church in America would be happy to supply with much-needed German books any of their pastors whose libraries had been lost or ruined through bombings. In the course of our conversation I asked the leaders of these two confessional bodies a forthright question: Since both were free churches, which held to the Lutheran Confessions, why did they not sit down together and try to reach doctrinal agreement? I knew that in the past they had had a number of sharp disagreements.

My question at once was given long and thoughtful discussion. Later I was able to discern that the Lord had His own purpose in view when He led me to ask it. Before I left them that day, they agreed to make arrangements for mutual talks for the purpose of seeking doctrinal concord on the basis of Holy Writ and the Lutheran Confessions.

This story had an even happier sequel. Some two years later God had blessed the conversations of the two churches to the point where they had declared themselves in full doctrinal accord, and they were joining hands to open a seminary at Gross-Oesingen in temporary barracks that our church helped them acquire with relief funds. That summer I happened to be in West Germany with Dr. Martin Graebner for a series of theological conferences arranged in the interest of establishing closer ties with the evangelical churches. It was only fitting and proper, the committee of the two cooperating churches insisted, that I should preach for the seminary dedication and the installation of its first faculty, made up of two instructors from each church body.

Dr. Walter Günther, president of the Breslau Synod, and Dr. Heinrich Stallmann, acting president of the Free Church, assisted at the installation. It was an occasion of genuine joy. After the service a deeply moved Dr. Günther pressed my hand and said, "I thank God that He permitted me to see this day." A few years later this theological institution was transplanted to Oberursel, near Frankfurt, where we found it possible to buy a piece of land with suitable buildings. Since that time the Oberursel school has trained about 100 young pastors for service in the German Free Churches, and some also in the *Landeskirchen.*

## *Surprise in Munich*

From Berlin we dropped down to Munich, which had also been heavily bombed. There we saw Chaplain Henry F. Gerecke, who not long after gained renown as the "Nuremberg chaplain" who ministered to the Protestants among the Nazi "war criminals" during the Nuremberg trials. Chaplain Gerecke took us to visit the Bavarian *Landesbischof,* Dr. Hans Meiser, a man whom I learned to know more intimately a few years later when he and Mrs. Meiser visited us several days at our home in Oak Park. The day I met him in Munich Dr. Meiser was quite insistent that I come to one of the still intact church halls, since the local clergy had planned a little welcome for me.

When I arrived with Chaplain Gerecke and Rev. Hartwig Dierks, then pastor of the Lutheran Service Center at Frankfurt, imagine my astonishment to be greeted by an assembly of no less than 50 pastors, a choir that sang beautifully, and an address in classic German by none other than the bishop himself. To add to my consternation, I was called on for a response, which of course had to be given in my Texas and Missouri brand of German. I am sure they understood me, however, and I appreciated the opportunity to explain the purpose of our visit, to offer a word of Christian sympathy and encouragement, and to tell them of our Synod's interest and intention to aid in the physical and spiritual rehabilitation of their ravaged land.

I took occasion also to tell these pastors of our church's conviction that the Bible in all its parts is indeed the inspired Word of God. I added the plea that they, too, should insist on sound Scriptural doctrine in the face of the efforts of Reformed and liberalistic groups to involve them in a union without unity. Dr. Meiser rose to say that he had often heard about the Missouri Synod's insistence on orthodoxy but that it had generally been pictured as a dead and sterile orthodoxy. This stricture, he stated, he now knew to be completely groundless; we had demonstrated that orthodoxy can be very much alive and active in deeds of love.

Our visit to Dr. Meiser's office on a cold and windy November 19 was another unforgettable experience. The building showed heavy bomb damage, and bone-chilling cold penetrated even the bishop's small office. We sat shivering in spite of our heavy overcoats. I can still see Chaplain Katt feeding a chunk of the rationed wood into the stove, though the little heater was plainly unequal to the battle. Our conversation, however, was warm and cordial, filled with deep concern for the cause of sound Lutheranism. Together with Dr. Meiser, taking a lively part in the discussion, were two of his faithful advisers, Dr. Wilhelm Bogner and Dr. Christian Stoll. As we bade these men farewell, Dr. Bogner placed his arm on my shoulders and said with deep earnestness: *"Herr Präsident,* you have my assurance: I will fight for conservative Lutheranism."

Only a few months later we learned that both Dr. Bogner and Dr. Stoll were killed instantly in a collision with an American military truck. Their tragic loss was certainly a heavy blow to the cause of conservative Lutheranism. I somehow cannot but feel that the Lutheran scene in Europe would be vastly improved today if these two stalwarts could have continued their fight for confessional Lutheranism during those critical years.

## *Godsend from the PX*

Our stop at the old university town of Erlangen was one we eagerly looked forward to, since the theological department at the university had the reputation of being one of the strongest and most conservative in Europe. We were especially anxious to meet Drs. Hermann Sasse and Werner Elert, two of the faculty's outstanding theologians.

We found only the Sasse family at home. The older son, Wolfgang, just 16, had just been released from a prisoner of war camp. Hans, the younger son, was then an alert and lively boy of nine, who at the time had developed the uncanny ability of being able to identify by make and model all the various vehicles being used by the American Army. An American officer had given him a cast-off tire, which he pretended was his official car until one day it got away from him and rolled off the river bank into deep water. He showed us the historical marker he had erected to mark the scene of the disaster. Both younger Sasses are now scholars in their own right, having earned PhD degrees at the University of Adelaide in Australia. Both have done graduate work in our country on fellowships from Eastern universities.

The Sasses gave us a most cordial welcome. Frau Sasse quickly prepared afternoon coffee (*Ersatzkaffee*, faux coffee of course, for which she offered profuse apologies), while the genial doctor soon had us deep in a discussion on the state of the Church and current doctrinal issues. Conversation inevitably turned to the doctrine of the Holy Scripture.

Dr. Sasse knew our Missouri position on verbal inspiration. What seemed to bother him more than anything else was the term "verbal inspiration." "One should find a happier expression for it," he remarked. His concern was that so many immediately wanted to equate verbal with mechanical inspiration. Our Synod of course has always rejected any view that would reduce inspiration to a mere mechanical level. We reminded Dr. Sasse of the explanation of verbal inspiration given by Dr. Pieper in his *Christian Dogmatics,* and with this he voiced agreement.

Before going to Erlangen we used our PX privileges to purchase a big box of groceries for delivery at the Sasse home. What joy and expressions of gratitude to God and to us greeted the arrival of this box! The two boys jumped and skipped with pleasure as they feasted their eyes on goodies they had not tasted in weeks and months.

I was able to get in a visit with Dr. Elert on another trip through Erlangen. I enjoyed a lengthy theological conversation with him, though I must admit that he did most of the talking, while I was a good listener. From a number of questions he asked about the Missouri Synod it was evident that he had gotten some incorrect information and had drawn some wrong conclusions. Some of these wrong impressions, I am happy to say, I was able to clear up for him. To the delight of the Elerts and our own great joy in seeing their happy faces we also bade them *auf Wiedersehen* with a well-filled box of PX provisions.

### *All-Texas Table*

While our mission to Europe had been undertaken largely in the interest of bringing spiritual aid, every day it became more apparent that the most immediate need was for physical relief. Tens of thousands were sure to perish of hunger, disease, and exposure that winter if steps were not taken immediately to stem the tide of human misery with vast quantities of relief materials of every kind. After talking the matter over with a number of chaplains, we came to the decision that I should fly back to the US without delay—two weeks earlier than originally planned—in order to seek an audience with President Harry S. Truman to urge that channels for charity and relief effort be opened up to the churches of our country.

Homeward bound on the train from Frankfurt to Paris to catch an Air Force plane to the States, I closed what were no doubt the seven most eventful weeks of my life on a "small world" note. I happened to be the only civilian on the train. When I entered the diner, the only place available was at a table occupied by three colonels. They naturally wanted to know all about me, who I was, how I got there, what I was doing. When I mentioned, among other things, that I had been a pastor in Houston for 29 years, all three announced that they hailed from Texas too, one from Austin, one from Dallas, and one from Houston. And the Houston man, after asking about the location of my church, recalled: "Sure, I've been there and heard you preach, once for a funeral and again for a wedding." From that moment the atmosphere at our all-Texas table warmed appreciably.

Only a few hours later our big transport plane put down in New York. As I stood once more on our shores amid scenes of peace, plenty, and prosperity, all that I had seen and experienced seemed to return to my mind with new and crushing force. I arrived home among my dear ones just a few days after Thanksgiving Day. The family waited until my arrival to welcome me with a good old American Thanksgiving feast. As we sat down to a table heaped with all the "trimmings" of a typical American Thanksgiving, the scenes I had witnessed of human woe and want were still much too recent and too vivid for me to enjoy it. I just couldn't eat.

### *Help from the White House*

I received an appointment with President Truman at the White House on December 14, again arranged through the kind offices of Herbert Waltke. Dr. Meyer had flown in from Europe earlier in the day and joined us in Washington for the 30-minute interview. The president received us most graciously and showed a marked interest as we unfolded our story and laid before him our request that our church and others be permitted to extend the hand of Christian charity to our late enemies.

The president, who himself had seen the indescribable misery that prevailed in devastated Germany, assured us that he would do all that he could to facilitate relief efforts. It seems we were the first church body to present a direct appeal, although as the dire need in the war-torn lands became more generally known, other church groups, too, entered pleas for an opportunity to undertake relief measures.

Within a few months most restrictions were lifted, and it became possible to mail parcels of food, clothing, and medicines first to the American Zone and later to practically any destination in Europe. How it made my heart swell to witness the wonderful response of our good people, who poured in an increasing volume of gifts into Europe's battle against hunger and despair over the next few years! Our Emergency Planning Council office in St. Louis was deluged by thousands of letters of tearful thanksgiving from people who received help, often in the nick of time, from Missouri Synod Lutherans. No one will ever know how many lives were saved by these gifts, nor what a tremendous impact this evidence of love made on our former enemies.

*{Chapter Eight}*

# THEOLOGICAL MISSION— EUROPE 1947–57

CONDITIONS WERE GROWING noticeably brighter when I got back to Germany two years later, although the previous winter had still been one of widespread suffering and privation. The problem of caring for the 13 million refugees besides several million war wounded, widows, and orphans was still tremendous, and the need for life's necessities, especially housing, was still acute.

My 1947 mission was to strengthen the cause of confessional Lutheranism in Germany. The previous summer Synod's *Praesidium* had asked Dr. Frederick E. Mayer, professor of systematic theology at the St. Louis seminary, to go to Europe as a kind of theological goodwill ambassador to continue contacts and foster closer relations with both the Free Churches and the territorial churches. He had the opportunity to address the theological faculties and student bodies at the German universities concerning doctrinal issues facing the Church in that time of disillusionment. He naturally used these occasions also to set forth the Biblical theology championed by the Missouri Synod and its sister churches. Dr. Mayer reported that he was warmly received and that he was asked many questions that betokened deep interest in Lutheranism in America.

To follow up these contacts, it was decided that a commission of two, Dr. Martin Graebner, professor at our St. Paul, Minnesota, Concordia, and I should meet with groups of pastors and church officials in various sections of Germany, not only to discuss doctrinal issues but also to offer them some of the theological books published by our church. Hundreds of pastors had lost their libraries along with their other belongings and were unable to purchase more, even if they had been available. Dr. Mayer had worked out the itinerary for us, which turned out to be rather strenuous. We appeared before quite a number of large conferences as well as at several mass meetings. Dr. Graebner, who wielded a forceful German, was particularly effective in his presentations.

### *Walther Returns to Germany*

On this trip we had a number of unforgettable experiences. One that impressed me in particular happened at Nuremberg, where I spoke to some 50 pastors of the Bavarian Church. I had just offered them some of our books, notably Dr. Walther's *Law and Gospel* and Dr. Pieper's *Christian Dogmatics,* when one of the older men got up to speak. "Brethren," he said, as closely as I recall his words, "I already have *Law and Gospel.* I have now read it through twice. Every evening after my family has retired I sit down and treat myself to the pleasure of perusing another chapter. Brethren, my sermons have taken on an altogether new character since I have been doing this. I can assure you that the Missouri Synod had something 75 years ago that we need in Germany right now."

To hear that spontaneous and straightforward testimonial surely thrilled my heart and crystallized anew in me the resolve to commend the study of Walther's classic to our own clergy more earnestly than ever. Concordia Publishing House has again reprinted Dr. Dau's translation of the Walther classic in English. It would be tragic if through sheer neglect such priceless treasures of our own heritage should be lost to us.

One morning, driving with Dr. Graebner and Pastor Hermann Eikmeier to Hannover, where I was scheduled to preach at a refugee camp, we had a flat tire. Shortly after changing this, we had a blowout. Somehow we had to get another tire. But how to manage this there in the British Zone without "inside" help of some kind had us stumped. Then we remembered that Rev. Horace H. Erdman, executive secretary of Synod's Ontario District, was in that area as a representative of the Canadian Christian Council and was helping to screen refugees for resettlement in Canada.

Dr. Graebner decided to walk to the nearest telephone—a good two miles away—to enlist his aid. Meanwhile Pastor Eikmeier and I waited patiently in the car. As the hour crept past noon, Pastor Eikmeier said that he had brought a lunch along and offered to share it with me. Assuring me that he could always get more if necessary—which I seriously doubted—he apologetically produced a few pieces of *Schwarzbrot* and two shriveled apples. I have had many a dinner and banquet invitation in my day, but none, I can assure you, has touched me more deeply than this one did. And few, I may add, have I eaten with greater relish. Incidentally, Dr. Graebner succeeded in reaching Pastor Erdman, and before too long we had our tire and were on our way again.

## *Counsel for the Bishop*

Another incident that often comes to mind was the time the *Landesbischof* of Bavaria and his official staff called on us for pastoral counsel. The problem troubling Bishop Meiser and his associates at the time concerned the large number of refugees affiliated with Reformed churches in the East who were settling in Bavaria and were now requesting the privilege of Holy Communion in the Lutheran churches. The fact that there were so many of these people raised the problem to emergency proportions, and apparently both pastors and officials were quite perplexed over how best to handle it.

A solution suggested itself when Dr. Graebner and I learned that the Bavarian churches still had the fine Lutheran custom of conducting special confessional services for those attending Communion—a practice I have always strongly recommended to our own congregations. We suggested that they advise the pastors to use each of the confessional services to set forth fully and clearly the distinctive Lutheran teaching of the real presence of Christ's body and blood in the Sacrament and then very frankly to announce to the refugees that if they sincerely accepted and believed this doctrine, they could be permitted to attend the Lord's Table. If, however, they did not accept this truth, the privilege of receiving the Lord's Supper at Lutheran altars would have to be denied them.

Bishop Meiser thanked us sincerely, and we gathered that they considered it sound advice. However, I never heard whether they followed it and have often wondered whether the solution we proposed turned out to be the answer to their dilemma.

Almost from the outset of our 1947 trip it became evident that if our purpose of helping conserve and strengthen confessional Lutheranism was to be realized, a more effective approach would be needed than the brief appearances we were making that year. After consulting with Dr. Lawrence Meyer, who also went back to Europe that fall to survey our church's rather extensive relief operations, we came to the conclusion that we should propose holding free theological conferences. While Dr. Graebner and I were carrying out our speaking schedule, Dr. Meyer undertook the task of presenting our proposal to leaders of both the *Landeskirchen* and the Free Churches.

Assured of their approval and cooperation, he at once set about expediting plans to hold a doctrinal seminar of at least a month's duration the following summer. He had a formidable job on his hands. To make arrangements not only for an effective program but also for a meeting place, transportation, housing, food, etc., for a sizable group in the sorely dislocated and impoverished Germany of that day posed some real problems.

## *Spa for Theology*

However, Dr. Meyer soon had committees hard at work. Happily, Dr. Karl Arndt, a son of Synod's first missionary to China, had been named chief of religious affairs in the US Military Government at the time and was able to render our committees invaluable help. We rented the facilities of Bad Boll, a health spa in the foothills of the Swabian Alps, some 40 miles south of Stuttgart, for the 1948 meetings and continued to hold our free conferences at Bad Boll for several years. Thus the name "Bad Boll Conferences" became the usual designation for all subsequent meetings of this kind, even though in later years they were held in various other places.

The committee decided that each conference should consist of a nine-day series of three sessions daily. All the topics, taken from the Augsburg Confession, were to be presented by an essayist and a co-essayist, one from the Missouri Synod, the other from one of the German churches. Since facilities were limited, the heads of the various territorial and Free Churches selected the pastors and professors who were to attend each session.

The Missouri delegation at the first Bad Boll meeting, which opened June 23, 1948, consisted of Drs. Walter A. Baepler, Paul M. Bretscher, Alfred O. Fuerbringer, Theodore Graebner, Frederick Mayer, Lawrence Meyer, and I. It was my privilege to have the opening and closing sermons, to conduct the morning devotions, and to preside at the sessions. Attendances at the three sessions were 110, 79, and 120. Some pastors, especially in the East Zone, found it impossible to accept their invitations. Others hesitated to make the trip because they feared the possible dire effects of currency reforms instituted by the military government just at that time.

Judging by the high level of interest on the part of all concerned and the many genuine expressions of appreciation over blessings received, I can only call the meetings an unqualified success. Bishops Hans Meiser of Bavaria, Julius Bender of Baden, and the venerable Theophil Wurm of Wuerttemberg attended part time; also a number of Lutheran chaplains and officials of the National Lutheran Council attended. Dr. S. E. Engstrom, an Augustana Synod man on the NLC staff, was especially enthusiastic and informed me that he would do his best to arrange a conference of this kind among the Lutherans of America.[1] The presentations were scholarly and stimulating and the discussions lively. Among the essayists were some of the finest theological minds in Europe, including Dr. Werner Elert of Erlangen, Drs. Edmund Schlink and Peter Brunner of Heidelberg, Drs. Adolf Koeberle and Helmut Thielicke of Tübingen, Dr. Eugen Gerstenmaier and his brother Ernst. Though our Missouri essayists in all humility wondered whether they were measuring up, there is no question whatever that all turned in excellent work.

## *In the American Manner*

The evening programs were designed to give the German churchmen an insight into the practical side of Church life in America. Our

---

[1] See the section, *Confessional Priority*, in chapter thirteen, pages 158–60.

talks, many of them presented with visual aids, stirred a great deal of interest, at least judging from the barrage of questions fired at us. Without going into details, I should explain that congregational activities in the German churches are markedly different from ours in America. This difference stems chiefly from the fact that the *Landeskirchen* are supported by tax moneys. The government levies a church tax, which everyone is required to pay unless he officially registers with the authorities as one who has renounced his church membership. Few ever do this, since it is tantamount to declaring oneself an atheist or unbeliever. Consequently, almost all consider themselves church members, whether they attend church or not; the church is required to carry their names on its rolls and to serve them whenever they request it. Even those who with some degree of regularity attend services can by no stretch of the imagination be called active members.

Hence our German friends at the Bad Boll meetings were rather astonished over our American manner of raising funds for our congregational work, our many mission activities, our parish schools, and pastor- and teacher-training schools. Very few seemed to have a grasp of the practical applications of the doctrine of Christian stewardship. Even the term "stewardship" was new to most (they usually adopted our English word when speaking on the subject). Also such familiar American institutions as the Sunday school, vacation Bible school, organized youth work, adult Bible classes, and evangelism committees were quite foreign to them.

For a few years after the war there was growing sentiment in favor of loosening the ties binding the church to the state. Several movements, led especially by the younger clergy, were started with just such reforms in view. Also Dr. Frank Northam, treasurer of the World Council of Churches, strongly urged such a step. However, Bishop Hanns Lilje of the Evangelical Church of Hannover took quick issue with the proposal, stating that the church tax system "best suits the *volkskirchlichen* (people's church) concept of both (Evangelical [Protestant] and Roman Catholic) confessions. From the organizational viewpoint it is the most economical, because the state largely bears the cost of the work of administration." One can well understand why ecclesiastical officialdom would take this view, but one must also seriously question any kind of church polity that, while it may bring in the money, can only result in indifference and inactivity on the part of the vast majority of church members.

An unforgettable feature at each Bad Boll session was known as the *"geselliger Abend,"* a kind of ministerial "amateur talent hour." For years these men had had little opportunity for any kind of social life or activities, and they were more than willing to work up an evening's program. The singing, instrumental music, dramatizations, addresses, and original poetry, both humorous and serious, were great. To me it was a marvel that these people, who had for years experienced so much anguish, woe, and privation, could still retain such a keen sense of humor. A number of their stories reflected the growing East-West tension of the time, as, for example, a story about a little dog that somehow stuck in my mind.

It seems that one night a thin, scrawny dog from the East sneaked across the border to the West Zone, where he was soon confronted by several sleek dogs of the West.

"What do you want here?" they growled at him. "You just want to fill up on our food."

*"Ach, nee,"* whimpered the little Red Dog, "I just wanted to hear myself bark once."

## *Cigarette Magic*

Four East Zone pastors managed to come to Bad Boll by crossing the border *schwarz,* as they said. That is, they slipped across without passes. While they certainly appreciated the good, plentiful food and the doctrinal discussions and fellowship with their separated brethren, they were quite worried about getting back home without serious consequences. Once again I made use of my PX privileges and gave each of them two packages of American cigarettes. Thus armed, they assured me, they would have no trouble whatever.

The magic of the little American cigarette in those early postwar years was certainly uncanny. A tip of two cigarettes assured one of courtesies and service far beyond the call of duty.

Once when we slipped a policeman two cigarettes for giving us road information, I noticed how carefully he stowed them away, saying, "One I shall smoke tonight, the other I shall save for Sunday."

In 1945 when we were returning from Berlin, the Russian border guards at the Helmstedt checkpoint would not let us through even though our papers were all properly drawn up in English, German, and Russian. Either these men could not read, or else they pretended that there was something wrong with the documents. At any rate, as soon as our driver flashed a package of cigarettes, the road gate was lifted immediately.

The Bad Boll conferences were continued annually for a full decade, with the exception of 1952, when the Lutheran World Federation held its third assembly at Hannover. Vice-President Herman A. Harms served as the representative of Synod's *Praesidium* at all except the 1948 and 1957 conferences. Since the latter was the tenth anniversary year, I was asked to return to help observe the occasion. In more recent years the European conferences have been held every two years.

I cannot put into words all that has been accomplished and is still being accomplished through these free conferences. Year after year the papers and discussions centered attention on vital theological truths. The focus was always on the Holy Scriptures and the historic Lutheran Confessions. Our church not only brought its testimony to bear on every issue but also made its witness felt. Throughout Europe and far beyond, the Missouri Synod came to be known—and appreciated—as a church that unflinchingly upheld high and soundly Lutheran confessional standards. I am convinced that hundreds of pastors and their flocks, especially those curtained off in East Germany, struggling amid the demoralizing effects of doctrinal confusion and political uncertainty in the postwar period, received untold encouragement and renewed strength from these very conferences. If expressions of gratitude and wholehearted appreciation are any criterion, then certainly the Missouri-sponsored free conferences must be scored as a success.

*{Chapter Nine}*

# EXPERIENCE OF A LIFETIME

O<small>F ALL THE SWIFT CHANGES</small> I have lived to see, none amazes me quite as much as the way our planet has shrunk in just a handful of years. Had anyone, even as late as the 30s, suggested (they didn't, of course) that I would ever get to Europe, or see the Holy Land, or visit Australia and the Orient, or even our neighbor continent of South America, I would certainly have considered him the wildest kind of visionary. But it all happened, and I am grateful to God that He permitted me to store a "world view" among my treasured memories.

My visit to the Holy Land came quite by accident. When in 1953 the Lutheran Laymen's League travel bureau, directed by T. G. Eggers, arranged its first tour to the Holy Land, plans called for Rev. Armin C. Oldsen, then the regular Lutheran Hour speaker, to accompany the tour as pastoral counselor. For reasons of health, however, Pastor Oldsen felt obliged to resign as Lutheran Hour speaker and also to withdraw from the tour.[1] Just before the Houston convention Mr. Eggers extended a surprise invitation to Mrs. Behnken and me to be guests of the LLL on this thrilling tour.

Busy as I was with convention preparations, the very prospect of such an opportunity excited the imagination. Our children shared our elation, and they, like everyone else who heard about it, urged us by all means to accept. I "owed it to myself," they said, to take a good, long vacation trip after the strenuous demands of a convention.

After the convention we stayed in Texas for the first reunion with my brothers and sisters and their families in many years. Since all our children and grandchildren were together, we remained a few more

---

[1] Pastor Oldsen followed Walter A. Maier and preceded Oswald C. J. Hoffmann as Lutheran Hour speaker.

days for a glorious visit with them. During this time I had a chance to go over the itinerary and do a little preparing for the tour. My assignment included having daily devotions with the tour group and special services on the four Sundays. In preparing for this assignment, the deeper I delved into the Bible record of the places we would visit, the more fascinated I grew with my task, and the more enthusiastic I became.

I shall not regale readers with descriptions and details of all we saw and did. In recent years, I realize that trips to the Holy Land have become somewhat commonplace, and the chances are that practically everyone interested enough to read this will by this time have listened to more than one account, complete with pictures or movie films, by friends or relatives who have been there. None, I am sure, however, will want to deprive me of the pleasure of making a few personal observations on what both my wife and I considered one of our grandest experiences.

## *Puzzle at St. Peter's*

On our first Sunday we happened to be in Rome. In our service, held at the hotel, we recalled the past glory of the "Eternal City," still evident in the ruins we had seen, and the important part the city had played in the life of St. Paul and the early Christian Church. Before the service Mr. and Mrs. Eggers, with my wife and me, decided to go back to St. Peter's, the largest and without doubt the most beautiful church in the world, to see a celebration of the Mass. We timed our visit for 8 o'clock, expecting that at this hour there would be a fairly large attendance. It came as quite a surprise, therefore, to see in that immense edifice at most 250 people, including a goodly number of visitors. There were many altars, yet only six were being used. The officiants were in full regalia at all the altars except two. At these the altar boys were wearing only what we would call T-shirts and shorts. To this day I don't know how to account for this startling bit of Low

Church style in the very citadel of ecclesiastical pomp. Had I not seen it myself, I would not believe it.[2]

At historic Athens, as we viewed remnants of "the grandeur that was Greece" in the storied ruins of the Acropolis, I certainly wasn't going to miss the chance to stand where the apostle Paul stood on Mars Hill when he delivered his powerful address to the Athenian philosophers (Acts 17). In my tour preparations, it seems, I had neglected my hill-climbing training, for I found the slopes of the famed hill almost too rugged for me. With the kind help of Pastor Carl J. Schuette, a fellow tourist, I finally made it, and both of us relished the experience of standing on what was reputed to be the selfsame spot from which the apostle delivered his stirring Mars Hill address.

The few days we spent in and around Cairo were just at the time of the Nile Festival. The mighty Nile was almost at flood stage, and we came to a fuller appreciation of how much this land of drought and desert, which once supported the mighty kingdoms of the Pharaohs, depended on the waters of the river. We saw something of old Egypt's long-departed glory on our visit to the Tutankhamen Museum. And, of course, we took the inevitable camel ride out to see the great pyramids and the Sphinx.

From Beirut, the very modern capital of Lebanon, the Eggers took us on a side trip to the site of the ancient Mediterranean cities of Tyre and Sidon. Here amid a rather incongruous scene—the construction of an ultramodern oil refinery with huge pipelines snaking across the desert hills and out to tankers offshore—we recalled the tender story of the "woman of great faith" who in that place encountered the Savior, pleading in her great need only for the crumbs that fell from the Master's table.

## *Up to Jerusalem*

To see the still thriving cedars of Lebanon and the remarkable ruins of the ancient heathen temples at Baalbek on the way to

---

[2] The term "Low Church" comes from Anglican circles, meaning a very simple, unadorned, and evangelical style in contradistinction to the pomp and ceremony of "High Church."

Damascus was marvelous, but not to be compared with walking down the "street called Straight" in the world's oldest inhabited city. Here newly converted Saul of Tarsus once surely walked, and the wayside chapel we visited on the Damascus Road may well mark the authentic site of his miraculous conversion. In my sermon at our hotel service—this was our second Sunday—I preached on the question in Acts 9:6 (KJV) that marked such a tremendous turning point in the career of Paul and, indeed, in the history of the Church and the world: "Lord, what wilt Thou have me to do?"

Once we had entered the Holy Land proper, trailing by car caravan over the mountain pass through which Moses very likely led the wandering Israelites to the border of the land "flowing with milk and honey," thrill followed thrill in eager succession. We stopped at the Jordan (somehow I had expected a much larger river), at the Dead Sea (salty but not silty and murky as I had pictured it), and at the site of old Jericho in the hot, almost tropical valley, some 1,200 feet below sea level.

On the ascent to Jerusalem, which lies at an elevation of some 4,500 feet, some recalled such expressions of the Savior as, "Behold, we go *up* to Jerusalem," and in the parable of the Good Samaritan, "A certain man went *down* from Jerusalem to Jericho."

### *Where Jesus Walked*

Crossing the so-called neutral zone between the Israeli and Arab sectors of the city, we observed that it was widely bomb and shell pocked and that there were heavily armed guards on both sides—a cruel reminder that war's unholy curse still hangs heavily over a land that is called holy by the millions of adherents of three major faiths, Christian, Jew, and Muslim.

How wonderful, however, was the undeniable feeling of inner peace as we walked the way the Savior walked and reverently contemplated the scenes at which He won our peace with God and an everlasting inheritance in heaven's glory—the Upper Room, the Brook Kidron, Gethsemane, Pilate's Judgment Hall, the Via Dolorosa, Calvary, the Holy Sepulcher, and Bethany, the place of His ascension.

To be sure, there was also our pilgrimage to the "little town of Bethlehem," nestled on a hillside six miles south of the Holy City. The commercialism, traditionalism, ecclesiastical trappings, as well as the squalor evident in the Arab-held town, have a rude way of disturbing the romantic picture we may have built up concerning the Savior's birthplace. But filing into the subterranean grotto where, we are told, the manger once stood can still be a moving experience. Undoubtedly it is as close as we shall ever come to the actual scene of the Nativity.

The shepherds' fields, however, are still there, real and natural and authentic, and it is not too difficult to picture them ablaze with the glory of the Lord and echoing with angelic music as they did when the awestricken shepherds took part in the first Christmas service. We could picture the shepherds, too, stumbling in the darkness over the rough ground as they came "with haste" to find the Babe wrapped in swaddling clothes and lying in a manger.

## *Church-free Galilee*

The Sea of Galilee, too, is still to be seen in all its wonderful natural beauty. Some of us took a launch trip on the lake, and I remember that, midway across, one of the ladies remarked: "Here at last we have an authentic spot over which no one was able to build a church." We could understand why Jesus often sought the shores of lovely, though at times treacherously stormy, Galilee. We remembered His many crossings of the sea, His walking on its waters, His seaside sermons and miracles, particularly the two great catches of fish told in Luke 5 and John 21.

Arriving at the town of Tiberias, we found a delectable fish dinner awaiting us. The fish, we were told, had been caught in the sea that morning. By stretching our imaginations somewhat we could think of our tasty trout as lineal offspring of some who figured in the Bible miracles, perhaps even of that particular fish whose mouth held the piece of money that Peter used to pay his own and his Master's taxes (Matthew 17).

Our stop at the Sea of Galilee was certainly one of the tour's highlights. But we had to hurry on to make Tel Aviv by evening. I noticed that our fellow tourists turned again and again for a last lingering look at the sea. At beautiful and very modern Tel Aviv we had our last open-air devotion in the Holy Land. Once again we lifted up our eyes unto the hills. I spoke of old Mount Carmel, lifting its head above the blue Mediterranean, of Mount Tabor, which we had seen that afternoon, of Caesarea, the coastal town, also brimming with sacred history. I again stressed especially—since there were a goodly number of Jewish people listening—how much it meant to us to visit the places where our Savior and Lord had lived and suffered and died for us and risen again to make us His own forever.

Together we thanked God for all we had seen and heard, for His gracious protection along the many miles we had come. Wrapped in our prayers also was the wish all of us had again and again expressed during those thrilling weeks: that our fellow Christians at home might someday also share that privilege.

*{Chapter Ten}*

# CEMENTING AUSTRALIAN TIES

M‍Y TRIP TO AUSTRALIA really started with a rumor. In 1955 I received an urgent invitation from our sister church in Australia to attend its convention to be held in the early part of 1956. I informed them that this would be out of the question; we would be tied down with preparations for our own convention in St. Paul, Minnesota. Then by all means come after the convention, they urged in their reply.

Our brethren in Australia had been hearing strange rumors about our Synod that were quite disturbing to them, they explained. They had also read in certain periodicals from America a number of statements and predictions that "Missouri" would soon be relaxing its former position and moving out into the mainstream of world Lutheranism. That, they felt, could only mean moving into the orbit of the Lutheran World Federation, a move that they feared would indicate that Missouri was inclined to pull away from her old doctrinal moorings.

## *Lutherans in the Antipodes*

To understand the deep concern of the Australian brethren we need to recall a bit of their church's history. About the same time that many of our synodical fathers left Germany to free themselves from the crass liberalism then rampant in the church of their homeland, several groups also emigrated to Australia for the same reason. Already in the early years a rift developed in this small band of colonists over the question of the millennium and a number of other points of doctrine. As a result of the split two Lutheran bodies developed side by side in the Commonwealth of Australia. Today they are known as the Evangelical Lutheran Church of Australia (ELCA), which for some 80 years has been in fellowship with our Synod, and the United Evangelical Lutheran Church of Australia (UELCA).

In recent years these two bodies have made a very serious effort to compose former differences and achieve full doctrinal unity. The outcome of their discussions looked very hopeful when mutual agreement was reached on a good, sound doctrinal statement. One or two practical issues, however, particularly in the area of religious unionism, remained unresolved. The UELCA is a member body of the Lutheran World Federation; the ELCA believed that membership in the LWF, under the constitution then in force, necessarily involved member churches in unionism. Accordingly, the two bodies drew up a joint request to the LWF to make certain changes in its constitution that would remove the ELCA's objections. The request was duly presented to the 1957 LWF assembly at Minneapolis, but the hoped-for action was not taken.

Another point at issue came to the fore when the two Australian bodies approached the question of jointly conducting their mission operations on New Guinea, where both churches had been active for some time. The UELCA, in addition to its own workers, had called European-trained missionaries to this field without requiring them to pass a colloquy. The ELCA properly insisted that these men should first be colloquized to determine whether they were, in fact, one with them in doctrine.

Later other complicating factors entered the picture when the UELCA at its 1959 convention voted to enter into pulpit and altar fellowship with the American Lutheran Church, a body with which neither the ELCA nor the Missouri Synod has had fellowship relations.

Having taken this decisive confessional stand on the unionism question, our Australian brethren were naturally concerned over the rumored possibility that their sister church in America was itself becoming indecisive and was softening in its attitude toward membership in the LWF. This accounted for the urgency of their invitation.

Synod's Board of Directors not only encouraged me to accept but also told me to be sure to take my secretary along. My regular secretary at the time was my daughter Helen. I had good reason to be grateful over and over again for this thoughtful gesture by the board, for on a trip as long and as closely scheduled as this one turned out to be no one could have asked for more efficient service than that which Helen rendered as secretary, traveling companion, and all-around "girl Friday."

For, you see, Australia was not to be my only destination. As soon as the Board for World Missions heard that I intended to cross the Pacific, it made sure that I would not bypass our Far Eastern mission fields. Drs. Otto H. Schmidt and Herman H. Koppelmann, the board executives at the time, immediately began to work out an itinerary for me. Board and staff members insisted it was high time that a president of Synod pay an official visit to the young churches our Synod had mothered on the other side of the globe.

## *Limp Back to Canton*

I of course would not have missed the chance for anything. To me the story of how God had led our church to carry His Word and build His kingdom in country after country during the decade since the close of the war was the most thrilling of all my years in office. Though I had often retold the stirring story of our church's mission advance at district conventions and elsewhere, I could do so only by way of reports and hearsay. However, as I soon found out, there is no substitute for having seen with one's own eyes the power of the Gospel in action in lands steeped in centuries of heathenism. Nor is there a substitute for hearing personally, from the lips of those who have been turned from idols to the true and living God, how thankful they are that He has moved the Christians of America to share the message of His love with them. As those who had been there had predicted, this trip was a revelation for me.

Our first stop on the long transpacific hop from Los Angeles to Sydney was Honolulu, where we stayed 24 hours. Our fellow Lutherans certainly gave us a royal Hawaiian welcome. I never realized that so much seeing and learning and wonderful hospitality could be crowded into such a short time. In our sightseeing we enjoyed our visits to some of the famed beauty spots in the delightful islands. But our greatest joy was to see the new churches, Christian day schools, and missions and to hear about the splendid progress with which God had blessed our work in the ten or twelve short years since we first began there.

The only serious trouble encountered on the entire journey came after our next refueling stop on Canton Island. About an hour's flight from the island one of the plane's engines "conked out." We were thankful that it happened when it did and that it was no worse. Our pilot had a comparatively easy decision: to jettison most of the fuel and limp back to Canton for repairs. The airline people took good care of us during the delay, even arranging a tour of the island.

We had one more stop before Australia—in the Fiji Islands, where we had our evening meal. Our barefoot Fiji Islander waiters reminded us that we were getting our Wednesday evening meal on Thursday, for we had now crossed the International Date Line. Shortly after we took off into the night, we also crossed the Tropic of Capricorn—a reminder that we had moved well "down under" in the Southern Hemisphere.

## *Leap into Winter*

Despite our 2:30 a.m. arrival in Sydney caused by the delay en route, we were met at the airport by the wife and son of Rev. O. F. Noske. After a few hours' rest at the parsonage the Noskes also saw us off on an early morning plane for Corowa. Here we were met by Dr. Clemens Hoopmann, president of the ELCA, and Rev. Theodore Harms, a cousin of Vice-President Herman Harms and my host during the conference. They drove us to Jindera, New South Wales, where the ELCA pastoral conference was in session.

Any strangeness we may have felt was quickly diffused by the hearty welcome the Australians gave us. Perhaps the one persistent odd feeling was due to the fact that on August 25 it was still winter in South Australia. Many of the men, I noticed, were wearing topcoats in church, and we were very glad that we were equipped to be in style. To make sure we would suffer a minimum of discomfort after our overnight leap from summer to winter, Pastor Harms provided an electric heater for us.

When the chairman called on me to address the conference, the brethren accorded me their rapt attention. I am sure the reason was more than the extra bit of concentration needed to follow my "outlandish" English. It was evident they were anxiously waiting to hear whether Missouri was beginning to drift from its doctrinal moorings. As I spoke and answered questions, I could sense the relief these men felt when I showed that neither at the Houston convention in 1953, nor at the St. Paul convention a few weeks before, had Synod given any indication of veering away from its historic position, as some had hinted and even predicted it would. Many expressed their gratification over having received correct information and were ready to lay the worrisome rumors at rest as the creation of wishful thinkers.

A unique feature of the conference was a one-day joint meeting with the UELCA pastoral conference, which was in session at Wagga Wagga, not too far from Jindera. The spirit prevailing at this meeting was friendly and cordial. I was also given a spot on the program, which I used to present in a friendly yet candid way the position of Missouri on the question of inter-Lutheran fellowship relations. I was grateful that I had the opportunity of attending this most interesting meeting. More than ever I have cherished the hope and prayer that God will find the way to lead these two bodies to full and God-pleasing unity both in doctrine and in practice.[1]

As an added pleasure of a most enjoyable conference it was my privilege to be a fellow guest for five days with President Hoopmann at the Harms parsonage at Burrumbuttock. Through this association I learned to know and to appreciate this very capable and devoted leader of our sister church.

As was to be expected, some of the Australian pastors scheduled me for speaking engagements, which also gave us the opportunity to

---

[1] The two churches did merge to become the Lutheran Church in Australia (LCA). It is in fellowship with the LWF-member Evangelical Lutheran Church of Papua New Guinea and the International Lutheran Council (ILC) member Gutnius Lutheran Church, a daughter of LCMS mission work. The LCA is also in fellowship with the Lutheran Church — Canada, a sister church of the LCMS, but not with the LCMS itself. It is an associate member of both the LWF and the ILC.

see something of this vigorous and picturesque island continent. The first was at Melbourne, where in spite of the very inclement weather a sizable group of fellow Lutherans turned out to hear the visiting Lutheran from North America. Pastors W. H. Noske and Walter Paech also arranged a tour of the bustling south coast metropolis, which was then at the height of its preparations as host of the 1956 Olympic Games.

## Praise Valley

A wonderful flight on the last day of August over the southeastern highlands and up the coast brought us to Adelaide, the center of the ELCA's work, where we were guests of Dr. Hoopmann. The next day, a Saturday, we went to Port Lincoln, a short plane ride down the coast, for the weekend convention of the Australian Luther League, the youth organization of the ELCA. These dedicated young people were "all ears" and full of questions to learn all about our Walther League and its activities. Not content with my brief talk and greetings from America, they also placed Helen on the conference program. It was the first time I heard her do any public speaking, and I must say that she certainly surprised her dad.

Near Port Lincoln we got a glimpse into the life of the Australian aborigines. What poverty and squalor! For many years the Australian Lutherans have been carrying on mission work among these "bushmen," particularly at Koonibba and Yalata. Difficult as it is to work among these nomadic people, some are being led to find the true riches in Christ.[2]

Sunday afternoon we flew back to Adelaide for a preaching engagement at Bethlehem Church. Monday and Tuesday morning Dr. Hoopmann guided us on tours of the historic Lutheran spots in and near the city. We visited Lobethal (German for Praise Valley), the cradle of Australian Lutheranism; the original seminary of the ELCA, quite similar to the log cabin seminary of our Synod in Altenburg, Perry County, Missouri; the present seminary, which incidentally also bears the name Concordia, at Highgate, a suburb of Adelaide; and the

---

[2] Behnken referred to the bushmen as "primitive" in the original edition, but that judgment is obsolete by modern standards of cultural anthropology.

graves of pioneer pastors August Kavel and Gotthardt D. Fritzsche, who led the first contingents of Lutherans to Australia in 1839 and 1841. I also enjoyed a fine visit with my old St. Louis seminary mate, Dr. Henry Hamann, who was still president of the Adelaide seminary at the time, and also with my friends of those dark days in postwar Germany, Dr. and Mrs. Hermann Sasse, who meanwhile had left Erlangen for a teaching post at Immanuel Theological Seminary (UELCA), Adelaide.

## *Contagious Story*

Our tight schedule, to my regret, did not permit a visit to our mission field in New Guinea. However, the Mission Board had asked Missionaries Erwin Spruth and Ian Kleinig, the latter a product of the Adelaide seminary, to meet me in Adelaide to give me a word picture of the work among the Enga people in the interior highlands of that huge island. The story unfolded by these young men is about the most fascinating I have ever heard. The enthusiasm and dedication revealed in the graphic report they brought of their trailblazing Kingdom work was contagious. Hearing their pleas for more manpower in this field, which after eight years of patient planting was beginning to show the firstfruits of a bountiful harvest of souls, I told them—and I meant every word—"You make me wish I were 50 years younger. I would certainly volunteer for a mission assignment in New Guinea."

Our last stop in Australia, after an afternoon flight from Adelaide, was at Perth, on the far west coast. Here we spent a delightful evening with Pastor R. M. Graebner, a nephew of the gifted Dr. August L. Graebner, who was still professor at St. Louis when I entered the seminary. Our visit with him recalled a significant bit of history. Back in 1903 his father, Dr. Carl F. Graebner, left his Bay City, Michigan, parish to accept a call to become "director" of the struggling Australian Lutheran seminary, then called Concordia College, at Murtoa. After a year the school was moved to Adelaide, with Dr. Graebner serving as president from 1905 to 1941. Still today our Australian brethren speak in glowing terms of Dr. C. F. Graebner's many contributions to their church. Nor have they forgotten that for a period of many years most of the members of their seminary faculty and also the president of their church, the sainted Dr. Theodore Nickel, were graduates of our seminary in St. Louis.

*{Chapter Eleven}*

# FRATERNAL VISIT TO THE FAR EAST

OUR TRAVEL PACE, already brisk, increased in tempo as we began our round of visits to the Asiatic missions. To get to Ceylon we flew by way of Singapore. Here we had an overnight stopover, which gave us our first taste of an Oriental city. What amazed us even more than the strange mixture of people was the traffic. On the way to the hotel we were part of a madly rushing stream of cars, trucks, motorbikes, pedicabs, and bicycles. Pedestrians took hairbreadth chances as they dashed across just anywhere. I remember a fellow passenger remarking: "It's a wonder they manage to stay alive."

Awaiting us at Colombo the next day at the end of a long flight across the Bay of Bengal were Rev. Andrew Fritze, our only missionary on Ceylon [now Sri Lanka] at the time, and Dr. Robert Zorn, of the seminary in Nagercoil, India, who was then on an official visit to the field. Here in Ceylon's capital I witnessed for the first time a scene that had a strangely shocking effect on me.

### *Right with Buddha*

Pausing to look into a Buddhist temple, we saw a mother with two children kneeling before and praying to an image of Buddha. I remember how in that moment the words of the hymn I had so often sung and quoted flashed home to me in all their piteous and appalling meaning: "The heathen in his blindness bows down to wood and stone."[1] This woman left a coin or two at the statue. There had been a death in her family, one of the Buddhist monks informed us, and she

---

[1] Quoted from the hymn, "From Greenland's Icy Mountains," by Reginald Heber.

had come to make it right with Buddha. In contrast I could not but reflect on the blessed hope we Christians cherish in our hours of bereavement. Then we too come before our God, not to "make things right"—Christ has already done that completely and perfectly when He gave Himself for us—but to seek comfort, strength, and healing. And He never fails us.

At Colombo I also had my first experience addressing a group of fellow Lutherans through an interpreter. During the remainder of the trip this was to be an almost daily experience. I must say that I rather enjoyed it. I had to take for granted, of course, that the interpreter was faithfully transmitting to the audience what I was saying. At a later occasion I was told by a missionary that because I speak slowly and use simple sentences an interpreter referred to me as "the interpreter's dream," while another speaker, who liked to use a rapid-fire delivery and oratorical flourishes, he called "the interpreter's nightmare."

Although we had a full week to visit the various areas of our South India mission field, Synod's oldest (1895) and largest, it soon became plain that we would have trouble squeezing in everything our several hosts had hoped and planned. But it was also plain that they were going to try!

## *Indian Bishop*

Alighting from the plane at Trichinopoly, we were met by Missionary Erwin Meinzen, one of our India veterans, and immediately whisked to the home of Bishop Rajah B. Manikam of the Tamil Evangelical Lutheran Church. The bishop, the first in India to be accorded this rank, was a grand host (the dinner Mrs. Manikam served was a real masterpiece) and also quite a conversationalist. A leading topic of his conversation was that the Lutherans of India must be sure to get together. The way to meet the ever-mounting problems confronting the Church in Asia, he stressed, was to combine forces and present a united front. When I sought to introduce the subject of also holding fast the sound doctrine committed to the Church by her Lord, it became apparent that his interest lay rather in the direction of numbers than in doctrine.

A highway trip of some 200 miles through the very interesting India countryside brought us to the seminary compound at Nagercoil, where we were guests of the Robert Zorns. It was a crowded weekend. In addition to inspecting the seminary, addressing the student body, and meeting with faculty members to bring a firsthand report of the St. Paul convention and to discuss doctrinal issues confronting the India church, I attended a Tamil-language service on Sunday, preached at a service for the missionaries and their families, and also addressed a large afternoon gathering of fellow Lutherans from that area. We also squeezed in a trip to Cape Comorin, the southernmost tip of India, with several stops en route to visit mission stations.

A Sunday evening social gathering by the Nagercoil people gave us a wonderful send-off for our trip to Trivandrum with Missionary Gerhard Stelter and his wife. Trivandrum, in Kerala State, though only 35 miles from Nagercoil, took us into a new language area. Here the people speak Malayalam, an altogether different tongue than Tamil, the language used in Madras. On the way we stopped at the missionary compound to which my son Kenneth had been assigned upon his graduation from the seminary in 1953. When God called my wife home in January 1954, she still expected Kenneth and his wife Eunice to be leaving for India in the near future. In fact, some weeks later Kenneth was commissioned for India service at St. Andrew's Church in Chicago. But neither he nor the three other men assigned to India that year got to go there. The India government had tightened restrictions and would no longer grant entrance visas to mission personnel except those engaged in medical, social-service, or other specialized work.

## *Look Out Below*

As at Nagercoil, our stay at Trivandrum included a visit at the higher school, an address to the student body, a Communion service for our mission personnel in that district, and an unforgettable social and get-acquainted evening. The next morning, before catching a noon plane for Bangalore, I had the opportunity of watching a large elementary school in action at the Nilamel compound served by Missionary Kurt Zorn.

At Bangalore, some 350 miles to the north, we got in some hurried sight-seeing among the city's ancient temples, teeming marketplaces, and growing industries before addressing (via interpreter) our fellow Lutherans of the area who filled the chapel to overflowing. As at other speaking appearances in India I had to keep a sharp lookout so that I did not step on any of the little folks when I was being escorted to the front of the church. It is the usual custom in the Indian churches for the children—and sometimes for the entire congregation—to sit on the floor.

Bright and early the next day we were on our way to Ambur with Missionaries John G. Naumann and Samuel G. Lang and their wives. On the way we stopped to breakfast with the Theodore Michalks at historic Krishnagiri. Here we saw our church's first mission chapel in India and paused for a few moments at the grave of Missionary Theodore Naether, the first Gospel ambassador sent overseas by our church. Profoundest respect and reverence filled my heart as I again recalled how Naether and his co-laborers Franz Mohn and O. Kellerbauer had patiently worked on for eight years in the face of massive discouragements before the first Indian convert was baptized. About a year afterward, in February 1904, Pastor Naether fell victim to the bubonic plague, contracted in ministering to some of his flock who were stricken with the dread disease.

Ambur stirred our interest since it is the home of the India church's teacher college, of Bethesda Hospital, founded in 1922 by Dr. Theodore Doederlein and now an efficient 175 bed institution, and also of our largest congregation, served by very capable Pastor N. J. Ezekiel, currently the general secretary (president) of the India church.

A highlight of the warm welcome given us by the Ambur Concordia Teachers College was a ceremony that included special guards of honor, one of men and another of women students, which I was called on to review, just as if I were a visiting dignitary. When later I was addressing the large and attentive audience that crowded the Ambur church, I spotted a very familiar face. Unbelievable as it was, there sat Dr. Alfred Rehwinkel. The tall, white-haired professor, on sabbatical leave from the St. Louis seminary, had been lecturing at seminaries and various churches of Australia and the Far East. Our paths happened to cross here in Ambur, where Dr. Rehwinkel was visiting his sister, Nurse Angela Rehwinkel, who then was nearing the close of a richly blessed career of 38 years dedicated to the service of Christ and the relief of human need at Bethesda Hospital.

## *Quick Shrinkage*

To beat the heat my host at Ambur, Dr. Wolfgang E. Bulle, then superintendent of the Ambur Hospital, insisted on an early start for the 120-mile trip to Madras. This also gave us time for a visit with Missionary J. G. Steinhoff and his fellow workers at the Lutheran Hour branch office in India. Though government restrictions do not permit Christian broadcasts on India stations, Lutheran programs are recorded in several languages by Indian nationals and sent to powerful stations outside the country to be beamed to listeners in India.

After getting our police clearance preparatory to leaving the country, we were off for Calcutta and a change of planes for the Philippines. To our dismay, as our papers were being checked for final clearance by officials at the Calcutta airdrome, we were politely informed that we could not be allowed to leave the country unless we were inoculated against cholera. This, they told us, would require a stay of 48 hours. And our plane for Manila was due to leave in less than six hours!

After some hurried consultations we gathered that a doctor could be made available—at a special fee, of course—who would provide the necessary shots and clear us for departure. Though we were glad to pay the fee, we have never quite figured out just why this should cause the 48 hours suddenly to shrink to less than six.

Our plane left at 2 a.m. As we droned into the Oriental dawn across Southeast Asia to a breakfast stop at Bangkok, Thailand, and on to the Philippines, what memories, both sad and glad, crowded in on us of our week in India! We had seen unspeakable poverty and the hopelessness of heathenism, but we had also seen convincing evidence that the Gospel is the "the power of God for salvation." Though emerging India has seen fit to bar its doors to new missionary forces from the West, we may be confident that under the leadership of our faithful and conscientious corps of veterans and especially of the growing numbers of national pastors, teachers, and evangelists, our church in India will continue its courageous witness to God's saving power in the India of tomorrow. Just about a year after our visit the India congregations formally organized as the India Evangelical Lutheran Church, the first of our missions to become a self-governing sister church. Since it is still small (some 14,000 communicants) and without financial resources to meet its almost unlimited opportunities, the IELC must continue to look to "mother Missouri" for subsidy for many years to come.

## *Rock of Memory*

At Manila practically the entire mission force was at the airport to greet us, since the missionaries had scheduled their conference in the city that day. After convoying us to the home of Missionary Rudolph Prange, our host for the three-day stay, they were eager to resume their sessions and hear all about the home church. They in turn reported on the progress and problems of their work on the islands. Time and again they stressed the need for more manpower. The number of reinforcements mentioned, as I recall, was 25 or 30. Though I had to shake my head at this outsize figure for a single field in view of the chronic shortages plaguing Synod's manpower resources and mission budgets, I had to admire the eager and aggressive spirit these men displayed in wanting to exploit to the fullest their opportunities to lengthen the cords and strengthen the stakes for the extension of Christ's Church in the Philippines.

Manila, as we found on a Saturday afternoon tour of the area, has its beautiful residential sections, especially along the ocean front, but we also saw many large sections marked by desperate poverty. In one of the latter a carnival was in progress from which, we were told, the Roman Church received a share of the profits. On the tour we took occasion also to view the little offshore island with a name that will long stir the memories and emotions of Filipino and American alike—Corregidor, familiarly known to GIs as the "Rock." Manila missionaries, no less alert to public relations possibilities than their stateside brethren, had also arranged a radio interview for me that afternoon on the Far East Broadcasting Company station.

Sunday morning we found it possible to attend both an early service at Bethel Church, conducted by Missionary Louis Dorn, and a later service at Grace Church in Pasay City, where we heard Missionary Prange. Grace is the mother church of the Philippine Mission, organized in 1946, shortly after our first two missionaries, Alvaro Carino and Herman R. Mayer, arrived in Manila.[2]

It was at this service in Grace Church that I had the privilege of baptizing the first Igorot baby brought into the Kingdom through our church's missionary efforts. The honor really should have gone to Missionary Louis Nau, who had done the pioneer work among these people in the Mountain Province of Luzon. Both he and the mother, however, insisted that I perform the baptism as a representative of the church that had sent the Gospel to her people.

Sunday afternoon I had the opportunity to meet and greet many of our Luzon Lutherans at a mass service in a large church. The service was followed by a reception. Before bidding us farewell these grand people presented us with some lovely gifts as mementos of our visit.

## *Bamboo Curtain's Edge*

Noon of the next day found us some 600 miles across the China Sea, being greeted by our missionaries in Hong Kong. This British crown colony, set like a gem on the South China coast, was literally swarming with people. Refugees from Communist China had in a short time raised the population tenfold, to more than three million. At the Shamrock Hotel, where we stayed, the service was excellent, except that, during the prevailing dry season at the time, the use of water was restricted to the hours from 4 to 9 p.m.

Forced out of China by the communist takeover, in 1950 a number of our missionaries had remained in Hong Kong to work

---

[2] The Lutheran Church in the Philippines became a sister church of the LCMS in 1971.

among the hordes of Free Chinese refugees, most of whom were left in desperately poor circumstances. God has blessed their work mightily ever since then. Concordia Lutheran School in Kowloon, to cite one instance, is by far the largest Lutheran elementary school in Synod, with an enrollment of about 1,500. Hong Kong is the only place I ever heard of where admission to Sunday school at times had to be restricted to ticket holders. Because chapel facilities were crowded to the bursting point, children who had attended previously were given tickets to make sure they could gain admittance when they returned.

Missionaries were very kind in interrupting their busy schedules to show us the various mission installations and points of interest about the hilly city. Quite exciting was the ascent by cable car to the famed peak on the island, which gave us a strikingly beautiful view of the city lying on both sides of the bay. Anchored in the bay was the cruiser *USS Los Angeles* with Old Glory waving from her mast—a thrilling reminder of home.

Since our itinerary did not permit a stopover on Taiwan, Dr. Roy Suelflow and Missionary Michael Trinklein flew over from that island to give us a firsthand briefing on the work in the Lutheran Church in Free China and to take back with them news and greetings from the church at home. The development of our work on Taiwan had largely paralleled that in Hong Kong. Workers banished from the China mainland had gone there to follow up the thousands of Nationalists who had fled their homeland to live under President Chiang Kai-shek's Free China government. It proved to be a favorable climate for mission work. To serve and expand the budding congregations that were soon planted, Dr. Suelflow had opened a training school for national pastors in Taipei, later transferred to a more favorable location at Chia Yi. Today a dozen ordained Chinese pastors are carrying an increasing share of the responsibility to reach out with the Christian message among both Free Chinese and native Taiwanese.

While in Hong Kong I had the privilege of speaking at what I do not hesitate to call the most impressive anniversary service in all my years of preaching. Our Chinese fellow Lutherans turned out in great numbers to honor Missionary Elmer H. Thode and Deaconess Gertrude Simon, both of whom had completed 30 years of mission service among the Chinese. During the more than 20 years they had served in the interior of China they had carried on in the face of staggering difficulties growing out of the almost constant turmoil, warfare, and political upheaval engulfing the country. It was not only the event and the place that stirred me so deeply but particularly the love and kindness these new Christians showed toward their servants in the Lord. I saw convincing evidence of the deep regard and appreciation they felt toward the faithful messengers from the Christian West who had brought them the Gospel of God's marvelous love in Christ.

After Dr. Thode had voiced his thanks, he suddenly turned the tables on me by announcing that the year 1956 also marked the 50th anniversary of my own ministry. In behalf of the Hong Kong Lutherans he presented me with a beautifully carved ivory fisherman. I shall always cherish it as a reminder of a very thrilling occasion and a remarkably brave and consecrated band of fellow Lutherans in the Orient.

## *Tokyo Beehive*

The next morning we were off for Tokyo. The Hong Kong runway, as we noticed when the plane taxied out, is unusually short. As we poised for the takeoff, we overheard an evidently nervous lady passenger remark: "Well, pilot, there it is. You get us up, or we have had it!" Our expert pilot, however, not only made the liftoff seem very easy but also gave us a delightful "ride." He took us over Okinawa, which looked so beautiful and peaceful as if to belie the fearful bloodshed and carnage that had occurred there during the American assault scarcely a decade before. Another beautiful sight as we were approaching Tokyo was the sky view of Japan's sacred Mount Fuji-San, its symmetrical, snowcapped peak bright in the rays of the setting sun.

Quite a number of missionaries and their wives were at the airport to greet us that evening. They at once escorted us to the Bancho Hotel, where we had our evening meal together and enjoyed a fine get-acquainted evening. It was the start of an extremely busy five-day visit in the "Land of the Rising Sun." Populous Japan was the country in which Synod back in 1893 had decided to open its first foreign mission. This decision was changed the next year, however, when attention was directed to the opportunity to begin work in South India with two experienced missionaries and also because of the threatening Sino-Japanese War. "Missouri" did not come to Japan until a half century later, when Missionary William Danker arrived in Tokyo in September 1948, three years and two weeks after the Japanese signed World War II surrender terms aboard the battleship *Missouri* in Tokyo Bay.

Tokyo is the world's largest city and it is densely populated. However, under such expert guides as Missionaries Elmer Bergt and Delwin Schneider, Chaplain Alvin Katt (the same who had been our ace military escort on our visit to war-ravaged Europe), and several others, we were able to get more than a good glimpse of it.

Especially interesting was the Yasukumi Shrine, the "Arlington Cemetery" of Japan. Really it is not a cemetery, since the Japanese cremate their war dead. But here the people come to pray for their fallen war heroes. Some bring flowers, others tie papers inscribed with prayers to the trees. They perform these services, we were told, to pacify the spirits of the departed so they do not return to trouble them.

We naturally spent quite some time at the Lutheran Center—a veritable beehive of activity. Included in the building is the mission's theological training school, headed at that time by Dr. Otto H. Theiss, for many years professor at the Oakland, California, Concordia College and later executive secretary of the Walther League. Dr. Thomas Coates, on sabbatical leave from his post as president of the Portland (Oregon) Concordia, also taught a number of courses to the dozen students enrolled that year.

The mission business office is also located at the center. But by far the busiest place was the Japan Lutheran Hour office. We were informed at the time that 140,000 listeners had enrolled for the Bible correspondence course and that 13,000 had requested baptism. To prepare such inquirers for baptism would naturally require additional instruction, but the missionaries found it possible to follow up only a very limited number. Some of the men told me that their conscience sometimes troubled them because they simply could not reach so many who expressed a desire to learn more of the Christian message.

We have since placed additional men in that field, but the situation, sad to say, has not changed much. The call is still for more workers. Recently the Tokyo Lutheran Hour office reported that it had received its millionth response from listeners, a remarkable testimony both to the effectiveness of the broadcast Word and of continued listener interest. What an opportunity if we had the workers, both American and national, to take advantage of it!

On another day, filled to the brim with sight-seeing and visiting some of our hard-working missionaries, we saw the so-called Great Buddha at Kamakura, a huge image that goes back to 1252, and also the Hachiman Shrine, dated almost a century earlier. At these places we again saw the saddening scene of large groups of children and young people, as well as older men and women, bowing down in worship before their graven images. The youth groups, many in the uniforms worn by all university students, were evidently being regimented into the practice of pagan rites by Buddhist leaders who escorted them.

Our chats with Rev. Kosaku Nao, now a highly respected member of the Tokyo seminary staff, and Missionary Ralph Phipps, who devotes much of his time to Lutheran Hour programing and operations, gave us some revealing insights into the problems and difficulties Christian workers must face in today's Japan.

## *Sermon Without Shoes*

It is very apparent that the ancient heathen faiths and particularly the "new religions," offshoots of the traditional Shinto and Buddhist systems, are putting forth tremendous efforts to recoup the losses sustained when the dream of "invincibility" built around their emperor-god cult collapsed in 1945. If only we had been in a position to move a large missionary force into the "spiritual vacuum" that existed in those years! I well recall General Douglas MacArthur's urgent plea when he headed the military government in postwar Japan that the churches of America send not tens but hundreds of missionaries to these disillusioned people.

Among the special events that I attended during my stay was the dedication of a new school in one of the Tokyo suburbs. Dr. Herman H. Koppelmann, then on a field visit in his capacity as Assistant Executive Secretary of the Board for World Missions, was the preacher. Since I was also expected to say a few words, I had to join in the procession. Japanese custom dictates that only soft slippers be worn for sacred functions in temples, churches, and the like. When I was introduced to this custom in connection with an address I gave before the student body of our high school at Hanno, I got along reasonably well with the slippers provided. However, at the school dedication all the slippers were much too small. The only thing to do was to march in and appear on the platform unshod. Some remarked later that they would just love to have a picture of Synod's president preaching in his stocking feet. Fortunately no one thought of aiming his camera at me at the time.

The brethren decided that I should preach at the regular Sunday worship service at the Lutheran Center even though this meant a sermon via interpreter. It was my last experience of speaking through an interpreter and a wonderful privilege it was to share the Word of God with an audience of Japanese. That evening Dr. Theiss and his staff had arranged a reception at the center so that I could meet some of the leaders and missionaries of other Lutheran bodies who are at work in Japan. For this opportunity, too, I was most grateful.

Monday was another gala day. The entire mission staff met in Tokyo for a conference. Dr. Koppelmann and I were supposed to be the "headliners." For this special occasion most of the missionaries brought their wives. Sessions continued throughout the day. I must say that I became so thoroughly engrossed that the time flew by.

Once again I could not escape the fervent wish that all our people back home could spend a few days with their missionaries at least once in their lives. I know we would all think more often of our representatives who are doing the Lord's work for us in the far corners of the world. I know we would be praying for them more fervently, and the matter of contributing to support their work would be far more joyful and spontaneous than it often is.

## *Longest Day*

That evening at the Tokyo airport, as we prepared for the last long leg of our journey, everything was in good order except for one little problem that, I understand, others too encounter at the end of an overseas visit—overweight luggage. Charges for excess weight, we were told, would be $52. We quickly sorted out enough items to get down to the weight limit and left them in the kind hands of our good old standby, Chaplain Alvin Katt. He later mailed them to us for something like $2.50.

The next morning we alighted for a "stretch" stop at Shimya on the Aleutian Islands. Though this was US territory, somehow we did not have much of a "back home" feeling with a long transoceanic hop still ahead. Since we had re-crossed the International Date Line, we were back to Monday morning again, making this quite literally the longest day of my life.

Late that evening my son Kenneth and his family were on hand to meet us at the Seattle airport. Catching sight of their beaming faces convinced us that now we were really "back home" again. Chatting away at Kenneth's parsonage (he was pastor of Atonement Church in Seattle), Helen and I just couldn't believe that only five weeks had elapsed since we left St. Louis. How much, how very, very much we had seen and done in that time! After adding it all up, Helen said we had traveled at least 24,000 miles, an average of almost 5,000 miles a week—surely more than ample reason for profound thanks for God's gracious protection and undeserved blessings.

*{Chapter Twelve}*

# MISSOURI WITH A LATINO ACCENT

THOUGH I HADN'T the slightest intention of making another intercontinental trip so soon, only a few brief months after my return from the Far East I was on official business in South America.

Our Synod has long had a vital interest in the other America, ever since our pastors and missionaries began answering the call to serve spiritually neglected Lutheran immigrants struggling to wrest a home and livelihood from the primitive wilds around the turn of the century. As a matter of fact, both Brazil and Argentina are part and parcel of the Missouri Synod, though many a South American must often have wondered what an "outfit" calling itself after a Midwestern state was doing down on their continent. The Brazil mission had been welcomed as an official district of Synod back in 1904 and its sister district, Argentina, in 1927. In recent decades, incidentally, the latter district has expanded its outreach into Chile, Uruguay, and Paraguay.[1]

I was aware that an official visit to these districts was long overdue. The only time a member of Synod's *Praesidium* had visited South American districts during the half century of their membership was in 1916 when Dr. Pfotenhauer made the long trip. If the brethren down there sometimes had the feeling that their districts were stepchildren in the synodical family, one could hardly blame them.

Time, distance, and costs, especially before the air age, were large factors to be reckoned with in arranging for official representation at South American district conventions. As these districts were properly

---

[1] ILC member churches, no longer districts of the LCMS, exist in Argentina, Bolivia, Brazil, Chile, Guatemala, Mexico, Paraguay, Peru, and Venezuela. The Universidade Luterana do Brasil (ULBRA) is one of the largest Lutheran universities in the world and these sister churches have reached maturity in their own right.

regarded primarily as mission fields, Dr. F. C. Streufert, Synod's first Secretary of Missions (1932 to 1953), and other missions executives so timed their survey trips that they could also be at the conventions. Earlier there had been visits by members of Synod's Board of Directors, notably Dr. Paul Schulz and Henry Horst, the latter at his own expense. Then, too, in order to maintain close personal contact with synodical affairs, the presidents and other delegates of the two districts usually attended Synod's triennial conventions.

What ultimately precipitated my visit to our southernmost districts, however, was a 1956 convention resolution calling for a reorganization and expansion of our pastor and teacher training program in Brazil. It involved the purchase of new campus sites, a matter of direct concern to both the Board of Directors and the Board for Missions in North and South America. The members of the Board of Directors who were to consult with Brazil District leaders on site acquisition problems were confronted with emergency situations that prevented them from going. As the time for the South American district conventions was now rapidly approaching, it was decided that I should act as the board's official "site-seer" and at the same time take the opportunity for a long overdue official visit to the Brazil and Argentina conventions.

## *Durable Dynamos*

Like most of our North American districts, the brethren "down below" prefer to have their conventions in the good old summertime. For the people on the other hemisphere this means January and early February. Accompanied by Rev. Harold Ott, then Secretary of Missions for Latin America, I left for Rio de Janeiro via Miami on January 13.

We took the occasion to make a stopover visit to Caracas, Venezuela, a rapidly developing city, where only a few years previously a thriving mission had been developed under the guidance of Dr. Theo. W. Strieter. Together with Dr. Strieter, a still energetic veteran of 68 who was about to retire and return to the States, and his successor, Rev. R. G. Huebener, we visited El Salvador (Savior) Church and its day school, beautifully located on a hillside. Both church and school were trilingual, sharing the Word with their community in Spanish, English, and German. We also visited Santa Trinidad Church, the all-Spanish mission shepherded by Pastor Hector Lazos. The approach of our flight time did not permit intended visits to some of the outlying stations.

In Rio we were welcomed by Dr. Rodolpho Hasse and his son Paulo. Dr. Hasse, then president of the Brazil District, was also speaker and director for many years on the Portuguese Lutheran Hour, editor of *Mensageiro Luterano*, a Portuguese publication of the church in Brazil. He also spearheaded the district's mission outreach to the cities of the north. At 67, in the 40th year of a demanding ministry, he was still one of the most youthful and zestful missionaries I have ever met, a veritable dynamo behind our work in South America. While on our site-inspection trips, we also took in some of the points of interest for which this beautiful metropolis of more than 2.5 million has become world famous. Our site surveying resulted in the choice of lots excellently located on a mountainside.

To view other possible sites Dr. Hasse flew to São Paulo with us, some 200 miles below Rio. This humming, highly industrialized city, sometimes called the Chicago of Brazil, has even outstripped Rio de Janeiro in population. In both of these huge cities there was an astounding amount of construction activity. While driving from site to site, I was much impressed with the many very beautiful modern buildings, which compared favorably with the skyscrapers of any city in the US. In fact, I felt at that time that the Brazilians had the better of the comparison, since they were adding bright color to the exterior of their buildings. In more recent years I have noticed that color is being used more extensively in our own new "high-rise" architectural marvels. It certainly makes them look much more attractive. Why, I wonder, wasn't something like that done long ago? In São Paulo our *site* seeking wasn't too productive, and we urged the brethren to carry on the search.

## *"Sprechen Sie Deutsch?"*

On January 19, a sweltering midsummer Saturday, we arrived at Porto Alegre, the home of our Seminario Concordia. Here we got a tremendous welcome from *Juventude Luterana,* the Brazil District youth organization, which was holding its convention on the campus. Informed that most of the young people could understand German, I addressed the convention in that language. But to make sure it wasn't all wasted effort, Dr. L. C. Rehfeldt, a seminary professor, repeated my remarks in Portuguese.

The next afternoon I again spoke in German as I delivered the sermon for the opening service of the Brazil District convention. A good 95 percent of the pastors and delegates, I was told, would have no trouble understanding me. Our churches in South America are passing through a language transition similar to ours in the US some 40 years ago. The professors' children, I noticed, always used Portuguese in their play about the campus, as did the younger men, both pastors and laymen, in their ordinary conversation at the convention. Many of the older men, however, still preferred German.

At the convention one day I greeted one of the pastors, a black man, in English. But he just looked at me somewhat bewildered. Then I asked: *"Sprechen Sie Deutsch?"* You should have heard how fluently he spoke German. His mother tongue, of course, was Portuguese.

The Brazil convention, like that in Argentina two weeks later, followed much the same pattern as our district conventions in the States. At Porto Alegre the doctrinal essay, delivered by Pastor Frederick Otten, was in German. Discussion, however, at times jumped over into Portuguese. In Argentina Prof. E. J. Keller's essay was both delivered and discussed in Spanish. At both conventions Pastor Harold Ott and I were given ample time to report on synodical affairs. In business sessions, as here at home, a great deal of emphasis was given to the work of missions and the recruitment and training of church workers. I was especially pleased to note that quite a number of laymen took an active part in the discussions.

After the Brazil convention we again spent considerable time looking at building sites in and around Porto Alegre. We of course also had a meeting with the faculty and an interesting visit to Casa Publicadora Concordia, our South American "CPH," established in 1923.

A few days' stay in Buenos Aires, Argentina's big, beautiful capital, gave us an opportunity to visit our other Seminario Concordia in South America and to meet with its faculty and Board of Control, as well as with the District Mission Board, before proceeding to the Argentine District convention. The seminary is really in Villa Ballester, a very nice suburb of the city that has become, as the proud residents reminded us, the third largest metropolis in the Americas, with an estimated population of five million. During our stay we were guests of Rev. Samuel H. Beckmann, at that time the district president.

### *Mission Barbecue*

On our trip to the convention, held at Almada, Entre Rios Province, some 200 miles to the north, we drove with E. Glaser, a lay delegate. For us *Norteamericanos* the trip to the hinterlands was a unique experience, particularly because it included a four-hour ride on a ferry up one of the broad, scenic rivers—the Parana—which give Entre Rios its name ("between the rivers").

We found Almada to be a very small village, and the congregation, about 350 communicants, typically rural. Since the Argentine District was incorporated in Entre Rios, it is required by law that conventions be held in this province. Efforts are under way to effect a change so that conventions may use the Villa Ballester seminary facilities.

While hosting a district convention places a strain on the rural Entre Rios congregations, they manage very well. The Almada people showed a gratifying kind of hospitality. Meals were served in a large tent on the church grounds—and what grand meals they were! The real test of their hospitality came on Convention Sunday, a kind of super mission festival. It attracts Lutherans from a wide area. At all three services the church was crowded beyond capacity, and all stayed to eat. The Almada men rose to the occasion by preparing *asado*, an outdoor barbecue with a special sauce—an Argentine favorite. My Texas-trained taste buds pronounced it a real *Delikatessen*.

At this convention, too, most of the men could understand enough German so that we had little trouble communicating with them. Much of the business was transacted bilingually. Besides the Spanish language the most noticeable difference from our conventions at home was the long noon recess. In keeping with the *siesta* custom common to Latin America, the afternoon sessions did not begin until about 3:30 and lasted until 7 o'clock. However, the extended noon recess allowed the convention committees to do their important work.

President Beckmann had the business so well organized that the delegates decided, with an extra session or two, they could close on Monday evening instead of the following day. By 7 o'clock Monday evening we were able to have our closing service. Mr. Glaser hurried us through the evening meal; his weather eye had spotted a storm moving up, and he knew that for the first 20 miles we would be traveling a highly uncertain dirt road. His timing was almost uncanny. No sooner had we reached the improved road than the rain started.

We arrived at the ferry landing that night at 11 o'clock, only to learn that no boat would be leaving until 5:30 in the morning. Since there was nothing resembling a hotel, the four of us did the next best thing—we dozed and catnapped in the car till daylight. We were a happy foursome, needless to say, when we got back to Villa Ballester at about 10:30.

## *Panama by Whirlybird*

I felt sufficiently rested the next day to start the long trip homeward by way of Santiago, Chile, and up the Pacific coast. Crossing the rugged, towering Andes, the pilot pointed out to us the "Christ of the Andes," the gigantic statue on the Argentine-Chilean boundary, erected by the people of the two republics to mark perpetual peace between them. En route to Brownsville, Texas, we made stops at Antofagasta, Chile; Lima, Peru; Panama City; Managua, Nicaragua; and Guatemala City. I made use of my in transit pass at each stop to alight for a short walk, so that, in real globetrotter fashion, I could later say that I had "traveled" in these countries.

In Panama I actually did some traveling, though I was there only a half day. Landing there at 4 a.m., I was met by two Army officers. I had a special entry permit to the Canal Zone, where I was to address a gathering of military chaplains. After arranging for me to get a few hours rest, they whisked me off by helicopter to Fort Koppa for my meeting—my first ride in a "whirlybird."

In speaking to the chaplains I again stressed a theme that I seldom fail to mention in speaking to God's servants anywhere: the need for good, sound, sanely balanced Law-and-Gospel preaching.

On the return trip my pilot gave me a helicopter view of the entire canal from Colon on the Caribbean to Panama on the Pacific. I hadn't expected to see much of this famed waterway, and seeing it in this panoramic way was an exceptional pleasure. It was beautiful.

Before catching the plane homeward bound, I had a chance to see Redeemer Church, excellently located in nearby Balboa, and to visit with some of our fellow Lutherans from the zone. Redeemer's pastor at the time was Rev. Robert F. Gussick, who has devoted his entire ministry to Latin American missions and is now Synod's resident mission counselor for the Caribbean area, with headquarters in Guatemala City.

Quite often on these flying trips, as I marveled at the blessings of the air age, my mind went back to the seminary classroom and the Old Testament exegesis lectures of Dr. George Stoeckhardt. Coming to Genesis 1:28 (it was just at the time the Wright brothers were attempting their first "hops" in their flying machine), the professor stressed that the passage indeed meant that man should subdue the earth and have dominion over all creatures on land or sea—then added, as he transfixed us with a sharp gaze: "*Aber er soll aus der Luft bleiben!*" (He should stay out of the air.) I have tried to picture what the good doctor would be saying in this age of jet travel and manned earth orbits. Knowing him as I did, I don't doubt he would have quickly rechecked his exegetical bearings and would, as occasion demanded, be flying off "into the wild blue yonder" along with the rest of us.

*{Chapter Thirteen}*

# IN PURSUIT OF UNITY

During my seminary days and early years in the ministry, as I recall, Lutheran unity efforts in our country were practically nonexistent. Still smoldering at the time was the unhappy controversy over the doctrines of election and conversion that had shaken the Synodical Conference and led to the withdrawal in 1882 of a large segment of the Ohio Synod and the "temporary" withdrawal of the Norwegian Synod.

Debate over the issues continued in the various church periodicals. Some rather sharp and caustic repartees were fired back and forth. Sometimes these seemed to be in the nature of a name-calling contest. At times we seminary students in reading the periodicals would amuse ourselves—perhaps a bit irreverently—by picking the winner of the month according to the most colorful and vitriolic expressions he was able to hurl at "the opponents." This sort of polemics naturally contributed nothing to Lutheran amity, to say nothing of Lutheran unity.

There can be no question, however, that our early synodical founders and fathers were very much unity minded. As evidence we need to recall only that the desire to establish sound Lutheranism in America was one of the big reasons that led Dr. Walther and his congregation (Trinity, St. Louis) to begin publishing *Der Lutheraner* in 1844. This well-edited publication was instrumental in drawing like-minded Lutherans together, thus leading to the founding of the Missouri Synod in 1847.

As Synod's first president, Dr. Walther later issued an invitation to all Lutherans who accepted the Holy Scriptures and subscribed to the Augsburg Confession as a correct interpretation of the Scriptures to hold a series of free conferences "with a view toward the final realization of one united Evangelical Lutheran Church of North America."

Between 1856 and 1859 four such conferences were held—at Columbus, Pittsburgh, Cleveland, and Fort Wayne. Among those who attended were representatives of Eastern synods (New York and Pennsylvania) and of several synods in the Midwest. Another conference had been set for 1860, but the Ohio Synod, until this time an interested participant, announced through its church organ *Lutherische Kirchenzeitung* that it would no longer take part. Hence the 1860 meeting was dropped, and the outbreak of the Civil War prevented resumption of further efforts.

## *Divisive Term*

After the war and its dislocations a renewal of doctrinal talks among the Ohio, Missouri, Wisconsin, Norwegian, Illinois, and Minnesota synods ultimately led to the organization in 1872 of the Evangelical Lutheran Synodical Conference of North America along strictly confessional lines. Among the purposes of this federation, according to the original constitution, were these: "Expression of the unity of the spirit existing among the respective synods; mutual encouragement in faith and confession; promotion of unity of doctrine and practice."

The first Lutheran unity effort I took a keen interest in was that undertaken from about 1910 to 1917 by three Norwegian groups—the United Norwegian Church, the Hauge Synod, and the Norwegian Evangelical Lutheran Synod. While not personally involved, I was particularly interested in this effort because the last-named body was supporting a college at Clifton, Texas, and also because the Norwegian Synod still had close fraternal bonds with the Missouri Synod, although it was no longer a member of the Synodical Conference. I also counted some of the Norwegian Synod pastors who completed their training at the St. Louis seminary among my personal friends.

Most of the doctrinal discussions in these merger negotiations centered in the doctrine of election, specifically whether God's election took place *intuitu fidei* (in view of faith), that is to say, whether God from eternity chose certain persons as heirs of eternal life because He foresaw they would come to and persevere in faith. Some Norwegian Synod pastors maintained that this term should not be used since it implied that man's faith was a cause of his election, whereas the Scriptures clearly teach that God's eternal election was *solely* by His grace.

After a long series of meetings the three bodies decided in 1917 to consummate a merger on the basis of a document known as the *Opgjør* (agreement). A small minority of the Norwegian Synod, however, refused to accept the *Opgjør* as a settlement of the issues. The very language of the "agreement," they insisted, expressed a doctrinal compromise, an agreement to disagree. The *Opgjør* stated: "We hold that this fact [that two divergent "forms of presentation" on the manner of God's election were being used] ought not to cause any division in the church nor disturb that unity of the spirit in the bond of peace which God desires should prevail among us."

This minority, which during the course of the negotiations had consulted with such theological leaders of our Synod as Dr. Franz Pieper, Dr. W. H. T. Dau, and Dr. Theodore Graebner, staunchly maintained that for conscience' sake they could not enter the union. In this conviction they determined to continue as the Norwegian Synod. This small body, which later dropped the "Norwegian" from its name to become the Evangelical Lutheran Synod, joined the Synodical Conference in 1920.

## *48-Synod Merger*

Another merger I remember very well was the formation of the United Lutheran Church in America. This union involved three bodies whose strength was concentrated largely in the East and Southeast: the General Synod, the General Council, and the United Synod of the South. It was an outgrowth of the quadricentennial observance of the Reformation. Though at first opposed by a few leaders as premature, the merger became a reality in November 1918. It brought together a total of no less than 48 individual synods (corresponding to our Missouri Synod's districts) which made up the three bodies. Only the Swedish Augustana Synod, the largest in the General Council, voted to remain aloof. Other synods, notably Iowa and Ohio, were invited to join the merger but refused.

Doctrinal issues and matters of church practice did not play too important a role in the ULCA merger negotiations. Dr. Frederick H. Knubel, president of the ULCA for its first 26 years, once told me when we were discussing doctrinal matters in his New York office that the pastors of his church were not so concerned about doctrine as were the men of our Synod, since the former had not passed through any grave doctrinal controversies.

The ULCA constitution, in fact, did not require unanimity in doctrine and practice, and seldom were such matters taken too seriously. Doctrinal discipline was left to the individual synods and could not be exercised by the general body. The synods themselves took disciplinary action only rarely. A notable exception was the recent heresy trial of two pastors of the Northwest Synod who had denied the Virgin Birth.

Some of the same casualness concerning doctrine appeared when our Synod's Committee on Lutheran Union met with representatives of the ULCA for doctrinal talks following an invitation extended by the ULCA in 1935. In its report to the 1938 convention our committee stated that it had held two meetings in which the doctrine of inspiration was made the starting point. "However, it was impossible," the report notes, "for the two parties to come to an agreement." Synod encouraged the committee to continue its efforts. But in 1941 the committee reported that, because of the wide disagreement of the ULCA's fellowship commission with our Synod's position on the basic doctrine of inspiration, meetings had been discontinued. Dr. Knubel himself expressed the view that further meetings "seemed useless."

Meanwhile the American Lutheran Church commission on Lutheran union, which had also been holding doctrinal discussions with the ULCA committee, reported that at a meeting in Pittsburgh agreement had been reached on a number of issues, including the doctrine of inspiration. Two of the ALC leaders, Dr. M. Reu and President Emmanuel Poppen, met with Drs. Theodore Engelder,

William Arndt, and me to give us an oral report on what had been accomplished. Without doubt these men were firmly convinced that the "Pittsburgh Agreement" would settle the issue. We, however, informed them that we could not share their optimism.

A statement to settle an issue so basic and of such far-reaching consequence, we felt, should be put into clear, definite, yes, unequivocal language. Our misgivings proved all too real when the Pittsburgh Agreement was presented to the 1940 ULCA convention in Omaha. Though the adoption resolution ultimately carried, it did so by a narrow margin. A large number voted against it. This gave a clear indication of the position of the ULCA regarding inspiration and rudely shattered high hopes held by many in the ALC.

## *Status Controversiae*

Unity stirrings in the post-World War I era were not confined to the groups that formed the ULCA. The 1920s saw an earnest renewal of efforts to establish closer ties among the so-called conservative Lutheran bodies, whose strength lay largely in the Midwest. Participants in these talks and conferences were representatives of the Ohio, Iowa, Buffalo, Wisconsin, and Missouri synods. Working patiently and without fanfare in an atmosphere of growing cordiality, the negotiators made a good deal of progress. In fact, it seemed that a good basis for agreement had been reached when the intersynodical conferees produced a document known as the Chicago Theses.

Among Missouri Synod pastors and conferences that studied the theses there were mixed feelings. This reaction was also reflected in the action taken at the 1929 convention in River Forest, which devoted considerable time to a review of the document. The convention resolution acknowledged with gratitude "the diligent and faithful work of our representatives, especially in view of the difficulties connected with their meetings." It also voiced "heartiest thanks toward God that some progress in the presentation of doctrine on the basis of the Scriptures and the Lutheran Confessions" had been made. "We recommend, however," the resolution continued, "that Synod do not accept the theses in their present form."

Two reasons were cited for not accepting the theses: (1) that "many serious objections have been raised by members of Synod" which should be carefully considered, and (2) that "all historical data" had been omitted in working them out. Future deliberations, the resolution stated, should proceed "from the exact point of controversy *(status controversiae)* and take into account the pertinent history."

I know that some of those who had worked painstakingly to produce the Chicago Theses, including men of our Synod, were rather deeply disappointed at the largely negative action taken by the convention. The very next year (1930) three of the bodies—the Ohio, Iowa, and Buffalo synods, which had reached agreement on the Minneapolis Theses already in 1925—announced that they would merge as the American Lutheran Church. I have never been able to escape the feeling that our Synod's somewhat summary refusal to accept the Chicago Theses helped to precipitate the organization of the ALC.

Almost immediately after organizing, the ALC joined with the Augustana Synod, the Norwegian Lutheran Church (later known as the Evangelical Lutheran Church), the United Evangelical Lutheran Church (Danish), and the Lutheran Free Church to form the American Lutheran Conference. When I think of the American Lutheran Conference, I recall the time I was invited to address the 1946 convention of the conference on the topic "Fellowship Among Lutherans." Perhaps it was in the nature of a "feeler" toward a closer approach between our Synod and the conference. In this address I sought to be kind, considerate, and evangelical, but at the same time firm in setting forth that the most urgent need among Lutherans in America—and for that matter anywhere—is agreement in doctrine and church practice on the basis of Holy Writ and our historic Lutheran Confessions; then pulpit and altar fellowship will follow as a matter of course.

At the request of Synod's College of District Presidents this address was printed and sent to all Lutheran pastors in North America. As was to be expected, my remarks were not received with equal favor in all quarters. Some, in fact, leveled very sharp criticism at what I said. Others, however, wrote to express warm and sincere thanks for having stated our church's position clearly and definitely.

Nothing further happened, however, to bring our Synod into closer ties with the American Lutheran Conference. By the fall of 1954 the conference voted itself out of existence, since by this time the five member bodies had moved well along in the direction of outright merger. The Augustana Synod soon withdrew from the proposed merger, giving as a reason that it preferred to work toward a union of all Lutherans in America rather than just a segment. The small Lutheran Free Church also decided to remain out of the proposed new ALC, after a referendum vote by the individual congregations showed that too many were not in favor of a merger.

## *21 to 3*

To pick up the main thread of our story, we need to go back to 1935, the year Synod decided I should be its new president. Before turning the gavel over to me President Pfotenhauer announced that from the American Lutheran Church and from the United Lutheran Church in America he had received invitations asking our church to confer with them in the quest for a closer fellowship. The convention voted to accept both invitations and instructed the president to appoint a Committee on Lutheran Church Union (renamed the Committee on Doctrinal Unity in 1941) to hold bilateral discussions with representatives of each body.

Thus from the very beginning of my incumbency as president, the Missouri Synod—and I along with it—became deeply and directly involved in the union question. It was a live (sometimes almost *too* live) current and recurrent issue throughout my presidential years and confronted the church with many a knotty problem and weighty decision.

As an interesting sidelight let me recall that in 1935 the convention floor committee assigned to review intersynodical and doctrinal matters was known as Committee 21. At the next convention in 1938 this committee became Committee 16. And by 1941, so voluminous had business under this category grown, this committee was raised to Committee 3, right behind the always vital

Committee on Missions and the equally important Committee on Seminaries and Colleges. Ever since then the Committee on Doctrinal and Intersynodical Matters has held the No. 3 spot.

In consultation with the vice-presidents, I appointed as our first union committee Drs. Theodore Engelder, William Arndt, Carl F. Brommer, Frederick H. Brunn, and Karl Kretzmann. During the next triennium this committee met six times with representatives of the ALC and twice with representatives of the ULCA. Each time it used as a starting point for discussions *A Brief Statement of the Doctrinal Position of the Missouri Synod,* adopted by Synod in 1932. But talks with the ULCA commissioners got little farther than the opening paragraphs of the *Brief Statement:* "Of the Holy Scriptures."

Talks with the ALC's church fellowship commission proceeded far more optimistically. Every article of the *Brief Statement* was thoroughly discussed. The committees found wide areas of agreement, even on points that in the past had been under dispute. The ALC commissioners, however, felt that the *Brief Statement* should be supplemented in a number of articles, particularly those on inspiration, objective justification, the Antichrist, and a few points regarding the doctrine of the 'last things." Accordingly, they prepared a supplementary document known as the ALC *Declaration.*

After weighing everything, the two committees decided to present both Missouri's *Brief Statement* and the ALC's *Declaration* to the 1938 conventions of their respective church bodies as a basis for future church fellowship. Our Synod's convention of that year, held at St. Louis, adopted the union committee's suggestions but added a number of safeguards, known as the St. Louis Resolutions, to ensure that the remaining divergent points would be fully settled and also that the churches already in fellowship with the Missouri Synod and those in fellowship with the American Lutheran Church would likewise become parties to the agreement between Missouri and the ALC. The 1938 convention of the ALC at Sandusky, Ohio, in turn, approved the *Brief Statement;* however, the adoption resolution noted that the *Brief Statement* was "viewed in the light of our *Declaration."* This phrase aroused the suspicions of quite a number of individuals both in Synod and in the Synodical Conference, and many registered protests.

## *Omission or Oversight?*

Perhaps this is the place to state that it was extremely unfortunate that the Wisconsin Synod did not receive an invitation to participate in the ALC-Missouri union discussions. Our Committee on Lutheran Union was definitely under the impression during the 1935–38 round of talks that such an invitation had been issued. We did not learn otherwise until after 1938 and at once proposed to our Wisconsin Synod brethren that we would urge the ALC commission to extend them an invitation. However, the members of the Wisconsin Synod's Union Committee felt constrained to decline this offer.

Later we sought to ascertain from the commissioners of the ALC whether an invitation had been extended to the Wisconsin Syond, and if not, what the reason might have been. At the next meeting we were given the information that the invitations had been written by hand and hence there were no carbon copies on file and that meanwhile the man who had written them had died. The only other information I have run across bearing on this matter was a reference in an article by Dr. M. Reu in *Kirchliche Zeitschrift* (Oct. 1941), which indicated that the ALC commission had not been counting on representatives of other synods being present at "preliminary negotiations" between ALC and Missouri. Negotiations with Missouri's sister synods would be in order "after results have been attained," the article said.

Whether it was an omission or an oversight, the failure to call in the Wisconsin Synod was most unfortunate. Much as I dislike to indulge in suppositions or probabilities, it is my sober opinion that the whole situation both in the Synodical Conference and in the entire area of Lutheran union would be altogether different today if the Wisconsin Synod had taken part in the discussions from the outset.

As an indication of how warm the union issue had become in Synod, no fewer than 52 memorials were addressed to the 1941 convention when it met in Fort Wayne. "Viewed in the light of our *Declaration*"—the phrase used in the ALC's Sandusky Resolutions— was not acceptable to some in our Synod, even though the ALC commission took pains to explain that the expression merely meant "a supplement to" the *Brief Statement.* To eliminate this obstacle and other areas of possible misunderstanding, the convention instructed our Committee on Doctrinal Unity to frame one clearly written document instead of the two presented in 1938 as a basis for agreement.

By 1944 the two committees, working jointly, had completed their task, though not in time for our Synod's convention at Saginaw. (This was the wartime convention that had first been postponed and later rescheduled after war-imposed transportation restrictions had been relaxed.) Copies of this document, entitled *Doctrinal Affirmation,* were sent to all pastors and teachers of our Synod, to sister synods of the Synodical Conference, and made available also to pastors of the American Lutheran Church.

While the *Affirmation* was given a good deal of careful study, it did not meet with general favor in either body. A big reason no doubt was because it tried to synthesize the *Brief Statement* and the ALC *Declaration.* Some ALC conferences felt it had too strong a "Missourian" accent, while a number of Missourians felt that it was weighted too heavily in favor of the ALC. The 1946 convention of the ALC declined to vote on the *Doctrinal Affirmation,* since, as the resolution stated, the "attempt to formulate a unified doctrinal statement has not produced a document generally acceptable."

## *Fresh Start*

When Synod met for its Centennial Convention (1947) in Chicago, the union question was burning more vigorously than ever. Committee 3 had to deal with some 60 memorials relating to the issue. In accord with the committee's recommendation the convention decided that the 1938 St. Louis Resolutions should be set aside as a basis for establishing fellowship with the ALC. The committee made it clear, however, that this did not mean that the *Brief Statement* was being set aside. In fact, the committee introduced a resolution reaffirming that the *Brief Statement* was a correct expression of Synod's doctrinal position. The convention not only adopted the resolution unanimously but also ordered that the *Brief Statement* be incorporated in the official convention *Proceedings*. The convention then instructed the Committee on Doctrinal Unity to prepare jointly with the ALC committee "one document which is Scriptural, clear, concise, and unequivocal."

Thus assured of a fresh start, our committee, which by this time consisted of Drs. William Arndt, John H. C. Fritz, Frederick H. Brunn, Walter Baepler, Rev. Werner H. Jurgens, Rev. George J. Meyer, and Mr. Herbert Knopp, patiently and conscientiously went to work. Well before the 1950 convention at Milwaukee they had hammered out the *Common Confession* and submitted it to our church for approval.

Committee 3 at Milwaukee went over the document with utmost care and permitted all critics and defenders to present their cases. Convinced that the doctrines treated were in harmony with the Scriptures, the committee recommended its adoption. When I called the motion, it carried overwhelmingly, though I heard a scattering of about six or eight nays. Later I was severely criticized by some for declaring the motion adopted, principally on the claim that such a vote on matters of doctrine and conscience had to be unanimous.

In order to be clear on the contested point, I consulted Synod's Committee on Constitutional Matters. The committee ruled that doctrines are not established by the vote of synodical conventions but only by the Word of God; synodical resolutions merely have the purpose of declaring whether a statement or document is in harmony with the Scriptures. The committee furthermore pointed out that the resolution on the *Common Confession* made provisions for further clarification of the doctrines presented and for supplementing them with a statement of principles covering church practice, particularly in the areas of fellowship, unionism, and lodgery.

While working on the supplementary document, called *Common Confession,* Part II, during the 1950–53 triennium, the doctrinal unity committee met repeatedly with representatives of our sister synods in the Synodical Conference to weigh all objections that had been voiced against Part I of the document. In addition, a conference of the union committees, presidents, vice-presidents, and district presidents of both bodies was held to thoroughly assess the whole situation in a very frank and friendly manner. On the groundwork of these consultations the joint committees drafted *Common Confession,* Part II, a thorough and clear-cut statement, solidly buttressed with Scripture and setting forth how "the Christian faith as expressed in the *Common Confession* must express itself in the life and corporate activity of the church."

The pronouncements of this document on anti-Christian organizations and religious unionism are particularly noteworthy. Those who level charges that "Missourians" are the only ones who are against fraternal organizations ought to read what the *Common Confession,* in which the American Lutheran Church officially concurred, has to say not only about the evils of lodgery but also about the disciplinary action to be exercised by congregations and by the church body. They ought, in fact, to examine the official pronouncements of all Lutheran bodies on this question, and they will realize that, on paper at least, the Lutheran churches of America have consistently expressed themselves as opposed to the anti-Christian tenets of lodgery. As for religious unionism, the *Common Confession* will show clearly that the Synodical Conference bodies are by no means the only ones who recognize and condemn any religious fellowship by which the truth of God's Word is compromised or error is condoned.

Unfortunately, *Common Confession,* Part II, did not appear in finalized form until mid-April 1953. Since many pleaded that the belated appearance of this important material had not allowed sufficient time for congregations, conferences, and individuals to study and evaluate it before the June convention at Houston, the delegates voted that Parts I and II of the *Common Confession* be treated as one document for purposes of study and that final action be taken at the 1956 convention.

### *"The Spirit Triumphed"*

It had taken 18 years—the very years that had been packed with the crises and complications of depression, war, and postwar readjustments—but it was now apparent that the American Lutheran Church and our Synod had moved very close to the goal of agreement in both doctrine and practice. To a large degree this remarkable progress may be attributed to the very friendly and cordial spirit that characterized all the discussions, and in particular to the evident desire of the committee members to reach their conclusions wholly on the basis of the Scriptures and the Lutheran Confessions. Where such an atmosphere prevails even the sharpest differences must disappear, as indeed they did. Time and again conflicting viewpoints vanished as we exposed them to the clear light of the revealed Truth. And when they vanished, there was no gloating over personal triumph or defeat, but humble submission to God's Word. I well recall a remark made at a committee session by Dr. Reu after consensus had been reached on a controversial issue. "Now let no one boast: 'Here we gained a victory,' " he said, "but rather let all exult: 'Here the Holy Spirit triumphed!' "

At the 1956 convention in St. Paul, Synod declared that it recognized the *Common Confession*, "one document composed of Parts I and II," as a statement in harmony with the Sacred Scriptures and the Lutheran Confessions. This selfsame resolution then declared the approved *Common Confession* should no longer serve as a functioning union document. Normally we would have expected this latter part of the resolution to state: Therefore we declare with thanksgiving to God that The Lutheran Church—Missouri Synod is now in pulpit and altar fellowship with the American Lutheran Church. What had happened?

As mentioned earlier, the bodies forming the American Lutheran Conference decided that the time had come to consider merger. On the basis of a doctrinal statement called *United Testimony on Faith and Life,* three of the member bodies, the Evangelical Lutheran Church, the United Evangelical Lutheran Church, and the American Lutheran Church, had by 1956 crystallized plans to form a new body, which took the name The American Lutheran Church (as distinguished from the 1930-vintage American Lutheran Church, with a small "the.")

This development presented a real problem for several reasons. The former ALC, with which our church had reached agreement, would no longer be in existence. Furthermore, the "old" ALC would be united with churches with whom we had had no doctrinal discussions. Then, too, this merger had been formed on the basis of the *United Testimony,* a document that our church's unity committee could not fully approve.

The members of the ALC Committee on Union and Fellowship realized that this development introduced a new element into our efforts to arrive at complete unity. They were fair and honest with us in keeping us informed on developments. We in turn were fair and honest in informing them that there were a number of points in the *United Testimony* that we felt were still unsatisfactory.

Hence we mutually agreed to suspend unity talks between our two bodies pending the completion of the three-way merger. Our 1959 synodical convention at San Francisco authorized the Committee on Doctrinal Unity to invite The ALC to resume talks after it began to function as a new body in January 1961. The committee reported to the 1962 convention that The ALC had accepted the invitation and that a preliminary meeting had been held to explore what the next steps should be.

This exploratory meeting was particularly needed, since by this time a number of new and far-reaching developments had occurred among Lutheran bodies in America. These new developments included a breach in the Synodical Conference, another even larger merger involving four Lutheran bodies, and the initiation of intersynodical talks with a view toward forming a possible successor agency to the National Lutheran Council.

## *"Impasse"*

Throughout the period of some 25 years that our Synod had been holding unity discussions with the ALC, it was apparent that relations within the Synodical Conference were becoming progressively strained. Already in 1938 the Norwegian Synod and the Wisconsin Synod had taken strong exception to Synod's "St. Louis Resolutions." Again in 1944 these two synods severely criticized the *Doctrinal Affirmation* and repeated earlier protests and "warnings" that Synod should revoke its resolutions and suspend further negotiations with the ALC until that body gave up its "unionistic position."

Both sister synods also took issue with two resolutions passed at the Saginaw convention (1944), one recognizing a Scriptural distinction between "joint prayer" and "prayer fellowship," the other sanctioning Lutheran Boy Scout troops under supervision and control of the local pastor and congregation. The Wisconsin Synod also objected to our Synod's position on the military chaplaincy, contending that the chaplaincy was essentially unionistic and involved a mixing of church and state.

Relations between these two synods and ours became quite strained after both our Synod and the ALC adopted the *Common Confession*, Part I, as a doctrinal basis for fellowship. Both sister synods declared that the *Common Confession*, even with the addition of Part II, did not settle past differences between the ALC and the Synodical Conference and was therefore inadequate. The Norwegian Synod went so far as to accuse our Synod of accepting a false position in the doctrine of objective justification. Our Committee on Doctrinal Unity had a series of conferences with committees of the sister synods to go over all the issues but could come to no agreement.

There followed during 1953 and 1954 a "fraternal exchange" of position documents—*A Fraternal Word; A Fraternal Word Examined* (Wisconsin Synod); *Another Fraternal Endeavor; Continuing in His Word* (Wisconsin Synod); *Our Relations with The Lutheran Church—Missouri Synod* (Norwegian Synod); *A Fraternal Reply*—all circulated among the clergy and congregations of the Synodical Conference in an attempt to remove misunderstandings. But neither this approach nor efforts to solve the issues at Synodical Conference conventions seemed to contribute positively toward healing the breach. In June 1955 the Norwegian Synod suspended fellowship relations with our Synod (though continuing membership in the Synodical Conference), and the Wisconsin Synod declared itself in "a state of vigorously protesting fellowship" with us.

Tensions were relieved somewhat when our 1956 convention shelved the *Common Confession* as a functioning union document. To place our intersynodical discussions on a more promising footing, a Joint Union Committee of the four member synods of the Synodical Conference was created to reexamine the specific points under controversy and to seek agreement on them in common doctrinal statements. This procedure seemed to be working out well. Several fine doctrinal statements were formulated. But when the joint discussions focused on the church fellowship question, in which many of the differences converged, the committee encountered trouble in reconciling the divergent views.

In 1959 and again in 1960 theologians from overseas churches in South America, Europe, Australia, and India that are in fellowship with the Synodical Conference came together to review and counsel with us on the fellowship question. The Wisconsin Synod union committee, however, informed the 1960 Synodical Conference convention that the theologians' conferences had not resolved the differences and that an "impasse" had been reached.

In a last-ditch effort to hold the Synodical Conference together, a committee of theologians from the overseas churches was asked to reevaluate the church fellowship statements submitted by the four Synodical Conference synods. Although the overseas committee report, which was presented to a special session of the Synodical Conference in May 1961, urged the synods to seek agreement by restudying and reformulating their fellowship statements "in the necessary context of the doctrine of the Church," the Wisconsin Synod three months later voted to suspend fellowship with the Missouri Synod.

Later that year, I directed a personal appeal to the president and Commission on Doctrinal Matters of the Wisconsin Synod in behalf of our Synod's *Praesidium* and Committee on Doctrinal Unity to reopen the discussions. We were ready to take this step even though the Wisconsin Synod resolution stipulated that any future discussions would have to be conducted "outside the framework of fellowship."

This effort too proved futile. The reply of the Wisconsin Synod's commission stated that it found "no indication of developments that would assure a profitable meeting." The (Norwegian) Evangelical Lutheran Synod at its June 1963 convention voted to withdraw from the Synodical Conference, and in August by a 138 to 28 vote the Wisconsin Synod followed suit.

IN PURSUIT OF UNITY

## *Rallying Point*

I find it difficult to express in words the deep sadness I feel that our sister churches felt constrained to sever the ties that for 90 years had bound us together in a blessed and fruitful fellowship. Their decision is the more regrettable since the differences between us lie almost entirely in the area of practice rather than doctrine, in the application of Scriptural principles rather than in the principles themselves. Their action in withdrawing from the Synodical Conference was certainly premature, for the course advocated by our overseas brethren that we mutually approach the goal of agreement "by the traditional highway of the doctrine of the Church" offered a promising opportunity for the Holy Spirit to lead us into the true unity in the bond of peace, which He desires and for which we pray.

Throughout the years of tension the fourth member body of the Synodical Conference—the (Slovak) Synod of Evangelical Lutheran Churches—maintained most cordial relations with our Synod and also continued fellowship ties with the two protesting bodies. Leaders of the SELC, several of whom were named to the Synodical Conference presidency, worked valiantly to compose its internal difficulties and to keep the federation—the longest continuous Lutheran alliance in America—intact.

Recently Dr. John Daniel, conference president since 1960, announced that the Synodical Conference will continue its work and that plans were envisioned to expand it into an international Synodical Conference, a "meaningful rallying point" for Lutheran churches in Europe and on other continents who wish to remain faithful to the Word of God and the Lutheran Confessions.[1]

## *Changed Map*

At the close of 1961, statistics showed that the Missouri Synod had grown to be the largest Lutheran body on the American continent, a ranking that since 1918 had been held by the United Lutheran Church in America. It was already evident at that time, however, that

---

[1] The Synodical Conference ultimately disbanded when the SELC merger was effected and no partner churches remained. Nevertheless, the germ of this idea grew into the present ILC.

Synod would be holding the top place only a matter of months. During 1961, the same year that saw the birth of The American Lutheran Church, four other Lutheran bodies ratified a merger agreement that would join them in by far the largest Lutheran body in America. This new body was constituted in June 1962 as the "Lutheran Church in America." Its choice of a rather sweeping name can perhaps be forgiven, since it brought together churches of four different ethnic and linguistic backgrounds: the United Lutheran Church in America, largely of German origin; the American Evangelical Lutheran Church (Danish); the Augustana Lutheran Church (Swedish); and the Finnish Evangelical Lutheran Church, also known as the Suomi Synod.

The next year (1963) the Lutheran Free Church merged with The American Lutheran Church, and the National Evangelical Lutheran Church (Finnish) merged with our Missouri Synod. Thus at this date 95 percent of America's 8,500,000 Lutherans have been drawn together in three major bodies.

Looking back, I can only marvel at the vast change in the "map" of American Lutheranism in little more than a generation.

When I was ordained to the ministry, there were no less than 67 different synods in our country. One despaired of even trying to distinguish between them. Even as late as 1930, when there were some 20 different bodies bearing the Lutheran name, their various designations, boundaries, alignments, and interrelationships were a source of confusion not only to the public generally but to most Lutherans themselves. Few indeed are the Lutherans who will not rejoice that the once sadly shattered state of US Lutheranism has been blessed with such a steady and marked improvement.

Whether America's Lutherans will in the future attain the desired goal of one united church is more than I either dare or care to predict. But I do know that the desire among Lutherans not merely to unite but to seek unity on the foundation of sound Scriptural doctrine and correct practice has never been so deep or so genuine as it is today.

All eight bodies involved in the formation of The American Lutheran Church and the Lutheran Church in America had been members of the National Lutheran Council. Because of the mergers the council in 1962 was left with only two participating churches, a situation that led the NLC to restudy its role and to seek a broader base by involving other Lutheran bodies in the US.

The NLC had been organized in 1918 as an outgrowth of cooperative efforts among Lutheran bodies to publicize the 400th anniversary of the Reformation and also to provide spiritual ministration for Lutheran men in the armed services during World War I. By organizing as the National Lutheran Commission for Soldiers' and Sailors' Welfare, 13 bodies cooperated in appointing camp pastors to minister to their servicemen in the many camps and bases opened across the country.

Because the Synodical Conference churches realized that we could not participate in such a program without direct involvement in areas presupposing agreement in doctrine, we appointed our own Army and Navy Board to direct our work among those called to the colors. However, our Army and Navy Board cooperated with the NLC in certain "external" matters, that is, in areas that did not involve our pastors in the administration of the Word and the sacraments. Joint use of a service center at Camp Funston, Kansas, and at one or two other places is a case in point.

## *No Hitchhiker*

The NLC continued its activities for some years after the war, especially in channeling aid to the prostrated Lutheran churches in Europe. Relief and rehabilitation activities led to the organization of Lutheran World Service. Though its activity diminished following the war emergency, the council did not disband. Under a constitution revised in 1926, the council enlarged the scope of its action by launching into joint publicity work, campus work, welfare work, mission work among African-Americans, and a few other endeavors.

The Missouri Synod never saw its way clear to join the NLC. However, wherever Synod's confessional position was sufficiently safeguarded, it sought to cooperate with the council. In such "external" areas as Lutheran World Relief, joint service centers for military personnel, immigrant and refugee service, prisoner of war service, and to a certain extent in social welfare work the two groups have worked together with very satisfying results and little friction.

In these cooperative arrangements our Synod has always carried its share of the load and was ready and willing to do even more. I recall, for instance, the matter of caring for the so-called orphaned missions, that is, Lutheran missions which were cut off from the support of their home base by the exigencies of war. During World War I our Synod had the opportunity to aid orphaned missions in China. World War II brought hardships to even more such missions.

At a meeting with representatives of the NLC in Columbus, at which we discussed the policy of cooperation we would follow in ministering to Lutherans in military service, we also aired the subject of orphaned missions. Then and there we offered to take over one or more of these missions, and the suggestion was forthwith adopted. But to our deep disappointment we were later informed that it had not been found feasible to carry out this resolution.

I mention this because there have been those, also within our own ranks, who have charged Missouri with unwillingness to cooperate. Some have even said that we have gone along on joint programs to take a "free ride." That is not true. The facts are there, and here as elsewhere we would be spared such irresponsible statements if the facts of the case were first investigated and carefully considered. I can honestly say that I know of not a single instance in which our Synod did not pay its full share and sometimes even more than its fair share. The Missouri Synod has never been a "hitchhiker."

## *Confessional Priority*

When NLC leaders invited our church in 1960 to discuss the possibility of forming a future inter-Lutheran agency to replace the council, Synod's Committee on Doctrinal Unity offered the suggestion that the theological and confessional aspects of such an alliance be given priority in the discussions. The NLC officials were willing to proceed along these lines.

Accordingly, from July 1960 to November 1961 a series of exploratory discussions were held among theologians of the ALC, LCA, and our Synod, centering in the statement of the Augsburg

Confession, Article VII (Latin text): "For the true unity of the church it is enough to agree concerning the teachings of the Gospel and the administration of the Sacraments."[2] These conversations revealed, as a summary report of the entire group phrased it, "a far greater extent of consensus on the subjects discussed than had been generally realized." In connection with the report Dr. Oliver R. Harms, elected to Synod's presidency in 1962, stated: "The evident blessing of God rested upon the deliberations."

Our Synod no doubt would have been drawn into closer association with the NLC far earlier had the principle of giving priority to "the theological and confessional aspects" been recognized. In this connection I cannot but recall the time Dr. S. E. Engstrom, an Augustana Synod mission executive who later was also president of the American Lutheran Conference, visited our first free conference with European Lutheran theologians at Bad Boll shortly after the war. Dr. Engstrom, then in Germany as a representative of the Lutheran World Federation, was so impressed with the doctrinal discussions that he asked me: "Why don't we have such 'Bad Boll meetings' among the Lutherans of America?" I assured him that Missouri was very willing. He replied that when he got home he was going to pass along his Bad Boll impressions to other Lutheran leaders and see what he could do to have them arrange such a meeting. Evidently he wasn't too successful.

At his encouragement, however, officials and representatives of most Lutheran bodies came together in Chicago on September 28, 1953. It was most regrettable that, because of a heart attack that later caused his death, Dr. Engstrom himself was not present.

Two of the presidents at the meeting indicated that if such inter-Lutheran gatherings meant more doctrinal discussions, they were not interested and would not attend. They held that all Lutheran bodies in America subscribed to the Lutheran Confessions and that subscription to the confessions should suffice. In our reply we stressed that doctrinal discussions are essential to determine whether or not we are fully agreed on the doctrine set forth in the confessions, and wherever

---

[2] Theodore G. Tappert, ed., *The Book of Concord: The Confessions of the Evangelical Lutheran Church* (Philadelphia: Fortress, 1959), 32.

such agreement was lacking, to seek it under the Holy Spirit's blessing.

The meeting adjourned without attaining the objective so much desired by Dr. Engstrom and also by us who, like our synodical forebears, have ever been ready to seek and find confessional agreement with all who bear the name Lutheran.

As a result of the LCA-ALC-Missouri exploratory talks concerning the possibility of future cooperation, an Inter-Lutheran Consultation was formed, comprising seven members of each of the three bodies (later joined by the Synod of Evangelical Lutheran Churches), to work out plans and a possible structure of a successor agency to the NLC. In a small committee meeting to determine the direction that future planning should take and the foundation on which it should rest, some of the spokesmen who had previously voiced objections to doctrinal discussions now stated that such theological discussions must be given priority. We were delighted and most grateful when we heard this.

By early 1964 the consultation had completed a provisional constitution for the new agency, which was given the tentative name "The Lutheran Council in the United States of America." A feature of the proposed new council not found in the NLC is the provision that participating bodies should engage in a common program of "systematic and continuing" theological studies. The constitution will be submitted to the individual church bodies at their coming biennial conventions, which are scheduled to take place between October 1964 and June 1966.

What a blessing it would be if by means of such systematic and continuing theological studies all of America's—indeed, the world's—Lutherans could be united *on the solid foundation of Holy Writ and the witness of the Lutheran Confessions!*

*{Chapter Fourteen}*

# ROSES AND THORNS

During my 33-year service as an official of our Synod I experienced many wonderful joys and pleasures. To have had so many God-given opportunities to serve my church for so many years was in itself a singular privilege. I must marvel again and again that God deigned to use me for such service and must marvel even more that He granted a measure of success to my humble efforts. When I think of the many other rich and rewarding experiences that have come to me—the privilege of working together with outstanding leaders of our church in both the theological and the administrative fields, the opportunity of meeting and conferring with eminent men of our sister churches in America and in all the other continents, the many contacts with distinguished churchmen of other Lutheran bodies in America and in lands across the sea—all in all, I must acknowledge that through the years God has granted me exceptional, though undeserved, joys and privileges.

The years, however, also brought with them darker and at times difficult and discouraging experiences. My cup at times contained some bitter draughts. As happens in a growing church, complex problems arose that do not readily yield to solutions acceptable to all alike. Some felt dissatisfied with Synod's policies and actions and gave vent to their feelings in sharp criticism and often in bitter accusations. Some insisted on going their own way when things were not to their liking, regardless of how it affected their church body. Sometimes this contrariness stemmed from indifference to doctrinal principles; at other times it arose from attempts to enforce doctrinal principles in a legalistic manner.

This I Recall

## Volley from London

As indicated in the previous chapter, the various attempts made by synodical committees and commissions to arrive at a doctrinal basis for fellowship with the American Lutheran Church drew some rather heavy and sustained fire from individuals and groups. Among the early volleys was one from a rather unexpected source—London, England. It was a publication called the *Crucible,* launched by Rev. W. M. Oesch, then pastor of Synod's two member churches in London. A native of Colorado, Pastor Oesch had become a citizen of Germany when assigned to the Evangelical Lutheran Free Church of Saxony after his graduation from the St. Louis seminary. He then accepted the call to the London churches in 1935.[1]

The very first sentence in the *Crucible,* in an article titled "Quo Vadis, Ecclesia?" (January 1939), read: "Plainly our church is at the parting of ways." The bimonthly publication, which took sharp issue with the action of the 1938 St. Louis convention declaring the *Brief Statement* and the ALC *Declaration* (together with the resolutions added by the convention as safeguards) a doctrinal basis for future fellowship, was sent to all pastors in Synod without the previous knowledge of Synod's officials. The editor simply announced on the inside cover that its publication and dissemination were necessary because Synod's "internal situation" had deterred others "from the plain speaking which is necessary in view of the grave intersynodical situation; the waning of doctrinal control; the externalistic, legalistic, enthusiastic *Zeitgeist* among us"; and several other reasons.

Several numbers of the *Crucible* had been issued when threatening war clouds led Pastor Oesch to request American repatriation through my office. The State Department advised me that such a transaction could be effected only if the applicant would be a resident in our country for at least six months. I relayed this information to the pastor in London. Meanwhile he had gone to Germany to discuss our Synod's unity action with a conference of the Free Church. Just then the Nazis unleashed their invasion of Poland.

---

[1] Oesch became a professor at the Lutheran seminary in Oberursel. He helped to warn the LCMS about the dangers of the higher-critical majority on the St. Louis seminary faculty through his publication, "Memorandum inter Nos."

England and the Reich were at war, and Pastor Oesch could not get back to London. The *Crucible* came to an abrupt stop.

An editorial note in the *Crucible* stated that the editor would "yield the editorial pen to an abler writer in the US as soon as the organization is sufficiently complete." We wondered about this. But sure enough, "the organization," flying the banner "The Confessional Lutheran Publicity Bureau," soon appeared. Its "editorial pen," called the *Confessional Lutheran,* took up the polemical cudgels where the *Crucible* had left off. Writers took a vehement stand against the 1938 St. Louis Resolutions and continued to oppose all the other unity documents drafted by the Missouri Synod and ALC committees, including the *Common Confession,* which Synod in 1956 recognized as a statement in harmony with the Sacred Scriptures and the Lutheran Confessions.

## *Many Bosses*

Unfortunately, much of the criticism voiced in its pages was quite sharp and contained not a little invective. Earlier volumes of the paper stated that it was published "in the interest of ecumenical Lutheranism" (later changed to "in the interest of Lutheran unity"). Its stance throughout the 25 years it has appeared, however, was consistently one of opposition—with Synod and its leadership looked upon as the "opponents." Though unwarranted charges were made and at times cut deeply, we did not undertake to answer them directly. As the old German proverb puts it: *Wet am Wege baut hat viele Meister* (He who builds on the highway will have many bosses), I realized that anyone in an official position must expect criticism. I felt the vast majority of our people knew better and would understand—as indeed they did.

What really hurt more than the personal attacks was the harsh criticism leveled against the action taken by synodical conventions. At our conventions, floor committees (often also called review committees) devote hours upon hours to hear and discuss the pros and cons of each question. They are chosen with great care and represent all areas of the church. Everyone entitled to do so may take the opportunity to present his views. Then the convention itself spends much time on a thorough discussion of the recommendations proposed by the floor committee. As chairman I always made it a strict point never to call for a vote on an important issue until it was certain that all who had asked for the floor had had an opportunity to speak. Time and again when weary or overanxious delegates called for the "previous question," I cautioned the convention to drop or defeat such a motion because it has the effect of cutting off all debate.

And still charges were raised that conventions were "managed" or "rigged" or otherwise manipulated! I realize of course that sometimes, despite all precautions, mistakes can occur at conventions. A synodical convention is not perfect. It is composed of human beings. However, if a mistake should occur, it should be corrected in an orderly way. Rushing into print with dark insinuations or ill-considered charges is never a proper procedure and seldom, if ever, leads to a satisfactory conclusion.

## *Mistimed Antidote*

Another very difficult and soul-trying period for me was precipitated by the appearance of *A Statement,* which was released over the signatures of 44 pastors and professors of Synod after a meeting in Chicago early in September 1945. The signers, some in positions of prominence in the church, had met to determine what might be done to counteract "a strange and pernicious spirit, utterly at variance with the fundamental concepts of the Gospel and the genius of the Lutheran Church, [which] has lifted its ugly head in more than one area of our beloved Synod," as it was expressed in the invitation to the meeting. This Chicago statement was drafted as a series of 12 "affirmations," to each of which was appended a "deploration." Among the matters deplored were:

> A loveless attitude manifesting itself within Synod . . . expressed in suspicions of brethren, in the impugning of motives, and in condemnation of all who have expressed differing opinions concerning some of the problems confronting our church today; a tendency in our Synod to substitute human judgments, synodical resolutions, or other sources of authority for the supreme authority of Scripture; all

man-made walls and barriers which would hinder the free course of the Gospel in the world; any tendency which reduces the warmth and power of the Gospel to a set of intellectual propositions which are to be grasped solely by the mind of man; the tendency to apply the non-Biblical term *unionism* to any and every contact between Christians of other denominations.

Additionally they "deplored" the supposed misuse of certain Bible passages, as Romans 16:17–18 and 1 Thessalonians 5:22. The statement also affirmed the signers' conviction that "in keeping with historic Lutheran tradition" fellowship among Lutherans is possible "without complete agreement in details of doctrine and practice which have never been considered divisive in the Lutheran Church."[2]

The Chicago statement came to my attention just as I was preparing to leave on my mission to war-stricken Europe in 1945. I knew that it would spell trouble with a capital T, and I pleaded with the "continuation committee" organized by the signers to postpone further action until my return so that the vice-presidents and I might go into the matter more carefully. Despite our vigorous protests the statement was mailed to all of Synod's pastors.

I was told that disseminating the document would serve Synod's welfare and help me personally, as it would provide an antidote for the ultra-critical approach described above. I doubt very much that either group ever weighed very carefully whether jumping into print was the proper thing to do. Why, I have asked myself a hundred times, why did they not talk their differences over in a spirit of brotherly love? Both sides spoke glowingly of their love of truth and the need to speak the truth in love—why then did they not "speak to" rather than direct public printed barrages "against" each other? As it was, a charged atmosphere of pro and contra quickly developed, and a rather bitter controversy resulted.

---

[2] These topics were related to the Adolph Brux case. He was removed by mission director Frederick Brand after 1925 for holding unionistic services in India. In 1965, along with the "Mission Affirmations," the LCMS apologized to Brux. The Brux case was the crux of the 1935 electioneering deplored by Behnken, as the appendix shows. The case was unsealed circa 2002.

What should be done? This was the question that confronted us when I returned from Europe. We had noted that some in other Lutheran bodies had hailed the Chicago statement as a manifesto. We learned also that *A Statement* had gained other signers, some voluntary, some solicited—perhaps more than 200 in all. To ventilate the situation, I called a meeting of the College of District Presidents and the "Forty-Four." It was decided at this meeting that the issues be examined and resolved, if possible, by a joint committee—ten men from the signers and ten to be appointed by me to represent "the other side." (Let me add that if I had it to do over again I would never accept such an assignment.)

The "Ten and Ten" had a series of meetings under the chairmanship of President W. H. Meyer of the Kansas District, chosen by mutual agreement as an "impartial" man. It became apparent that the "Ten and Ten" could come to no satisfactory solution. Both the *Praesidium* and Chairman Meyer agreed that further meetings would serve no useful purpose.

Then the members of the *Praesidium* themselves took the matter in hand by meeting with representatives of the "Forty-Four." As a result the spokesmen of the signers agreed to withdraw *A Statement* as a basis for further discussion; the *Praesidium* in turn agreed that the issues that had been raised should be presented in a series of special study documents prepared by men whom I should choose.

During the next few years five such Scripture-based studies by unnamed authors were sent to Synod's pastors. How much and how thoroughly they were studied and explored by pastoral conferences I do not know, but this much is certain: Our pastors were given some very excellent and meaty material that should have sent them deeply into the Scriptures and evoked many a profitable discusion. The "Forty-Four" as an organized group has long since gone out of existence. Today one hears only an occasional reference to it.

## Painful Spots

Also the stresses and strains within the Synodical Conference were a source of no little concern and heartache to me personally and, I know, also to the others who served with me on the Intersynodical

Committee. I am thinking especially of the chairman, Dr. John H. Meyer, and Vice-Presidents Herman Harms and Henry Grueber. At practically every meeting we had to listen to charge after charge leveled against the Missouri Synod.

On the one hand, there were charges of doctrinal laxity or confessional compromise raised particularly in connection with the doctrinal statements Synod adopted in seeking agreement with the ALC. At such times the atmosphere of our fraternal consultations was rather heavily charged. On the other hand, I can vividly recall that often meetings were scarcely opened when those representing some of our sister synods would start in listing complaints and indictments of "unionistic practice" interspersed with insistent demands of what we were going to do about it.

These were, to say the least, unhappy occasions. The sad part of it was that in many an instance we had to admit that the complaint was warranted. This or that member of Synod had simply disregarded Synod's practice or had acted unthinkingly or irresponsibly without conferring with his brethren and without duly considering the effect his action would have on the church. Such ecclesiastical freewheelers all too often placed me and also their district officials on some very painful and most embarrassing spots. Instead of helping to relieve an already overheated situation in the Synodical Conference, they only added fuel to the fire.

## *New Theology*

Another deeply disturbing and disheartening experience that fell to my lot was the controversy within Synod concerning the inerrancy of the Scriptures. This dispute, as so many others, had its roots in European theological circles, where a movement known as neo-orthodoxy had developed in recent decades as a reaction to the rationalistic and liberalistic attitude toward the Bible that had long held sway.

The new emphasis that this movement placed on the Bible as God's revelation and on the centrality of Christ was all to the good. Neo-orthodoxy, however, stops a good way short of accepting the Bible in all its parts as the inerrant Word of God. Some hold the viewpoint that only those parts of the Bible that speak directly and convincingly to the individual are "Word of God" to him. Others hold that many Bible accounts, such as the early chapters of Genesis, the Book of Jonah, the recorded miracles, and other parts are mainly "story forms" that must be "demythologized" before their real meaning and intention can be arrived at. It need not be pointed out that these and other presumptions of the new theology constitute either open or veiled attacks on the inerrancy of Holy Writ.

Currents of such approaches to Scripture were soon touching American shores. Theologians—and I include also those whom our church has called to teach and to lead in theology—must concern themselves with these matters. For the sake of both their students and for the church in general, they must not only know what is going on in the theological world but must also be driven ever deeper into the Scriptures to evaluate such theological trends and theories in the light of Holy Writ, the unchanging constant, the clear-sounding "Thus saith the Lord."

Unfortunately, some who had made the problems connected with Bible interpretation their special concern advanced the opinion that perhaps the term "inerrancy" ought no longer to be used. They did this in consideration of the newer views regarding the nature of God's revelation and also because of certain difficulties and variations in the Bible records. This set off a sharp controversy, which led to some ugly name calling, accusations, and recriminations. Nothing during my 27 years in office caused me more heartache.

I am most grateful that the vice-presidents, the district presidents, and other synodical leaders supported me so staunchly. Together we made it crystal clear that Article II, paragraph 1 of Synod's constitution: "Synod, and every member of Synod, accepts without reservation the Scriptures of the Old and the New Testament as the written Word of God and the only rule and norm of faith and practice," dare never be weakened or slighted, and that the bylaw pledging professors at Synod's institutions to the Scriptures "as the inspired and inerrant Word of God" must be honestly and consistently upheld. May God ever keep it so.

## Roses and Thorns

### *"Not Up to Him"*

Quite often I have been asked why I ever accepted still another term of office at the 1959 convention, in view of the proliferating "thorns" among the presidential "roses." In 1956 when I assumed my eighth successive term, I fully believed that it would be my last. In fact, I announced this as my intention at the convention. As the San Francisco convention approached—I was then 75—some wrote me to urge that I do not permit my name to go on the ballot. A few even suggested that a younger man with a new outlook and fresh ideas should be elected. Why, then, permit my name to stand for reelection? And why accept if elected?

Actually it was a combination of reasons that influenced my decision. But chiefly it was my settled conviction, strengthened by the example of my sainted predecessor, that in such a decision one must let God decide and that God decides through His Church. As I told the editor of the *Correspondent,* the organ of the Aid Association for Lutherans, in an interview some months before the 1959 convention: "God lets a person know through His people." Their voice or their silence in the balloting would indicate whether God wanted me to continue to serve or to retire.

There were also other indications. Quite a number of kind brethren impressed on me either orally or by letter that I had no right to decline if the Church asked me to serve. Then, too, I was aware that God had been exceptionally gracious in granting me continued health and vigor. I had, it seemed, experienced little letup in energy or in staying power to keep abreast of my work. In this connection, an item in one of the regular columns of the *American Lutheran* (September 1956) seemed to have particularly a message for me. Let me quote it:

> When a successor was needed for the now sainted Dr. Pfotenhauer God led our people to elect this up-and-coming missionary with administrative ability from the far Southwest. For 21 years Dr. Behnken has been President of our great church body and has now been reelected for an eighth term. He says it will be his last. That is not up to him.

Gladstone was prime minister of Great Britain at 85; Edison was still taking out patents on inventions at 80; Titian painted some of his best works after 70. We have not as yet given in to the modern craze for putting fledglings in positions of authority—bishops with scarcely a gray hair on their heads and generals who do not need to use a razor.

Accordingly, when the fourth ballot at the San Francisco Civic Auditorium revealed the decision of the delegates, I knew there was only one thing for me to do. In my acceptance address the next day I said: "Since you have cast your vote as a representative of the Church, I interpret your decision to mean that God wants me to serve." Retirement, God knows, would have been welcome. I accepted His choice for me, however, expressed through the call of His people, as the one that would redound to His glory and the welfare of His kingdom.

## *Unconstitutional*

A general feeling of optimism at the San Francisco convention led many to feel that the 1959–62 triennium would be a reasonably quiet one. I was inclined to agree. The "venture of faith" spirit manifested by the convention gave high promise that Synod was in a mood to meet its missionary, educational, and financial challenges. The convention had also expressed itself clearly and with conviction on the doctrinal issues that had been causing some disturbance. Everything seemed to augur well.

But we were wrong. As it unfolded, the triennium proved to be the most difficult and most trying of all my terms in office. News commentators during that period often remarked that unrest, tension, and dissatisfaction seemed to be characteristic of the temper of the times. Occasionally I, too, felt that some of this had also filtered into the bloodstream of the Church.

One question, which soon erupted into warm debate in many corners of Synod, revolved about the constitutionality of a San Francisco resolution known as "Resolution 9." This resolution, adopted by the convention as a recommendation of Committee 3 (Doctrinal Matters), declared that Synod's pastors, teachers, and professors are held to teach and act in harmony with every doctrinal statement of a confessional nature adopted by Synod as a true exposition of the Scriptures. Individuals, conferences, and even entire districts contested this resolution on the claim that it raised doctrinal statements of more recent origin (such as the *Brief Statement* and the *Common Confession)* to the level of the historic Lutheran Confessions laid down in Synod's doctrinal platform.

Prior to the 1962 convention the question was submitted to the Committee on Constitutional Matters. Because Resolution 9 had the effect of amending Synod's confessional basis without following the procedure required for such an amendment in the constitution, the committee held Resolution 9 to be unconstitutional. The Cleveland convention resolution that upheld this ruling, however, clearly emphasized that "the doctrinal content or the Scriptural correctness of any doctrinal statements is not being judged or questioned in the consideration of the constitutionality of Resolution 9, but the question of constitutionality is *confined to proper procedure."* (Italics added.—J. W. B.)

Another very important but burdensome and problem-filled task that rested on me and the other officials during my final term was the implementation of the Survey Commission Report, calling for streamlining and restructuring Synod's administration. The Survey Commission (some called it the Little Hoover Commission) had been appointed by request of the 1956 convention because many maintained that our administrative setup had grown top-heavy and required a disproportionate amount of money for "overhead." Many expected great savings both in money and in administrative manpower to result from the commission's work.

The much-discussed report was duly implemented, and no doubt much greater coordination and efficiency was achieved in the process. But the great savings, to the disappointment of many, just did not materialize. The survey, in fact, revealed that some departments were heavily overloaded with duties and demands that Synod itself had imposed. Many members of Synod had forgotten that a rapidly growing and expanding church must reckon with a growing need for administrative personnel if it is to function efficiently.

Also during this triennium, difficulties arising from the inerrancy question flared anew. Charges and protests, claims and counterclaims, flew thick and fast. I and the others charged with responsibility for doctrinal supervision sought to pursue in an evangelical way the course we deemed necessary to clarify and settle the issue. The *Praesidium* and the College of District Presidents, together with the faculties of our two seminaries, thoroughly went over the accusations with the accused and arrived at what I believed was a full and satisfactory clarification of the issues. We reported the outcome to our pastors and teachers by letter, and to the church at large in the columns of the *Lutheran Witness*.

### "Crisis Convention"

Because of these tensions and signs of disturbance during the triennium, there were some who began to refer to the approaching convention at Cleveland as a "crisis convention." Already months before the convention I was fully aware that we would be facing an enormous amount of business and particularly that doctrinal and intersynodical matters would necessarily consume a very large portion of our convention time. Anyone who even glanced at the reports and memorials addressed to the convention realized that the doctrinal issues would demand earnest and prayerful deliberation, frank and open discussion, and firm action.

Both I and my associates worked with particular care in selecting the 40 men who were to serve on Committee 3, the floor committee on doctrinal matters. We made it our concern to pick men who were known to be doctrinally sound and intellectually capable. I asked these men to meet for several days about a month before the convention in order that they might organize, form subcommittees, and study in advance the reports and memorials assigned to them. Furthermore, I requested this committee not only to meet in Cleveland a full week prior to the convention opening but also, for the first time in Synod's history, to hold preconvention open hearings so that all the controversial issues could be fully aired.

Practically all the convention delegates—and hundreds of other interested persons as well—followed my plea to attend these open hearings. Dr. Theodore F. Nickel, the committee chairman, handled the hearings in admirable fashion. Everyone who so desired was given an opportunity to express himself—so long as he stayed with the subject under discussion. At the same time the committee members were able to get at first hand all the information they desired regarding the issues and complaints. As I think back to those days in Cleveland, I can only be deeply grateful that the Lord led us to arrange for these open hearings.

Constantly in my heart, as I presided over the Cleveland convention session, was the prayer that God would give me the gift of Christian patience. No matter how restive or over-anxious some delegates became, I was determined that all who had any opinions or arguments to present on doctrinal issues should have the privilege and opportunity to speak. Because the delegates were seated almost the entire length of the huge auditorium, I asked all speakers to identify themselves whenever they took their place at one of the eight floor microphones. On the chairman's rostrum I had a control panel at my side that flashed a red light whenever a speaker called for the floor. Before calling any vote I made doubly sure that the panel showed "all clear." I insisted also that no debate should be cut off by any parliamentary device, such as a call for the previous question.

Throughout the convention this system operated smoothly and effectively. At times, as is quite normal when there is a large audience and a live issue, speakers would get a bit too vehement and overemphatic, which would cause "mike blast." I would then have to interrupt with the request: "Move back a little from the microphone, please." Occasionally, when I had to do this several times, it would cause a ripple of laughter. This usually served as a "tension reliever," particularly when someone was heard adding: "Yeah, about two miles back, please!"

It was gratifying at the close of the convention to have one of the delegates, who had perhaps taken the "mike" more than anyone else, approach me and say: "I want to thank you for being fair and impartial. I may not always have agreed with you, but you were very fair." Much as I appreciated his remark at the time, I had reason to cherish it even more later on, when charges of convention "managing" were again placed on my doorstep.

The long and rather strenuous 1962 convention, which closed with the installation of my worthy successor, Dr. Oliver R. Harms, is now history. Yes, as I now view it from a perspective of some 20 months, I have no hesitancy about calling it historic. The gloomy and pessimistic predictions of "crisis" and "crackup" faded like fog before the morning sun. Many—and there must have been very many—members of our church must have been praying most fervently that God would bestow His Spirit in rich measure on their fellow members gathered in Cleveland.

To me it was decidedly evident that He, the Spirit of truth and power, was the Chief Delegate, leading, directing, persuading, and convincing all under-delegates. Thanks to His gracious presence, the members of Synod showed clearly that they wanted no part of liberalism, or of legalism, or of radicalism. By the action they took the delegates furnished convincing evidence that they wanted their church to continue in the "old paths" of strong evangelical confessionalism. They left no doubt that The Lutheran Church—Missouri Synod is unalterably committed to the cause of sound, solid, conservative Lutheranism.

Of course I am not so naive as to believe that every issue has now been settled completely. The Church, I know, always has and always will face issues, both old and new. And it is the mark of a strong confessional church to examine each issue and to reexamine itself in the light of God's holy Word and to be ready to accept or to condemn with a clear "Thus saith the Lord." In keeping with this principle the Cleveland delegates referred a number of the current issues to the Commission on Theology and Church Relations for expert and incisive study. Preliminary progress reports issued by the commission certainly give indication that it is working under the Spirit's evident blessing.

During the time our convention was in session in Cleveland, the Lutheran Church in America was holding its constituting convention just across Lake Erie from us, in Detroit. As this was only minutes away by plane, our convention requested me to drop in personally on June 30 to convey our Synod's greetings.

This was my last official act as president.

I shall never forget the warm—yes, I would even say enthusiastic—welcome given me by the more than 2,000 delegates in Detroit's great Cobo Hall. I was overwhelmed. Three times as I spoke this great crowd gave me a tremendous ovation. Perhaps you would like to know what I said:

Dear Friends in Christ:

You have been so very kind and gracious as to invite me to your wonderful meeting. You are in a decidedly festive mood. Success has crowned your efforts of the past few years. The Lutheran Church in America, for which you have been praying, to which you have looked forward with great eagerness, and on which many of you have spent hours upon hours, days upon days, weeks upon weeks, of earnest and intensive work, is now a reality. Another union of several Lutheran church bodies is an accomplished fact. Hence it is my privilege to bring to you as a new and by far the largest Lutheran church body in America, the cordial greetings and hearty felicitations of The Lutheran Church—Missouri Synod.

We realize that the union of your church came as a result of conversations or negotiations concerning doctrine, life, and church policies. This is the true foundation on which to build. Unity must be the basis for union. God wants His people constantly to endeavor to keep the unity of the Spirit in the bond of peace. Our Savior is concerned about the message which His Church is to proclaim. We are to be His ambassadors to the world in which we live. As ambassadors we must deliver His message. The Holy Spirit has given us this message in clear, unmistakable language. We have it in God's Book, the Holy Bible, divinely inspired and hence infallible.

God has been exceptionally gracious to the Lutheran Church. Through the Reformation we have the great God-pleasing slogan *sola Scriptura, sola gratia, sola fide*. What a precious heritage! Furthermore as Lutherans we have the precious heritage of the marvelous Lutheran Confessions, a faithful and correct exposition of God's holy Word. What a priceless treasure! No other church body among Protestants has anything like it.

You are well aware of the fact that The Lutheran Church—Missouri Synod has ever considered the issue of Biblical doctrine and Scriptural practice of paramount importance. We are thoroughly convinced that this is what we Lutherans in America and Lutherans throughout the world need most of all. Yes, we are persuaded that it is the witness which we owe to Protestantism, Catholicism, and paganism throughout the world.

We look forward with great anticipation to the firm resolve and wholehearted determination of your new church body, the Lutheran Church in America, to stand solidly on Holy Writ as the true foundation. We pray that God may grant you ever deeper convictions about the Lutheran Confessions as God's wonderful gift to the Lutheran Church. What the future may bring we cannot foretell, but we surely pray fervently that ultimately it may please God to bring about union on the solid basis of true unity. We plead with God to equip and strengthen all of us for the conflict raging today against Scripture, whether it be neo-orthodoxy, rationalism, atheistic communism, or any other issue.

I know that you will join me in the prayer that God may make us ever more faithful and loyal to Holy Writ. May we ever bear in mind that the very heart and core of all this is "Jesus Christ, and Him crucified." To that God-pleasing end The Lutheran Church—Missouri Synod greets you and congratulates you. May God graciously bless you!

The first round of applause given me was not too surprising. It acknowledged the historic first appearance of a president of the Missouri Synod at a convention of the Lutheran Church in America or of any of the churches that formed this new body. The final burst of applause was also understandable, for, after all, I had finished speaking and my talk had not been too long.

What was surprising to me—and no surprise could have been more agreeable—was the thunderous ovation that greeted the words in which I expressed the hope that God would bring about Lutheran union on the basis of true unity—unity on the true foundation of Holy Writ and the Lutheran Confessions.

If indeed I needed convincing, that day in Cobo Hall convinced me thoroughly that there is a deep, sincere yearning in America's rank and file Lutherans not merely for Lutheran union but for Lutheran unity—the only true and enduring foundation for union.

God speed the day when that unity will be realized.

# EPILOGUE

"How does it feel to be retired?"

Ever since Synod decided that I should bear the title "Honorary President," the question has greeted me everywhere I go.

My invariable answer is an unreserved "Wonderful!" To be relieved of heavy administrative duties and the responsibility of decision making—indeed just to be free from the demands of an office-hours regimen—is wonderful.

It is even more wonderful to be given the opportunity for continued active Kingdom service. Almost from the time I laid down the president's gavel, Synod has favored me with some very gratifying assignments. I accepted with deep pleasure the appointment to serve on the Faith Forward executive committee. Also the invitation extended to me to serve as chairman of the Board of Trustees of The Lutheran Church—Missouri Synod Foundation could not have suited me better. Both are areas of synodical service in which I am decidedly interested, and I have taken keen delight in bearing the message of these vital causes to hundreds in almost every corner of Synod.

I deemed it a particular favor to be requested to serve as Synod's representative at several district conventions. And it was the fulfillment of a long-cherished dream to be granted the opportunity, after 27 years, to serve once again as convention doctrinal essayist.

As God gives me health and strength I shall be happy to give every service possible to my beloved Synod, which throughout my years has given so indescribably much to me.

In conclusion, I cannot but recall for my fellow Missourians the frank appraisal of the Missouri Synod by a non-Missourian some 40 years ago. It comes from the pen of respected and scholarly Ohio Synod theologian Dr. R. C. H. Lenski and appeared in the official organ of that body. After pointing to the growth of the Missouri Synod at its 75th milestone, Dr. Lenski said:

## This I Recall

Here is a historical fact that refutes all talk trying to persuade us that we must be liberal, accommodate ourselves to the spirit of the times, etc., in order to grow externally. The very opposite is seen in the Missouri Synod. Missouri has at all times been unyielding; it is so still. In this body the Scriptures and the Confessions have been, and still are, valued at their full import. There was no disposition to surrender them.

With this asset Missouri has been working in free America, which abounds in sects and religious confusion, and now exhibits its enormous achievements. What so many regard as Missouri's weakness has in reality been its strength. This fact we might write down for our own remembrance. It is a mark of the pastors and leaders of the Missouri Synod that they never, aye, never tire of discussing doctrine on the basis of the Confessions and of Scripture. That is one trait that may be called "the spirit of Missouri."

That spirit of Missouri—long may it hold sway to bring new outpourings of the Holy Spirit's gracious blessings on her worldwide ministry in the future.

SOLI DEO GLORIA

# POSTSCRIPT TO *THIS I RECALL*

**William J. Schmelder**

# INTRODUCTION

*This I Recall* was published in 1964. With the exception of a few words about his involvement with the Faith Forward executive committee, about being chairman of the Board of Trustees of the LCMS Foundation, and about serving as synodical representative at several District conventions, the book ends with his greetings to the constituting convention of the LCA on June 30, 1962. John Behnken was called to glory on February 23, 1968.

Since no biography—definitive or otherwise—has been published, it seemed proper to ask if some of the information in the memoirs could be expanded with additional data or with comments not included in the published version. Since we are in possession of the original type script, those areas could be readily identified. A more important issue was to ask about the last six years of Behnken's life and how he was remembered after his death.

To do this we shall focus on five basic issues.

1. Materials not included or truncated in *This I Recall*, such as a broader view of the family into which he was born, the issues surrounding his election in 1935, and his evaluation of the ecumenical movement.
2. The conditions within the Synod after his retirement. Behnken's views can be seen most clearly in the questions that he addressed to the faculty of Concordia Seminary and that he shared with the Council of Presidents.
3. John Behnken as preacher. In dedicating the two volumes of *Sermonic Studies* to him on the occasion of the 50th anniversary of his ordination, it should be noted that first of all among the graces with which the Lord endowed him was "clarion clear, Christ-centered preaching;" that "throughout his ministry he has championed Biblical preaching and has urged the clergy of our Synod to search the Scriptures diligently for their sermon thoughts and thus let God speak to them and their congregations."

4. The person of John Behnken. What kind of a man was he? How did he interact with his family?
5. The end of his life. Did he die an unhappy, disappointed old man, as some have portrayed him? The funeral services and what was said about him and how he was remembered.

It might be thought that there are too many quotations of Behnken—some admittedly long. However, his ideas, positions, and views are better expressed in his own words rather than in what someone else thought he meant. It is hoped that in the end justice has been done to the man.

# LACUNAE

*Family Background*

In the preface to *This I Recall* John Behnken gave a sketch of his family background and noted that his maternal family tree had not been traced. In 1993, however, Roger Wunderlich, great-grandson of Johann Peter and Maria Katharina (Hofius) Wunderlich, published the detailed research of *The Wunderlich & Hofius Families of North Harris County, Texas 1852–1993 141 Years*. From this we now know a great deal more about John Behnken's family background. We know that love of Christ's Church on the congregational, district, and syndical level was a driving force in these families.

The story of Behnken's father is related in *This I Recall*. What was not told was that his father was not the only Behnken to emigrate to Wisconsin. Four other siblings did so.

Anna Meta came in 1871. Her intended husband, the Reverend Johann Meyer, came in 1870. They were married in May of 1871. Their son, the Reverend Johann P. Meyer, served from 1897 in congregations and institutions in the Wisconsin Synod. In 1920 he began his long career at Wisconsin Lutheran Seminary. From 1937 to 1953 he was its president. He served for many years on the Commission on Doctrinal matters. In 1963 at age 90 he still carried a full classroom load. What is significant about this is that first-cousins Behnken and Meyer were involved in the discussions between Missouri and Wisconsin that Behnken details in *This I Recall*. As noted, one of the issues was military chaplaincy. Wisconsin believed that the chaplaincy was essentially unionistic and involved the mixing of Church and state. Behnken's son was a military chaplain.

Johann emigrated in 1874 or 1875, George in 1876–77, Margaret in 1885, and Hannah in 1888.

With the exception of George, all remained in Wisconsin and the Wisconsin Synod.

## Postscript to *This I Recall*

The Wunderlich family has a fascinating history. Three Wunderlichs from the same family emigrated from Weide, a village near the town of Feudingen, in the province of Westfalen, Prussia. They could trace their ancestry to the Reverend Jodokus Wunderlich who was the first Lutheran pastor in Feudingen. He served there for fifty-one years, 1563–1614. He was succeeded by his son Wilhelm, 1614–36, he by his son Jodokus, 1636–91 and he by his son-in-law Jost Heinrich Klingspor, 1691–1712. The Texas Wunderlichs are descended from Wilhelm's son Johann. They were the ninth generation of Wunderlichs.

The first of the Wunderlichs to emigrate to Texas was Johann Peter, John Behnken's grandfather. He came early in 1852. On the same ship were Maria Katharina and Magdalena M. Hofius, also from Weide. On December 26, 1852 Johann Peter and Katharina were married. Peter died in a powder mill explosion in 1864, leaving Katharina a widow with six children.

*Elisabeth* was born in 1855. In 1872 she married teacher Herman Goldman. She died in childbirth ten months after her marriage.

*Wilhelm* was born in 1856. He married Wilhelmina Wilder, the sister of the Reverend August Wilder, pastor of Trinity, Klein, in 1882. They lived with her mother and farmed.

*Anna Theresa* married the Reverend August Hofius in 1876. He was pastor of St. John's in Little Cyprus. August was the son of Maria Katharina's oldest brother Johann Christ. Thus they were first cousins. Three of their sons, Emil, William, and Walter became pastors and one, Gottlieb, a teacher.

*Frederich* (Fred) married Bertha Klein in 1885. He was pastor at Trinity, Riesel, Texas (1884–1904); St. John in Lincoln, Texas (1904–1907); and St. John, Waco, Nebraska (1907–29). Of their thirteen children, three daughters, Ella, Renata, and Frieda were teachers; one, Alma, married a teacher; three sons, Lorenz, Harold, and Robert, were pastors; and three sons, Traugott, Theophil and Roland were teachers.

*Helena* was John Behnken's mother. Her life is presented in *This I Recall*.

*Peter* was born two months after his father's death. Peter farmed and raised cattle.

After the death of Pastor George Behnken, Helena married Pastor Gotthilf Birkmann. He served as the pastor of Trinity, Fedor, Texas for 43 years, 1876–79 and 1882–1922. Between those periods he served Zion, Dallas 1879–82.

He was the second child of the Reverend Johann George Birkmann and his wife Frederika. Johann was born in Bavaria, and following a growing interest in becoming a minister, he found his way to Neuendettelsau where J.K.W. Löhe had established a missionary school to prepare men for work in America. These students were called *Zöglinge* (apprentices). In 1846 Löhe sent eleven of them, including Johann, to the new practical seminary in Fort Wayne. The studies were a "crash course" in preparing men to shepherd the new immigrant Germans. In November of 1847 Birkmann was sent to minister to Lutheran families in Belleville, Illinois. In January of 1848 he was examined through C.F.W. Walther, the president of the newly-organized Missouri Synod and was authorized to be ordained and installed. He served a number of congregations in Southern Illinois, primarily Holy Cross, Wartburg (1850–65).

Gotthilf Birkmann, born in Wartburg in 1854, matriculated at Concordia Seminary and began his ministry in Fedor in 1876. In 1886 he married his first wife, Hulda Kilian, the daughter of the Reverend and Mrs. Johann Kilian. Kilian had become a friend of C.F.W. Walther during their student days at the University of Leipzig. He was the spiritual leader of the Wends who emigrated to Texas in 1854. He served as pastor in Serbin until his death in 1884. He joined the Missouri Synod in 1855. Hulda died of typhoid fever on October 14, 1892, leaving three young children, George (4), Paul (3), and Alma (1).

He married Helena Behnken on May 30, 1893. She brought three children to the marriage: John (9), Meta (7), and William (5).

Together they had seven more: Ernest, Gotthilf (the twin who died in infancy), Carl, Gotthilf, Ella, Frieda, and Herbert.

## Postscript to *This I Recall*

John and Paul became pastors; Herbert a school teacher; Ella's son Ray Martens was president of Concordia, Austin.

Gotthilf Birkmann served as interim president of the Southern District of the Missouri Synod (1889–91) and of the Texas District (1912–20).

While the emphasis has been on those who entered full-time service in the Church, the lay people of the family were also devoted to the faith. As Roger Wunderlich noted in the *Foreword* to his family history:

> During my research, I noticed the amazing dedication of the original settlers, especially their religious dedication. The distance some traveled to worship. Their feeding their farm animals early on Saturdays, and traveling a half day or better by buggy or wagon to get to the church, spending the night, attending church on Sunday mornings and then traveling a half day to reach home again.

Such was the larger family that produced a John Behnken. No wonder he would write:

> Just when I first entertained the desire to enter the holy ministry, I do not remember. God apparently implanted that desire into my heart very early. As I look back, it seems that both my parents and I simply took for granted I would become a pastor.

It should not be surprising that all of Behnken's children should enter full-time service in the Church. Four sons became pastors: Victor, John Jr., Lloyd, and Kenneth. One son, Donald, became a teacher. All three daughters, Ruth, Lois, and Delle, married pastors.

Of his grandchildren, three became pastors: Kenneth and Duane Behnken and David Droegemueller. Four became teachers: Marian and Judith Behnken, Sharon Droegemueller, and Donna Behnken.

In addition to service on committees, boards and commissions on the district and synodical level, his children were given special tasks:

> *Victor* was president of the Southern California District (1955–69) and third vice-president of the synod (1969–71).

*John Jr.* was a military chaplain, first in the US Army Air Corps and later in the US Air Force. He had assignments in Korea, Germany, and the Philippines, as well as numerous bases in the US (1943–77).

*Donald* was active in the Lutheran Education Association and served as its president (1959–62).

*Lloyd* was president of the Florida-Georgia District (1973–87).

*Kenneth* was a member of the synodical Board of Directors (1979–87).

*Son-in-law A.F. Droegemueller* was president of the Montana District (1966–69).

*Son-in-law William Schmelder* was professor at Concordia Seminary St. Louis (1974–95) and on leave was special assistant to the president of synod, Ralph A. Bohlmann (1991–92).

By any evaluation the family story of John Behnken is a remarkable testimony of how the Lord works through His people to keep the Gospel moving to the ends of the earth.

## *Election to the Presidency*

Behnken was second vice-president of the Texas District (1919–21), first vice-president (1921–26) and president (1926–29). At the River Forest convention he became second vice-president of the Synod, and three years later at Milwaukee, first vice-president.

At the convention in Cleveland in 1935 it was assumed that Dr. Pfotenhauer would be re-elected. After several ballots, Behnken asked Pfotenhauer to give him an opportunity to speak. "Not now, just wait." When it narrowed down to the two of them, he again asked, and was told, "You must not say anything. Let God decide the matter by the vote of the convention."

In the original draft of *This I Recall*, Behnken wrote:

> The final ballot placed the obligations and responsibilities of Synod's Presidency on my shoulders. No one realized this more than I did. Why should God have permitted me to be

elected? Like Solomon I prayed fervently that God might "give me an understanding heart." Even as Elisha prayed for a double portion of Elijah's spirit, so I prayed that a double portion of my predecessor's spirit might be upon me. I received much encouragement when in a special meeting during a recess period all the District Presidents by special resolution assured me of their prayers and co-operation and when also the Board of Directors received me so graciously and gave me similar assurances.

However, in all honesty I must say that if I had known at the time of the Cleveland convention what I learned about five years later, I would not have accepted the Presidency. From a man, whose reliability I cannot doubt, I learned that there was very much electioneering or propaganda. This occurred in the lobby and had also taken place through the mails. It is hardly believable that anyone would resort to such political tactics and maneuverings, against or for a candidate, in church elections. But it happened. The reader will understand, then, why I have warned repeatedly against electioneering at our conventions. It simply is improper and inexcusable in Synodical elections. May God graciously preserve our Synod from practices which would make a political football out of our elections. Where this is done the church body is on slippery paths, and these lead downward.

## The Ecumenical Movement

On July 10, 1961, Behnken sent a copy of *The Future Reunited Church and The Ancient Undivided Church* by Hermann Sasse to the officials of the synod. In the cover letter he wrote:

> The above excellent treatise, as you note, stems from the pen of Dr. H. Sasse. He was so kind and considerate as to send me a copy.
>
> I am sure that you will appreciate this thorough treatise which focuses our attention on a question which confronts Christian Churches throughout the world today. Also our Synod must face and find an answer to the tremendous

movement which seeks to unite all church bodies which claim to be Christian churches. This movement sails under the name "ecumenical." This is a wrong use of the term "ecumenical." True ecumenicity, which all of us accept, is something altogether different. In this day of much confused thinking and speaking and writing let us know and abide by the true Scriptural answer.

May the very excellent and pertinent treatise of Dr. H. Sasse be a genuine contribution and guide to all of us as we study and come to definite conclusions on the basis of God's Word concerning the so called "ecumenical movement."

During and as a result of his visits to Europe, Behnken became acquainted with many of the leaders of both Lutheran churches and the World Council of Churches. The Bad Boll Conferences continued for a decade.

In the original draft of *This I Recall*, Behnken reflected on his experiences:

Not only Lutherans throughout the world have put forth mighty efforts to unite, but also Protestants are doing their utmost to unite all Protestant churches. They would include also all Lutherans. They hold that all church bodies which profess to be Christians should not continue separately, but should unite and be a truly strong church. It is evident that the chief objective is not unity, but union, not growth in grace and in the knowledge of our Lord and Savior Jesus Christ, but rather growth in numbers.

When church bodies seek to unite, the question which must be asked is: On what doctrinal basis? Surely every church body has or should have some doctrinal basis. It must tell its members and others what position it takes on such important questions as, Are God's Word and the Sacraments means of grace? Is the Bible the divinely inspired Word of God and hence God's inerrant truth? Does baptism work forgiveness of sin? Should little children be baptized? Is the body and the blood of Christ truly present in the Lord's Supper and actually received under the consecrated bread and wine by everyone who partakes of it? Is Jesus Christ the true God-man because [He is] "begotten of the Father from eternity and born of the virgin Mary?" Is Jesus Christ our Substitute? Did He atone for the sins of the whole world? Are we saved solely by faith in Christ? Must the great truth of justification not by our works but solely by grace, for Christ's sake, through faith be taught and accepted? Is our coming to faith in Christ solely the work of the Holy Spirit without any cooperation on the part of man? What is the proper relationship between justification and sanctification? Etc. etc.

Surely when church bodies, whether Lutheran or Protestants in general, seek to unite one of the prime requisites is to come to bona fide agreement on Scriptural doctrines. Union should not, yes, dare not to be established on the basis of a compromise. When men resort to compromises, truth always suffers. We need only recall how some men in the old World Conference on Faith and Order of the last century realized that the difference between the churches on some very vital issues were far deeper than anybody had anticipated and how after years a proposal will be offered which may be understood correctly but also lends itself to another interpretation.[1] I have reference to the World Council of Church's proposal to the 1961 convention in New Delhi: "The WCC is a fellowship of churches which, according to the Scriptures confess the Lord Jesus Christ as God and Savior and therefore seek to fulfill their common calling to the glory of the one God, Father, Son and Holy Spirit." A person must know definitely what is meant by "the Scriptures." Again, what is the teaching concerning the person and work of Jesus Christ? When some in the WCC deny the deity of Christ, His vicarious atonement, His blood-bought redemption, etc. how can Christian churches—and even Lutheran churches—hold membership in it?

---

[1] The World Conference of Faith and Order was proposed at the World Missionary Conference at Edinburgh in 1910.

The same thing holds true of the NCCCUSA. The convention of this body in San Francisco, December, 1960, received considerable publicity. Even prior to the convention Dr. Eugene Carson Blake, (a Presbyterian) and Bishop James A Pike (an Episcopalian) had proposed a merger of four groups—Presbyterian, Episcopalian, Methodist and United Church of Christ. This body would then number more than 18,000,000 members. Dr. Roy G. Ross, National Secretary of the NCCCUSA said at the meeting that in many parts of the world the church faces political prejudice; that the message has become irrelevant in others and that its many divisions pose tragic difficulties on the newly developed nations. How true ... but why? Bishop John Wesley Lord was quoted as saying: "If carried out this proposal would release millions of dollars annually for humanitarian and world service agencies—money now consumed in administering our various denominations and communions.... As denominations we are complacent, parochial, proud. In an increasingly secular and deteriorating society the spiritual and religious forces must make a total impact to be effective. We can no longer afford the luxury of our separate ways."

A person feels constrained to say: What a great concern about outward numbers and finances! But what about concern for Scriptural doctrine? Should not Christian Churches, instead of seeking compromises, or striving merely to unite, consider that God's Word, both in the Old Testament and the New Testament on the one hand insists on sound doctrine (Jer. 23:28; Rom. 6:17; I Tim. 4:16; 6:3; II Tim. 3:10; Titus 2:1; 2:7; Jude 17, etc.) and on the other hand solemnly and earnestly warns against false doctrine (Jer. 23:31–32; Matt. 16:12; Romans 16:17; Eph. 4:14; I Tim. 1:10; Col. 2:22, etc.)?

This is not a simple and easy position to take, but it is the only correct one. Especially we Lutherans should remember it. Ours is definitely a doctrinal church. Our Lutheran Confessions of which we are convinced that they are the correct interpretation of Holy Writ, are of deep significance to us. We cannot be indifferent to them. Any yielding spells disaster. It means the sacrifice of our precious heritage,— nothing less than that. What will happen to Lutheranism if Lutheran bodies link up with those who deny Lutheran doctrines? We know that Lutheran doctrines are Scriptural. Is this not something which especially we of our Synod should remember? What would happen to the faithful insistence on purity of doctrine? Will it disappear? Will these present-day misnamed "ecumenical" efforts ultimately result in a watered-down national or even international religion? Will it come to such a pass that men will consider God's holy Word to be merely a collection of legends and myths? Will the deity of Jesus Christ, the vicarious atonement, the sinner's salvation solely by grace, for Christ's sake through faith, already attacked and denied by leaders in these movements, also become so diluted and adulterated until nothing is left but the hopeless religion of natural men? Will the faithful adherents and defenders of Biblical truth dwindle to little groups within churches, such as are found in European countries today?

All these are very serious questions which we must weigh and consider earnestly and conscientiously. The future of Lutheranism depends on it. One of the great theologians of our day asked me the question: "What will be the destiny of Lutheranism in this out-going 20th century?" He added: "The great question confronting our churches is whether also in the future there will be a Lutheran church, or whether Lutheranism will live on as a school of thought within the framework of a great Protestant union, whatever the name may be."

May God graciously grant the preservation of sound Lutheranism.

# THE GROWING DOCTRINAL CONTROVERSY IN THE SYNOD

John Behnken was not unaware of the growing doctrinal controversy within the Synod. He made frequent reference in *This I Recall* to issues that he confronted. The essayist at the San Francisco convention was Dr. Paul M. Bretcher of the St. Louis Seminary, the topic was "Take Heed unto the Doctrine." In his acceptance speech Behnken said:

> You know the position I have taken. On the one hand I am convinced that we must be ready always to give an answer to every man that asketh us for a reason of the hope that is in us with meekness and fear, as St. Peter expressed it. On the other hand I am convinced that we dare not become entangled in unionistic alliances. The matter is not simple and easy. It sometimes requires wisdom and courage and even diplomacy which only God can supply. I realize the enormous responsibility. Thank God! I shall not be alone. You are placing Vice-Presidents at my side. Then there will be the Committee on Doctrinal Unity. Above all, God will be at our side. I know that Jesus, at the very time when He told His church, "teaching them to observe all things whatsoever I have commanded you," assured her, "lo, I am with you always, even unto the end of the world."
>
> I want to plead with every one of you for your fervent prayer and for your wholehearted cooperation in this important task. Especially do I plead with our professors, both at our seminaries and at our colleges, to be true and loyal to the Scriptures as the divinely inspired and inerrant Word of God. Next to God I must depend on you. Furthermore, I plead with all our officials, boards and committees to recognize fully the great purpose God wants us to serve and in deep consecration and in gratitude to God for the way He has led

us to devote ourselves to the great assignment earnestly to contend for the faith once delivered unto the saints.

God grant that we may be found faithful. I pledge myself to my God and Savior and to my beloved Synod to do whatever God would have me do according to the ability which He supplies.

The careful planning of the Cleveland convention again demonstrated his determination to deal with the issues that had been the focus of attention during his last term in office.

On August 6, 1966, he sent to the faculty of Concordia Seminary "Some Questions Concerning Statements in God's Holy Word." It thus follows:

> Some present day theologians hold that God's account of creation is not to be taken literally, factually or historically, but must be understood as a legend, a parable, a symbol, a myth, etc. The term "Symphony of Creation" also has been used.
>
> Some other accounts in Scripture, even Books of Scripture, have been subjected to similar treatment.
>
> Modern discoveries, advanced learning in the natural sciences, the "refinement" of the term "evolution" to "theistic evolution" etc., are given as reasons for this new approach to the accounts in God's holy Word,
>
> Then there are those who hold that where the traditional and the new interpretations of Scripture are in conflict with each other we must grant the new interpretations equal rights, regard them as optional, mere alternatives, and hence permissible.
>
> In view of the above I have a number of questions concerning some of the accounts which God has given in the Pentateuch. I am especially eager to know what position the present day theologians of my dear Alma Mater, Concordia Seminary, are taking. My earnest request and fervent plea is that I be given frank, conscientious answers on the basis of Scripture, God's holy Word.

1) Must God's historical account of the world's creation in Genesis 1 and 2 be judged in the light of the theory of evolution? Or must the theory of evolution be judged in the light of Scripture? Is this an optional matter? If so, why? If not, why not? Please refer also to Ex. 20:11; Ne. 9:6; Ps. 19:1, 24:1–2, 33:6, 33:9, 95:3–6, 96:5, 102:25, 121:2, 146:5–6, 148:5; Is. 40:18–28, 45:12; Jer. 10:10–13, 32:17; John 1:3; Acts 4:24, 14:15, 17:24; Rom. 1:20; 1 Cor. 8:6; Eph. 3:9; Col. 1:16; Heb. 1:1–2, 1:8–10, 3:4, 11:3; Rev. 4:11.

2) Is God's account of man's creation, as recorded in Gen. 1:16–17 and Gen. 2:18–25 factual or must it be interpreted in the light of "theistic evolution?' Or is this optional? If so, why? If not, why not? Please refer also to Gen. 5:1–2; Deut. 4:32; Job 33:6; Ps. 100:3; Is. 51:13; Col. 3:10; James 3:9.

3) Did the devil actually speak through the serpent as recorded in Gen. 3:1–5? Cf. Rev. 12:9, 20:2. Or is this merely legend: Is this optional and permissible? If so, why? If not, why not?—Is there anything to the argument advanced against the serpent's speaking: "The serpent has no vocal chords?" Did Balaam's ass, which had no human vocal chords, speak to Balaam as recorded in Numbers 22:28–30? Did God's angels, who are spirits and have no vocal chords, speak and sing to the shepherds on Bethlehem's plains as recorded in Luke 2:8–14? Did God, Who is Spirit, (John 4:24) and has no vocal chords, speak to man again and again?

4) Did God actually plant a real "garden eastward in Eden" in which "He made to grow every tree that is pleasant to the sight and good for food" of which he said: "Of every tree of the garden thou mayest freely eat; but of the tree of the knowledge of good and evil, thou shalt not eat of it; for in the day that thou eatest thereof thou shalt surely die," Gen. 2:8–17 [KJV]? Please refer also to Gen. 3:23; Is. 51:3; Ezek. 28:13, 31:9, 36:35; Joel 2:3. Or is all this merely a legend? May the 'legend interpretation' stand alongside the clear statements of God's Word? Is this optional, permissible? If so, why? If not, why not?

## Postscript to *This I Recall*

5) Did Adam and Eve actually eat "of the fruit of the tree in the midst of the garden" (Gen. 3:3 [KJV]) and thereby bring sin, death and eternal damnation on all mankind? Please refer also to Gen. 3:19; Rom. 5:12, 6:23; 1 Cor. 15:21. Or is all this merely a legend? May the "legend explanation" stand alongside the clear Word of God? Is this optional? If so, why? If not, why not?

6) Is the Messianic prophecy in Eden, Gen. 3:15, factual or historical? Or is this merely a myth which must be demythologized, or merely a beautiful legend, or a part of the "Symphony of creation"? May both explanations stand side by side? Is this an optional matter? If so, why? If not, why not? Cf. Rom. 16:20; Heb. 2:14; 1 John 3:8.

7) Did Cain actually murder his brother Abel as recorded in Gen. 4:1–15? Please refer to Matt. 23:35; 1 John 3:12. Or is this a myth, a legend? May both interpretations be permitted? If so, why? If not, why not? If we permit such explanations of God's account in the foregoing questions, why not also here?

8) Is the account which God gives of the world's destruction by the flood in Gen. 7, actual history? Or is this merely a myth or a legend? Please refer to 1 Peter 3:19–22; 2 Peter 3:1–10. Are both interpretations permissible? If so, why? If not, why not? If we say, "It is optional" in answers to questions one to six, why not here?

9) Are the seven years of plenty followed by seven years of famine, as recorded in Gen. 41, history or legend? If the interpretation, "a myth, a legend" is permitted in answer to questions one to six, why not here?

10) Were Jacob and his sons and their cattle and their goods, which they had gotten in the land of Canaan, Gen. 46:5–7, actually brought down to Egypt because of the famine? Did Joseph provide for them by speaking to Pharaoh to grant them the land of Goshen? Please refer to Gen. 45:16–28, 46:28–34, 47:1–12. Or is this merely a legend or a myth? May we permit the latter interpretation to stand alongside of God's inspired account? Is this interpretation optional? If so,

why? If not, why not? Is not the answer, "It is a legend, it is a myth" just as proper here as it would be in questions one to six?

11) Did the children of Israel actually become slaves some time after Joseph's death, as recorded in Ex. 1:7–14? Or is this merely a legend? May the latter interpretation be accepted alongside of the account which God has given? If so, why? If not, why not? If we permit it in answer to questions one to six, why not here?

12) Is the marvelous deliverance which God provided through Moses, the so-called exodus, factual, historic? Please refer to Gen. 46 to Ex. 13. Or is this merely a legend or a myth? May the latter explanation be permitted alongside of God's account? If so, why? If not, why not? If it is not permitted in answer to questions one to six, why not here?

13) Is the account of Israel's passing through the Red Sea with the "waters a wall unto them on their right hand and on their left" because Moses, according to God's account "stretched out his hand over the sea", Ex. 14:15–22 [KJV], as well as the other miraculous help which God granted them, e.g., the pillar of a cloud or the pillar of fire, real, factual, historic? Ex. 15. Or is this merely a myth or a legend? If so, why? If not, why not?

14) Is God's account of the daily manna and quail in the wilderness—except on the Sabbath—according to Ex. 16:11–36, factual, historic, or is this a myth or a legend? Is it actually true that when some gathered more than they needed, v. 20, it "bred worms and stank" except when on Friday they "gathered twice as much" v. 22, and on the Sabbath "it did not stink, neither was there any worm therein" v. 24, or is this a mere myth or a legend? Could the latter explanation be permitted to stand alongside of God's account? If so, why? If not, why not? If it is permitted in answer to questions one to six, why not here? Cf. John 6:31, 6:49.

15) What about water out of the rocks when Moses smote them with the rod, and the quantities sufficient for the people and the cattle according to Ex. 17:1–7 and Number 20:11?

## Postscript to *This I Recall*

Please refer also to Neh. 9:15; Ps. 105:41, 114:8; Isaiah 48:21. Is this factual, historic, or merely a myth or a legend? May we permit the latter explanation to stand alongside to God's account? If so, why? If not, why not? If it is permitted to answer to questions one to six, why not here?

16) In Ex. 17:8–16 God gives His account of the battle against the Amalekites. Moses had the rod of God in his hand. When he held up his hand, Israel prevailed. When he let down his hand, the Amalekites prevailed. When his hands were heavy, Aaron and Hur stayed up his hands. Thus Israel defeated the Amalekites. Is this factual, historic, or is it a legend? May the explanation that it is a legend stand alongside of God's account? If so, why? If not, why not? If we permit it in answer to the first six questions, why not here?

17) Did God actually give the law as Ex. 19 and 20 have recorded it? Did God speak amidst lightening and thundering? Did the mountain smoke? (Ex. 20:18) Did the people stand afar off? (Ex. 20:21) Did God say, "Ye have seen that I have talked with you from heaven"? (Ex. 20:22 [KJV]) Is all this factual, historical? Or may we call it legend? May both interpretations stand side by side? If so, why? If not, why not? If we permit it in questions one to six, why not here?

18) Is God's account of the very large cluster of grapes, which the spies brought back from Canaan's Brook of Eshcol, as recorded in Numbers 13:21–24, factual, historic, or is this merely a beautiful legend? May the latter interpretation stand alongside of God's account? If so, why? If not, why not? If we permit an optional interpretation in answer to the first six questions, why not here?

19) What about the forty years' wandering in the wilderness until all had died, who were twenty years old and upward at the time when the spies brought back their report—all with the exception of Joshua and Caleb? Is this account which God has given in Numbers 14:21–34 factual, historical, or is it a legend? May the latter interpretation stand

and be accepted alongside of God's account? If so, why? If not, why not? If we permit an optional interpretation in answer to questions one to six, why not here?

20) Did the ten spies, who brought back an evil report and caused the people to murmur against God and against Moses, actually die of a plague before the Lord as recorded in Numbers 14:36–37, or is this merely legend? May the two explanations stand side by side and let the reader have his choice as to what interpretation he wishes to accept? If so, why? If not, why not? If we permit the explanation of "legend" in answer to the first six questions, why not here?

21) Numbers 16:1–35 [KJV] brings God's record of the rebellion of Korah and 250 princes of the assembly. It states that "the earth opened her mouth and swallowed them up", and that "they and all that appertained to them, went down alive into the pit, and the earth closed upon them; and they perished from among the congregation." Is this factual, actual history or a myth or a legend? May both interpretations be permitted? If so, why? If not, why not? If we permit the "legend of myth" interpretations in answers to questions one to six, why not here?

22) Did Aaron stay the plague, which took the lives of 14,700, by putting incense on the fire in the center, this making atonement for the people, as recorded in Numbers 16:46–50, or is this merely a myth or a legend? May the latter interpretation be permitted as optional? If so, why? If not, why not? If we permit the "legend of myth" interpretation in answer to questions one to six, why not here?

23) Did only Aaron's rod bud and blossom and yield almonds, as God has stated in Numbers 17:1–13? Was it kept for a token against the rebels? Or is all this merely a legend or a myth? If so, why? If not, why not? May both interpretations stand side by side? If not, why should we permit it in the answers to the first six questions?

24) Did Moses and Aaron, by smiting the rock instead of merely speaking to it, sin so grievously against God that they were not permitted to lead the children of Israel in Canaan, as

God has stated in Numbers 20:7–13? Or is all this merely a legend or a myth? Is the latter interpretation permissible alongside of God's statement? If so, why? If not, why not? If "legend or myth" is permitted in answers to questions one to six, why not here?

25) Is the healing from the deadly bite of fiery serpents by a mere look at the brazen serpent which Moses had made and put on a pole, as recorded in Numbers 21:1–9 an actual historical fact, or is it a myth or a legend? May I accept either the one or the other explanation? If so, why? If not, why not? If we permit the "legend" or "myth" explanation as answers to questions one to six, why not here?

26) Did Balaam's ass actually speak as we read in Numbers 22:28–30, or is this myth or a legend? May I permit the latter interpretation to stand alongside of God's clear account? If so, why? If not, why not? Must I permit it here if I permit it in the first six questions.

27) Did Balaam actually speak the prophecy concerning the "star out of Jacob" and the "Scepter out of Israel," as recorded in Numbers 24:17–19, or is this a mere myth or legend? If the latter, why? If not, why not? May I permit the latter to stand alongside of God's clear account? If I permit the "legend of myth" interpretation in questions one to six, why not here?

28) Did Moses actually see Canaan from Mt. Nebo? Did he die there though "his eye was not dim, nor his natural forces abated?" Did God actually bury him? Is this inspired record in Deut. 34:1–9 actual history, or is it a mere myth or legend? May both explanations stand side by side? If so, why? If not, why not? If we permit the "myth or legend" interpretation in the first six questions, why not here?

Other instances, inspired accounts, might be mentioned from the Pentateuch and the same questions asked which I have asked above. In fact, this applies to every account of the Old and New Testaments, especially those where we find God's account of that which to us is most marvelous, yes, miraculous, which our reason simply cannot grasp. I am not a so-called "literalist" or "fundamentalist." I know that there are parables in Holy Writ. I know that there is poetry. However, I cannot agree that everything, which our reason cannot grasp or understand, must be placed into the category of "parables, legend, myth, etc." in an effort to make it understandable and acceptable to human reason. The miracles of the Old and New Testaments are simply beyond—not contrary to—reason. This applies also to the miracles of our Savior. It applies to His coming into the world, to His life, His suffering, His death, His resurrection, His ascension into heaven. My reason asks: How could God's Son be born of the Virgin Mary? How could God "lay on Him the iniquity of us all?" How could He make Him, Who knew no sin, to be sin for us? How could the God-man suffer and die for my sin? How could He say, "Destroy this temple and in three days I will raise it up" and actually do this on Easter morning? How can St. John say of Him, "His is the propitiation of our sins, and not for ours only, but also for the sins of the whole world?" How can my Spirit-wrought faith assure me that Christ's perfect fulfillment of the law and His innocent suffering and death actually has reconciled me to God, that on account of it God forgives all my sins and makes me absolutely certain that I shall inherit eternal life? My reason does not grasp, nor can it explain these marvelous truths. I accept them and believe them because God's Word says so.

Should this submission to God's Word not apply to all parts of Scripture? Must I not be ready to say, "Thus saith the Lord?" Is this not true in every case unless Scripture itself compels us to interpret it otherwise? Must we not let Scripture interpret Scripture? Must we not accept the truths which God has recorded in Holy Writ as He has given them? Dare we, as one of the great theologians of our day has expressed it, "make a text of Scripture say what we want it to say?" God forbid! May we ever let God speak, let Him say what He wants to say, and wholeheartedly accept what He has said. God grant it.

## POSTSCRIPT TO *THIS I RECALL*

Some of these twenty-eight questions had already been proposed by Behnken on October 7, 1959, for use in interviewing prospective faculty members for synod's colleges and seminaries. These questions were no "child's play"—to use Luther's expression—but a serious call for the faculty to address the issues facing the synod. Correspondence between Behnken and seminary president Alfred O. Fuerbringer did not resolve any issues. Seminary officials told him all was well with the faculty. Later Behnken remarked that they had been "economical with the truth." One seminary official told him dismissively, "Behnken, you wouldn't understand."

The faculty never answered his questions.

On March 6, 1967 he sent the questions to all members of the Council of Presidents with this cover letter:

> Enclosed you will please find a mimeographed copy of "SOME QUESTIONS CONCERNING SOME STATEMENTS OF GOD'S HOLY WORD."
>
> After attending two meetings of the COUNCIL OF PRESIDENTS and the THEOLOGICAL FACULTIES I was troubled very much. I wrote down a number of questions and referred to the many passages of Holy Writ in which God gives His answers. Next I presented these to two good theologians of our Synod (not members of any faculties of our Seminaries or Colleges). These men urged me to proceed.
>
> On August 6, 1966 I mailed the questions, as I am presenting them to you, to the President of the Seminary, Dr. A. O. Fuerbringer. We have had some correspondence about them. Dr. Fuerbringer stated that he wanted to assure me that the Bible account of creations is not to be judged in the light of the theory or philosophy of evolution, and that the text must be interpreted as it stands there. But he then referred to Joshua 10:12–14, pointing out that there we depart from the literal sense just because it does not fit the Copernican theory. He also sought to explain why some of the professors have spoken as they did. But we have come to no conclusion by this correspondence.

The President is informed about my intentions to send copies of the questions to the COUNCIL OF PRESIDENTS, THE BOARDS OF CONTROL and the MEMBERS OF THE THEOLOGICAL FACULTIES etc. I should have mentioned also the BOARDS OF CONTROL and the DEPARTMENTS OF RELIGION at our TEACHERS COLLEGES. I called attention to the fact that this really is a "public" matter which has been discussed rather publicly. Some of it has appeared in print. Furthermore, some of the men have spoken in conferences in different parts of our Synod.

On January 1, 1967 I informed our Synod's President, Dr. Oliver R. Harms, what I have done. I also mentioned my intention to send copies to the persons mentioned above. I assured him that I did not want to interfere with him and his work in the least. In fact, just the opposite is true. I had a very fine letter from him.

The above as well as the mimeographed questions indicate that I am very much concerned. I know that this is true also of others in many parts of Synod. Of course, I realize full well that I am not an *official* of Synod. But I am a *member* of Synod. As such I am deeply concerned. I sincerely hope that these questions, especially the Bible texts, will be truly beneficial and of real service. May they move many to pray fervently and work earnestly and zealously that our Synod may remain unwaveringly faithful and unswervingly loyal to the precious, divinely inspired and hence infallible Word of God, and our Lutheran Confessions as a correct interpretation of this Word of God. May God graciously grant it!

Wishing you God's choicest blessings
Yours in Christ,
John W. Behnken

He received encouraging responses from many who received this letter.

# BEHNKEN AS PREACHER

John Behnken was a preacher. For twenty-nine years he served as parish pastor in Texas. He developed a reputation as an articulate proclaimer of the message of God's Law and Gospel. He spoke the language of the people entrusted to his care with clarity and directness, but always with the caring heart of a *Seelsorger*. His sermons are redolent with copious Scripture passages that underline the two themes in every proclamation: his absolute reliance on the Scripture as the Word of God and the centrality of the death and resurrection of Jesus Christ for the forgiveness of sins, that we are justified by grace for Christ's sake through faith.

Following the Houston convention of Synod in 1953, the Behnken-Birkmann families and then John's immediate family held reunions. At that time his brother Bill remarked that, following the death of his first wife Gertrude Geisler on July 27, 1910—six days after the birth of Victor—John's sermons changed. He became more caring and loving, preaching more to the needs of those entrusted to his care. These qualities remained throughout the rest of his life.

Behnken was one of the pioneers in the use of radio for the preaching of the Gospel. Station KPRC in Houston made arrangements with four churches, each to broadcast once a month. Trinity was the first congregation to make application. The cost was $15.00 per Sunday for the operator and for the transportation of the remote control instrument. Both the morning and evening services were broadcast. People with sets tuned to distant stations. Broadcasting northward from the South at night was especially good. Behnken noted that Trinity received letters from people in Minnesota and Iowa relating that they were "snowed in" and could not attend their own churches, but joined in Trinity's worship. Letters came from many other states and from ships in the Gulf of Mexico. These broadcasts continued for a period of six years. The privilege was suddenly denied Trinity when one of the other preachers began to preach "rank socialism." The owner of the station warned him and when he nevertheless continued his radical preaching, the owner gave orders: "Cut them all off!"

His reputation as a preacher grew within the Synod when in 1919 the Lutheran Publicity Organization of St. Louis engaged him to preach a week of sermons during Lent. The services were held in the American Theater. He participated in this for eighteen years. With each year he became more known not only to St. Louis Lutherans, but to people throughout the Synod. This exposure played a significant role in his becoming second vice-president of the Synod in 1929.

There are numerous references in *This I Recall* to his preaching at synodical and district conventions, at special celebrations in the Synod's life and at many events around the world. Many of these appeared in the official *Proceedings* of the respective conventions.

Other than *This I Recall*, another of his books was *Mercies Manifold*, a series of sixteen sermons delivered on the Lutheran Hour radio network during the summer of 1949 and published in 1950. The texts seem to be freely chosen and it is assumed by Behnken. They began with Pentecost, June 5, and ended on September 18. The fifth sermon *Our National Blessings* was delivered on July 3. The fourteenth, *The Divine Lesson for Employers and Employees*, on Labor Day weekend, September 4.

In the first sermon the two emphases of his preaching are evident:

The Scripture:

> Holy Scripture is the work of the Holy Spirit. Though men were the penmen, it was the Holy Spirit who selected and moved these men to write. St. Peter declares: "Holy men of God spoke as they were moved by the Holy Ghost," 2 Pet. 1:21 [KJV]. More than the, God inspired these men that which they wrote was "God-in-breathed." It was not the word of man, but the Word of God. I know that this is extraordinary. There is nothing else like it anywhere. In fact, the inspiration of Scripture is the miraculous work of the Holy Spirit. It is one of the marvelous blessings granted unto mankind. Since the Bible is the product of the Holy Spirit, we are assured that it is God's infallible truth (pp. 4–5)

The Gospel:

> The greatest and most miraculous thing that has ever happened on earth is that Jesus Christ sacrificed Himself on Golgotha's Cross for your salvation and that on the third day He rose victorious from the grave. The greatest and most miraculous thing that has happened since that day, as far as you are concerned, is that God the Holy Spirit by means of the precious Gospel has touched your heart to enlighten you, to convert you, to engender within you, implicit, childlike, faith in Jesus Christ. (p. 9)

To strengthen faith:

> In my vast audience of the great anniversary of Pentecost, there may be such as entertain all manner of doubts and misgivings with reference to the great truths of the Christian religion or with reference to their application to their own situation in life. Perhaps you were once a faithful and active church member, but something happened, and you were ready to throw everything overboard. Possibly the devil has been tempting you and is trying to drive you to despair. Or you have been in the throes of some heart rendering sorrow. Life's experiences have been hard and bitter for you, and there seems to be no comfort, no encouragement, no strengthening. Take heart, whoever you are. Turn to the Word of God. Let the Holy Spirit guide you into all truth. He is eager to supply every need of your soul. Even now He pleads with you to receive Him. Grieve Him not. Send Him not away. You will enjoy a wonderful experience. You will be strengthened, assured, convinced, comforted. (pp. 6–7)

He also had some direct words for the preachers in his audience:

> Since the Bible is the product of the Holy Spirit, we are assured that it is God's infallible truth. It is well for us preachers to remember this fact. If we want to speak with authority, if we want our hearers to be convinced of the truth of our message, then we much preach what the Holy Ghost has revealed in Holy Writ. I want to plead with all of you to

proclaim—not the wisdom of men, not political messages, not mere sermons on moral uplift, not sensational addresses on topics of the day, but the glorious truths of the inspired Word of God. Remember that blood-bought souls have been entrusted to your care. You are to preach to them what God wants them to hear, the precious Word of God, of which Jesus Christ declared: "Sanctify them through Thy truth. Thy Word is truth." (John 17:17 [KJV]) (p. 5)

Again, in a sermon on Luke 11:18, "Blessed are they that hear the Word of God and keep it":

> To all the preachers these words of the Savior have something very positive to say. We must not attempt to entertain men with all kinds of so-called sermons on social improvement. It brings no spiritual blessing to the hearts of sinners to hear discussions of political questions, or moral issues, of civic improvement, and for that matter, any other temporal issues. What God wants sinners to hear is His Word. He tells His preachers: "preach the Word; be instant in season, out of season." 2 Tim 4:2 [KJV]. You and I are to expose the sin and guilt of our hearer. With the hammer of God's holy Law we are to crush their hearts. We are to cause them to tremble that they may ask, "Sirs, what must I do to be saved?" Acts 16:30 [KJV]. And then we must tell the story of Jesus and His love. We must lead poor sinners to the Cross of the Redeemer and tell them, "The Lord hath laid on him the iniquity of us all," Is. 53:6 [KJV], "the blood of Jesus Christ, His Son, cleanseth us from all sin," 1 John 1:7 [KJV], "He hath made Him to be sin for us who know no sin, that we might be made the righteousness of God in Him," 2 Cor. 5:21 [KJV]. Are you proclaiming this message? Or are you wasting your own time and the time of your hearers with subject matter that does not belong in the pulpit? Unless we proclaim the Word of God we miss the mark altogether. Only the Word of God can save sinners. Only the Word of God is the power of God unto salvation," Rom. 1:16 [KJV]. (pp. 111–18).

## BEHNKEN AS PREACHER

This is fairly representative of Behnken's preaching, coming from the mid-point of his service as president of the Synod. When his son Kenneth preached one of his early sermons, his father commented, "Someday you will have more fire." Behnken's preaching is evidence that he had "fire," both in content and delivery.

His attitude toward preaching is reflected in the closing paragraph of the book, in the sermon *The Pearl of Great Price*:

> By the kind invitations of the Lutheran Laymen's league it has been my privilege to be the sermon speaker on the Lutheran Hour. I herewith want to thank them most sincerely for the privilege granted me. I have preached Christ crucified to you. I have offered you the pearl of great price. If these services have meant anything to you, I thank God for the privilege of serving. My prayer is that God may graciously bless you and keep you. Above all, may He grant you the immeasurable riches—salvation in Christ Jesus, the pearl of great price. Amen.

Three times—privilege.

After leaving the routines of the parish ministry, Behnken still longed for the regular contact with a congregation of people. Occasionally, he assisted with worship at St. John, Forest Park, where the family held membership. Once when he officiated at a wedding, the pastor at that time told him, "Remember all honoraria belong to the *pastor loci*." He wasn't joking; he meant it. And he got it.

During many of the Oak Park years, he was regular pulpit assistant at St. Andrew's in Chicago where Martin Frick was the pastor. A wedding even developed out of that relationship; son Kenneth married Fricks' daughter Eunice. In 1954, Kenneth was commissioned at St. Andrew's to serve as missionary to India. However, that was not to be. The Indian government declared that no new missionaries could enter the country. Appeals for exception to the rule went unheeded and Kenneth accepted a call stateside. On his visit to India in 1956, Behnken stopped at the compound where his son would have served.

After the move to St. Louis, he occasionally preached at Pilgrim where his classmate and friend Alfred Doerffler was pastor. But he served as regular pulpit assistant at St. Peter's in St. Louis where his friend from Houston days, A. J. Meyer was pastor.

Behnken appreciated the opportunity to preach to these congregations on a regular basis. Here he was not the president of the Synod marking an anniversary or the church executive urging people to support Synod work, but he was Pastor Behnken, preaching to people he had come to know over time, sharing in their joys and sorrows, greeting many by name, observing who was present or absent (since Lutherans then and now have the habit of always sitting in the same pew!). Here he fed the flock of the Lord with the riches of His Word. This he counted as a joyous privilege.

After his election to another term as president at the St. Paul convention in 1956, an interview by Lloyd Green, staff writer of the *St. Louis Globe-Democrat* was published in the July 22 edition. After the notice that he preached regularly at St. Peter's, he said he held the position to "keep my hand in." The article ends with this:

> Although he'll be 75 when he completes his present three-year term as president, which he says will be his last, he does not plan to retire from the ministry.
>
> "I have never lost home sickness for the wonderful personal contact a minister has in serving a congregation," he says, "My only hope is that I won't be too old to return to it when I finish my present duties."

Of course, the Synod decided that he should hold the presidency another term, and then asked him to serve in other capacities, as noted in the Epilogue of *This I Recall*.

In the copy of *Sermonic Studies*, which he presented to me as a beginning preacher, he wrote:

> May these Sermon Studies aid you in making the great summary which St. Paul expressed concerning all his preaching the slogan and motto of your ministry: "For I determined not to know anything among you, save Jesus Christ and Him crucified," 1 Cor. 2:7.

Your Dad

# BEHNKEN—PERSON AND FAMILY

"He's a rarity—a modest Texan." So read the caption under John Behnken's picture in the Lloyd Green article on him in the July 22, 1956 edition of the *St. Louis Globe-Democrat*. The article began:

> Pick the only man in St. Louis who's the administrative head of more than 2,000,000 people and you have—of all things—a modest Texan.

John Behnken was indeed a modest Texan. He was one of those rare people who are genuinely humble. Humility was not a cloak to be donned and doffed according to circumstances; rather, it described who he was. In 1955 he wrote a brief family history for the benefit of his children. At the end of this he wrote:

> Whether or not I shall add anything to this semi-biographical sketch is a matter of the future, and the future is entirely in God's hands. Should this be final, I want you to know that if the great apostle St. Paul felt constrained to say, "By the grace of God I am what I am," then surely such an undeserving sinner as I am must attribute everything, absolutely everything, to God's boundless grace. This holds true of every phase of my life and every position into which my beloved Church placed me. It surely holds true of my present position into which God called me to serve the Church-at-large. Who am I, and what have I done, that I should be given such an assignment? Knowing myself as I do, I am compelled to repeat what I said at one of the Synod's conventions, namely, that I am the most over-rated man in Synod. God's grace and only God's grace accomplished things. *Soli Deo Gloria!*

He never forgot his humble origins. As a young boy he assisted his mother in providing for the family during his father's illness, her widowhood, and her marriage to Pastor Birkmann. He worked in the garden, cared for the animals, chopped and picked cotton.

During his Winfield and St. Louis days, he could not go home for summer vacations because of lack of money for travel. One summer he worked on a farm near Independence, Kansas. Two summers he spent with his friend Henry Vesper and worked in the bakery for his father. One Christmas was spent with a friend and his family in Independence. Two Christmases were spent with the Vespers in Topeka. Finally, in 1905, his father insisted he come home for Christmas. He wrote "We have not heard you preach. I would like to have you come prepared to preach a Christmas and a New Year's Eve sermon." Of this Behnken wrote for his family, "I surely appreciated that very wonderful Christmas at home. I was an exceptional treat for me."

Pastor's salaries were modest. So life was frugal at home and when he began his ministry in Houston. His salary was $40.00 per month—for rent, furniture purchases, food and clothing. While salary and living conditions improved over the years, so did family and its obligations. Still, when Victor graduated from Winfield and St. Louis, the family budget did not permit the expenditures of a journey from Houston. The family lived in three different parsonages provided by Trinity. These homes were comfortable, but modest. So also was the home in Oak Park and the two in St. Louis.

Behnken was also a frugal man. His salary and expenditures were God's gift through his people. An elaborate life style was contrary to the pastoral calling. Since the railroads issued clergy passes, he did most of his travel as Synodical president by rail. He took a berth rather than a compartment, and liked the time rail travel gave him for uninterrupted work. He was very conscious that people sacrificed to support Synod. Once, when the two martini lunch was common, he spoke to a group meeting at the Lutheran Building as they broke for lunch. He told them that they could have a two martini lunch if they desired—although he did not recommend it. However, he insisted the lunch came from Grandma Schmidt's mission money, the drinks came from their pocket.

I came into the Behnken family by way of a wedding. I became the best man at the wedding of a seminarian I had known since Bronxville days. He was marring a young woman from Ascension, the church the Behnkens joined after the move to St. Louis in 1951. She asked Behnken's youngest daughter, Helen LaDelle (known to the family as Delle), to be her maid of honor—and we were paired off. We dated a few times, and after the wedding I went home to Connecticut for summer employment and to gain some preaching experience while area pastors took their vacations. Since Delle was also her father's secretary, she went to the St. Paul convention, a family reunion, and then accompanied him on his six-week visit to the churches of Australia and the Far East missions. We courted via US Mail, became engaged by Christmas and married June of 1957.

Since her mother's death on January 20, 1954, Delle was not only her father's secretary, but also managed the household for them. Since my vicarage assignment was Gethsemane in South St. Louis County, Delle continued her roles and we lived with him. Ever since his election as Synod's president, he had an office at home with a daughter as secretary. His routine was that he stayed at home in the morning—unless meetings demanded otherwise, dictated letters and other materials, and after lunch went to the Lutheran Building. Everything got typed in the afternoon and was ready for review and signature when he came home for dinner. It also meant work could be done on Saturday and Sunday and evenings if he would be going out of town!

With the completion of vicarage and a return to the Seminary, the routines of the household changed. We had been blessed with the gift of our first child—a boy named Bill—on September 9, 1958. Dad was as delighted as we were with the presence of a baby in the household again. He took great interest in his development, held him, and did what grandfathers do.

I completed my last year of seminary and received a Bachelor of Divinity degree, having written a thesis on the conflict between Walther and Löhe in the doctrine of the Church, on June 3, 1959. However, I did not receive a call. I received a fellowship to prepare a bibliography of the writings of Walther and study for the degree of

## Postscript to *This I Recall*

Master of Sacred Theology. Both were completed, with a thesis on the Altenburg Debate, and the degree was awarded on June 1, 1960. During that year I also served as graduate assistant at Hope, St. Louis, preaching, teaching Bible class, and visiting sick and shut-ins.

In the spring placement, I received my first call, to be associate pastor with the Reverend Erich V. Oelschlaeger, at Immanuel, St. Charles, Missouri. Immanuel was one of the oldest and largest congregations in the Synod. Since I had received the theological diploma on June 3, 1959, I was able to accept the call immediately. Since Immanuel provided a housing allowance, we began the search for a place to live. On May 27, our second child, Keith, was born and Delle resigned as Dad's secretary.

Then came the question. Where would Dad live? Would he stay at 6477 Murdoch and fend for himself? Would he take up residence closer to the Lutheran Building? Or would he move with us to St. Charles? It was his decision. His response—St. Charles.

So we set out to find a home to buy. We found a modest ranch with three bedrooms and prepared for the move. I was ordained and installed at Immanuel on June 26, with Dad as the preacher.

So John Behnken joined the ranks of commuters. For the last two years of his presidency he left home after breakfast, had a secretary at the Lutheran Building, and used dictating equipment at home in the evening.

After his retirement he accepted assignments to serve the Synod. This meant occasional meetings and travel, but free of administrative duties. And he had more time for his family.

In the fall of 1962 I received the call to Gethsemane in Fort Wayne, a mission of the Central District and across from Concordia Senior College. Dr. W. C. Birkner, Executive Secretary of the district and secretary of the Synod, urged me to accept since the congregation had been vacant for fifteen months and was in need of pastoral leadership. I decided that the Lord was calling me and I accepted the call. We moved, just before Christmas.

Again came the question—what would Dad do? Again, should he live in St. Louis? Dad decided to move with us. Whatever work Synod asked him to do could be done just as well from Fort Wayne as anywhere else. Since Gethsemane did not own a parsonage, a home was rented for us until we could determine where we might live. We decided to build a home not far from Gethsemane where Dad lived until a few weeks before his death.

Gethsemane had started with a school. So we worshipped in a junior-high sized gymnasium, with a chancel in the front. When the canvas curtain was up, it was a church; when it was down, it was a gym. The children knew which behavior was appropriate. The congregation sat on hard steel chairs. Here Dad worshipped and attended Bible class for five years. Dr. Birkner referred to Gethsemane as the church with all the children. We had almost as many unconfirmed members as communicant members. Dad loved the participation of the children and how they sang, especially at Christmas and during Lent and Easter. Dad was a fine example for the congregation—especially those new to Lutheranism. Where else would one be but in God's house? At one voter's meeting Dr. Oscar Walle—one of the founders of Gethsemane and faculty member at the Senior College—used Dad as an example to be emulated. He said, "If the Honorary President of Synod, now in his eighties, can sit through church on a hard steel chair and sit through Bible class for another hour, no man in this church has any excuse not to follow his example."

Two other children, Craig in 1964 and Lynn in 1967, were added to our family. As soon as they were able to negotiate stairs on their own, our boys usually ended up in the bedroom with Grandpa. He delighted in them and they in him. In 1965 Lois and Luther moved to Fort Wayne with their three, Beth, Paul, and Mary. And he made sure they got their share of Grandpa's affections.

Dad loved all twenty-four of his grandchildren:

Victor & Kathleen's four: Marion, Kenneth, Judith, and Duane

Ruth & Augie's two: Sharon and David

John Jr. & Evelyn's four: Jayne, Carol, John III, and James

Donald & Audine's two: Donna and Rosemary

L. Lloyd & Dora's two: Maureen and Lester

## Postscript to *This I Recall*

Lois & Luther's three: Beth, Paul, and Mary

Kenneth & Eunice's three: Sandra, Susan, and Amy

Helen & William's four: William Jr., Keith, Craig and Lynn

Another granddaughter, Kathi, was born to Helen in 1972. With the exception of Carol and John III, who died in infancy, Lynn who died in 2002, and Duane who died in 2013, all of the grandchildren are still alive.

In the later years of his life, Dad would periodically send a check to his eight children. His thinking was they could use the money now—no need to wait until he died. But there were always nine checks, each in the same amount. The ninth went to Synod's Church Extension Fund, his "ninth child."

As opportunities arose, he visited with his children as he traveled around the country. But the gatherings he most enjoyed were reunions with all present. The first was held in 1947—and he was not present. He was in Europe to "strengthen the cause of confessional Lutheranism in Germany." This is described in Chapter Eight of *This I Recall*. But thereafter he never missed one. They were held after seven Synodical conventions from 1950–67. While he was president, they served as great relaxation after the rigors of the convention. With the exception of J. W. Jr. when on military service overseas, everyone was there. He loved the gatherings, the stories, the memories shared, the growth and progress of the grandchildren. The grandchildren got to know aunts and uncles and one another.

In the tradition established by Dad, family reunions continued for many years. Toward the end only his children and spouses met. Over the years this group became smaller as the Lord called His own to Himself. The last gathering was at John Jr.'s funeral in Albuquerque in September of 2005. Since then the remaining five—Lois, Ken and Eunice, Delle and Bill—keep in touch via telephone. The bond of family remains vibrant.

Perhaps nothing tells better what family meant to John Behnken than a devotion he led at the 1953 reunion in Houston. In typical fashion it was thoroughly Biblical, Gospel centered, well thought through and well prepared with a typed manuscript. The text was Psalm 121.

Dear Members of our Family:

The Psalmist definitely recognized the need of God's help. He lifted up his eyes unto the hills. This has reference to the hills of Zion on which Jerusalem was built. He was convinced that from this source help could be drawn in abundant measure and that this help was certain. The Lord who made Heaven and earth never lacks power and ability to grant help unto His people.

By the very fact that the Psalmist speaks as he does, he acknowledges the great need of help. Without God and His gracious and powerful help he could not exist. The Psalmist's words certainly are of great significance for us on the occasion of our family reunion. One of the chief essentials is that we realize and recognize our own helplessness. We are helpless not merely in matters spiritual, but also in matters temporal.

Mother and I want to take this occasion to weave into this devotion a few thoughts which to us seem tremendously important. We realize that we have reached an important milestone in our lives. This does not mean that we are celebrating an anniversary. We are not. It means rather that when the last of our boys graduated from Concordia Seminary June 5, 1953, God had permitted us to live until all the children of our family were not merely reared, but also given that education which they needed and which they chose.

The first point that we want to make is that in all this we were altogether helpless. Some of you are now experiencing the truth that it is not a simple thing to follow the Lord's will with respect to our children, that we "bring them up in the nurture and admonition of the Lord." No one realizes more than mother and I do that we made mistakes, sometimes grievous mistakes. Permit us to acknowledge this at this time and take this occasion when we are gathered in family reunion to ask for forgiveness not merely of God, but also of you children. Where we did wrong we plead for pardon.

Another point mother and I wish to make on this occasion is that we owe deep gratitude to God, Whose help we implored, for all that He did for us in rearing our family. On the one hand we think of His gracious help in temporal matters. You know that there was a goodly number of mouths to feed, a goodly number of bodies to clothe and a goodly number of minds to educate. It was not always simple and easy. But God provided the help. To His glory we want to say that neither we nor you children every suffered want. We did not always have the choicest and the best, but we always had a genuine sufficiency. Yes, we enjoyed far more than we deserved. You know as well as we do that God provided not merely necessities, but also luxuries.

Mother and I want to express our gratitude to God for the gracious protection in which He was ever ready to afford us. Undoubtedly God's help in this direction is the chief thought of the Psalmist. When we think back to the nearly four decades of married life we must say that God surely was with us. He permitted you children to grow up healthy and strong. While at times there occurred the ordinary sicknesses and diseases, we must say in gratitude to God that there were no serious accidents which left any permanent after-effects. God gave you children healthy bodies and sound minds. What wonderful blessings! And throughout the years God preserved these blessings for you. In this connection let us center our attention upon the various statements of the Psalmist. They certainly apply to the life and experience of our family. We have reason to thank our good heavenly Father because He did not suffer our feet to be moved. When we slept and rested, He did not slumber nor sleep. He was our Keeper. He was our Shade upon our right hand. He saw to it that the sun did not smite us by day nor the moon by night. Let me say here that this is not by any means an exaggeration. Kenneth and Eunice will soon learn that there is not merely such a thing as sun-stroke, but also a moon-stroke. In other words, we want to say here that day and night God protected our family. He preserved us from all evil.

In view of these marvelous temporal blessings we certainly have reason to thank God. We did not deserve them. We are not worthy of them. It was God's grace which granted them to us.

More than that we want to take this occasion to express our gratitude to God for granting us the grace and the joy of keeping you faithful to Christ and His Church. Though we often failed to do what should have been done, God used our weak and humble efforts to give you children a Christian training, to lead you to a knowledge of your sins and transgressions and above all to lead you to the cross of our blessed Redeemer, there to receive forgiveness of all sins, to be washed and cleansed in His Holy precious blood and to be assured of adoption into His family and to be made heirs of God, joint heirs with Jesus Christ. As we look back today we note with special gratitude to God that He not merely granted help in this important matter, but that He was ever ready to turn even our bunglings into blessings.

In this connection we also want to mention with grateful hearts to God that we are decidedly happy that all of you are engaged in direct Kingdom work. I am sure that all of you realize that we are justifiably happy and proud of what you are doing. We see in this the marvelous fulfillment of God's gracious promises. Yes, wonderful blessings have been bestowed upon us. In view of such amazing and undeserved benedictions we certainly have every reason to thank God.

Mother and I want to emphasize on the occasion of this reunion that also in the years which lie ahead we lift our eyes unto the hills from whence cometh our help. The Lord Who made heaven and earth is our only help and will not leave us nor forsake us. We want to urge you ever to cling to this undeniable and reassuring truth. We want to plead that also you may continue to pray to God for His gracious help, guidance and protection. We are especially interested in this, that you do it not only for yourselves, but also for the other members of the family. You children are in church work, and yet not all this work is the same. You are working in different parts of the country and before long will be working in different parts of the world. You face different situations and different problems.

Our earnest and fervent wish and prayer is that this reunion may have served to bring all of you closer together than you have ever been. I am sure that you learned to know each other better and to know more about each other. After all, we must recognize that there is a span of twenty-two years between the oldest and youngest member of our family. Our prayer is that the reunion may have served to lead you to love each other all the more fervently, to pray for each other more regularly and to commend yourselves and each other to the help, guidance and protection of God more earnestly.

Mother and I realize that we are advancing in years. We want to assure you that while we are living we shall continue to take a very heartfelt interest in your welfare and shall ask God to continue to bless you in your hearts, your homes and your work. While we live, as God gives us grace, we want to continue to serve as the hub of the wheel which keeps the spokes of the family together. It is our earnest desire that all of you continue to manifest a very sincere and heartfelt interest in each other.

At this time it may be well to mention a few coming events in the life of our family which emphasize all the more the truths expressed by the Psalmist. Mother and I will soon make a trip to the Near East. Though we had never expected anything like that, we shall be permitted to visit some of the places where the early Christians worshipped God and by His grace established Christian congregations. More than that, we shall be privileged to see the places where Jesus lived, preached, performed miracles, suffered and died and rose again for us poor sinners. I know that we shall be thrilled beyond words. On our journey we shall be very much in need of God's gracious protection.—Ere long J. W. will be going to Korea. We know that this is one of the battlefields of the world today. We know that it presents dangers. We know that he will need the grace, the help and the protection of the Lord.—Before many months Kenneth and Eunice will depart for India and thus be far removed from the rest of the family. They, too, will need the help of God for their personal lives and for their work. I am sure that all of us realize that we have every reason to include all those mentioned, in fact, all of us in earnest, fervent prayer.

May God Himself, Who alone can do what is necessary, supply what we need, give strength for our weakness, forgiveness for our mistakes, success instead of our failures. May He write into our hearts in indelible letters the joys and pleasures which we had at our reunion, but above all the important truth expressed in the closing verses of the Psalm: "The Lord shall preserve thee from all evil: he shall preserve thy soul. The Lord shall preserve thy coming out and they coming in form this time forth, and even for evermore."

Amen.

What more needs to be said!

# LORD, LET AT LAST THINE ANGELS COME

By the middle of 1967 it was becoming obvious to the members of his family that John Behnken's physical condition was failing, but not his mind or his spirit—they were as sharp as ever. This became all the more obvious in his decision not to attend the New York convention of the Synod—the first he would miss in more than four decades. He thought the busyness of the convention and the bustle of New York City would be too physically taxing. This did not stop him from attending the family reunion at Flathead Lake, Montana after the convention. As it was, this was his last gathering of the family, and he enjoyed himself immensely.

During the fall of the year, Lloyd and Dora invited him to spend the winter with them in Florida—Lloyd was then pastor at St. Mark's in Hollywood. Members of the family encouraged him to accept. This would give relief from the cold of a Fort Wayne winter. He did so, but on one condition—he would come after Christmas. He wanted to spend Christmas with the grandchildren in Fort Wayne. This he did fully—attendance at our children's service on Christmas Eve, the Choral Service at Midnight, and the Communion Service of Christmas morning, with the traditional dinner on Christmas Day. In addition there were gifts exchanged and stories to share. It was indeed a marvelous celebration.

Shortly after New Year's Day he was driven to Chicago so that he could take a direct flight to Florida. Then he settled into Lloyd and Dora's comfortable home to enjoy the warmth of Florida. However, this did not last long. Within a month he was hospitalized with congestive heart failure. On February 23 Lloyd was with him when the Lord let His angels come to bear him home.

Lloyd contacted all the members of the family, and plans were formulated for the funeral service. It would be in St. Louis since that is where his Hilda was buried and where he intended to be buried.

## Postscript to *This I Recall*

In the family history he had prepared for his family in 1955, he left one concluding paragraph regarding his funeral:

> Should God call me home suddenly, I want to request a very simple funeral. Let there be one sermon by one of the Vice-Presidents (if my death occurs while I am in office). My choice of a text is 1 Timothy 1:14–17. If it is found necessary, let *one* man speak briefly for Synod and all its boards and committees. If you can do it diplomatically, emphasize memorial wreaths for Synodical purposes, especially the Church Extension Fund, instead of many flowers. Throughout let Jesus, our adorable Savior, be exalted.

With that to go on, Lloyd kept contact with the family and decisions were made.

Where? At first it was thought at Ascension, the church to which the Behnkens had belonged after their move to St. Louis, and the church from which Mrs. Behnken's funeral had been held on January 23, 1954. However, officials at Synod's headquarters insisted that Ascension was not large enough to accommodate the crowd they believed would attend. Dr. Paul Koenig, the pastor of Holy Cross in St. Louis graciously extended the invitation of Holy Cross to use its church for the service. He also served as officiant.

When? In order to permit the family time to gather and to have opportunity for visitations, it was decided to schedule the funeral for Ash Wednesday, February 28. He would lie in state at the Beiderwieden Funeral Home on February 27.

Who should preach? Although he had noted that if he died in office, one of the vice-presidents should preach, he later indicated that if he were able, he wanted his old friend Pastor Alfred Doerffler to be the preacher. He accepted, and used the text Behnken had requested, with the title, "God's Mercy Toward Us All." Pastor Doerffler had been the preacher for the service at the St. Paul convention on June 24, 1956 commemorating the golden anniversary of Behnken's ordination. In his sermon he noted:

> His was a life above reproach. He has the commendation of the church and of us who knew him intimately, to be a man of

his word, honorable and respected by all. He was a man without guile and deceit, upright in his dealing and sympathetic with the brethren, considerate and thoughtful and even-tempered. Never did anyone ever cast a shadow of suspicion upon his motives of conduct or question his nobility of character.

On the morning of February 28 the family gathered at the funeral home for a service conducted by Dr. Lorenz Wunderlich, professor at Concordia Seminary and Behnken's first cousin.

> As I think of our father and our grandfather, our brother, our cousin, our friend who has fallen asleep in the faith, there are two characteristics for which I thank God in his life more than any others. One was his steadfast and unmovable faith in the Lord Jesus Christ as his Savior and Redeemer. If there was one message that came through in his proclamation, it was always this implicit trust in the offer of God of the redeeming sacrifice of Jesus Christ our Lord. He never tired of proclaiming this message. He could say with Paul, even when he didn't speak these words, "I'm determined to know nothing among you except Jesus Christ and Him crucified."
>
> And then there was another characteristic which made him so beloved, which made him a true pillar of God in my humble judgment, and that was his Christian humility. His Christian humility. Much could be said about this because you see true humility is a humility which is born in God's love and exercised by God's grace. And when I think of this strong Christian faith, when I think of this Christian humility then I cannot but appraise him as one of the great pillars of God.

That afternoon the service was held at Holy Cross. The church was packed. The hymns were "For All the Saints" and "The Strife is O'er." The singing with many pastors present was tremendous. Mr. Luther Kolander was the organist. The Concordia Seminary Chorus under the direction of Dr. Wm. B. Heyne sang the Bach setting of "Jesus Priceless Treasure." Dr. Oliver R. Harms, his successor at

Trinity, Houston and in the synodical presidency, spoke for the Synod. The pallbearers were Dr. Harms, Lorenz Wunderlich, Arthur Wunderlich (Behnken's first cousin and the only layman to serve), W. Harry Krieger, George W. Wittmer, and Oswald C. J. Hoffmann. Honorary pallbearers were the presidents of districts of the synod. The committal service at Concordia Cemetery was conducted by Dr. Roland Wiederaenders, first vice-president of the Synod.

Dr. Harms commended John Behnken to the members of the Synod as a truly humble dedicated servant of the Gospel of Jesus Christ. Because he knew him as well as he did, he knew he would not have wanted his funeral to focus on him, but on his Savior. Nevertheless, he said that we would be remiss if we did not use the occasion to thank God for all that Behnken had done for the Synod.

Mr. and Mrs. Karl Meyer generously offered the use of their home in St. Louis as a gathering place for the family. When John Behnken was a seminary student, Mrs. Meyer's parents, Mr. and Mrs. George Bang, members of Grace in North St. Louis, were his "Sunday Family," that is, he worshipped at Grace, had dinner with them, and they took care of his laundry. Mrs. Meyer was a young girl, but the friendship between the families lasts to the present time. The Meyers were wintering in Florida when Behnken died, but returned to St. Louis for the funeral and were wonderful host and hostess to a large gathering of Behnken's children and grandchildren.

On Sunday afternoon, March 3, the members of Gethsemane in Fort Wayne held a memorial service for its most distinguished member. Pastors and parishioners from area congregations and the Senior College community joined in a service of thanksgiving for his life and work. Dr. W. C. Birkner, secretary of the Synod, was the preacher. In his sermon he noted:

> Dr. Behnken eagerly took every opportunity to speak the Word of God . . . Preaching the Word in all its fullness, its richness, instructing, warning, admonishing, consoling—*that was the thrill of his life* . . . Now what are we to make of all these references to our departed leader, Dr. Behnken? Our text says: "Whose faith follow." And what was that faith? . . . His faith was centered in the unchangeable Christ, the eternal

Son of God, Who is revealed to us in Scripture as Savior from sin and its consequences of eternal death; Jesus Christ who became the world's Redeemer, not by precept, not by example, but by sacrifice, shedding His blood for the atonement of sinners.

The April issue of *The Lutheran Witness* featured John Behnken on its cover, and carried this tribute:

## PRESIDENT BEHNKEN

*He stood in holy awe before God's grace*

Only once while he was honorary president of the Missouri Synod did Dr. John W. Behnken ask the LUTHERAN WITNESS to publish something he had written. That was shortly after his 80th birthday on March 19, 1964, almost 2 years after his retirement from the presidency and 4 years before his death on February 23. He submitted a message of thanks for more than 2,000 congratulatory letters, cards, and telegrams received on his birthday anniversary.

"It is due entirely to God's grace that I reached this age in life," the message said. "It is certainly due only to the marvelous grace of God that I was permitted to serve our beloved Synod for so many years. It was God who graciously blessed my humble efforts. With all my heart I confess: Soli Deo Gloria!" (To God alone be the glory!)

He meant it. The "marvelous grace of God" was the theme of his life and lifework. Whether he ministered to people during a 27 year pastorate at Houston's largest Lutheran church or headed the Missouri Synod for nine successive 3-year terms, John Behnken stood in holy awe before the miracle God's redeeming grace in Christ.

Speaking to the 1962 synodical convention in his last presidential address, he warned against boasting of great growth in numbers—though he saw the Synod grow during his tenure from 1.25 million to some 2.75 million members. "Are *we* building God's temple?" he asked. "Not we," he said, "but God builds the church. When we speak of it (growth of the church), may we learn to say 'by God's grace,' 'under God's gracious blessings.'"

His presidency spanned lean years and fat years—depression, retrenchment, and debt; prosperity, progress, and special offerings of $6 million and $13 million. While the Synod opened numerous missions at home and overseas, Dr. Behnken became an international figure. He was among the first American churchmen to visit war-ravaged Europe in 1945. He was a prime mover in establishing the Bad Boll conferences to strengthen confessional Lutheranism in Europe. He addressed the 1952 Lutheran World Federation assembly in Hannover, Germany. He visited young churches around the globe.

Yet when this renowned president of a vigorous international church body gave his farewell address at the 1962 synodical convention, he said: "I humbly thank God for permitting me to serve. That the good Lord deigned to use such an undeserving person as I am convinces me all the more of His marvelous grace and mercy."

What was his theme in life became by his own choice the theme of the February 28 memorial service for the Synod's honorary president. His 1906 St. Louis seminary classmate and lifelong friend, Pastor emeritus Alfred Doerffler, preached on 1 Timothy 1:14–16: "And the grace of our Lord was exceeding abundant with faith and love which is in Christ Jesus. This is a faithful saying and worthy of all acceptation, that Christ Jesus came into the world to save sinners, of whom I am chief..."

And so the long life and service of a man of God who made significant marks in the history of The Lutheran Church—Missouri Synod closed as he would have had it, on the joyous note of Soli Deo Gloria!

The family received cards and letters of sympathy and tribute from leaders of the church, from leaders of other Lutheran churches in America, and from rank and file members of the synod's congregations. It was also a way for the grandchildren to hear of the impact their grandfather had had on so many people.

One of the most touching tributes came in a letter from Dr. Hermann Sasse to Dr. Wunderlich:

> I hear just from St. Louis that our beloved Dr. Behnken has been called home and that you have been one of the pallbearers. I cannot say how deeply I am moved by this news though from his last letters I concluded that he was taking leave from his children. I shall never forget what this great and humble churchman has meant to me since we first met in 1945. I feel as if I have lost a father again. He stood by me in years of utter loneliness and we both knew that we, each in his way, were trying to save the Lutheran Church from being absorbed by the anti-Lutheran tendencies which have been sweeping through the Lutheran churches of the world. In some way he may have been the last Church Father of the Lutheran Church in your country.
>
> ... I assure you of my deep Christian sympathy with you all. It is my prayer that the heritage of our great Father in Christ is not lost.

Not all comments written after his death were so positive. In the May 1968 issue of *The Cresset* of Valparaiso University he was remembered with these words:

> In the death of Dr. John W. Behnken the Lutheran Church—Missouri Synod lost one of the most respected leaders in its history and, more importantly a great man of God.
>
> Dr. Behnken would not, during his lifetime, have considered any words of praise from *The Cresset* a compliment. Nor do we wish to be so hypocritical as to say, now that he is dead, anything that we would not have said during the twenty-seven years during which he was president of the Synod.
>
> He and we differed deeply and irreconcilably on many questions which, for both of us, went to the heart of our understanding of the nature of the Church and its proper role

in the revolutionary world of the mid-twentieth century. Differing as we did, both of us felt compelled to neutralize, as far as possible, the influence of the other. Neither of us fully succeeded, and the Church remains torn between the two opinions. For us—and we suspect for him also—this lack of unity in thought and word was the occasion for profound sorrow.

Having said all that, we must yet say one thing more that however limited his theology and however provincial his outlook, Dr. Behnken had an unwavering instinct for the evangelical. He was at his best—and his best was often very great—when the issue involved people rather than ideas. He had the power to destroy his opposition. He used power, often and skillfully, to defeat or sidetrack policies which he considered inconsistent with the Gospel or with the best interests of the Church. But he did not have it in him to destroy a man. No matter how hot the dispute, no matter how deeply engaged he was intellectually and emotionally, at the point where lesser men are tempted to clinch victory by destroying those who oppose them, Dr. Behnken's essentially pastoral nature asserted itself and he refused to strike the death blow. He was a hard fighter, but never a killer.

Next to a happy family and a few good friends, the best human gift that God can give any man is a worthy adversary. We are grateful to have known Dr. Behnken, both because to know him was to know a real man and because we learned from him, perhaps more than from anyone else, that the fellowship of the Church is not some sort of Rotarian good-fellowship or even the kind of live-and-let-live accommodationism which keeps civil society from falling apart but the kind of oneness that exists within a family—a blood relationship which cannot be denied, even though its members may find it difficult to understand each other or to live without friction.

And so may God grant him eternal rest, and may perpetual light shine upon him.

In the years since his death one reads reports that in his last years Behnken was depressed and in despair over what was going on in the church and that he died a disheartened and sad old man. The source of these kinds of remarks seems to be a visitor in our home one Sunday afternoon.

That Behnken cared deeply about what was going on in the Church in general and in the synod in particular is evident in the materials presented in this writing. A glance at his twenty-eight questions to the St. Louis faculty and his letter to the district presidents reveals the level of concern.

But disheartened? Depressed? Despair? Sad? Absolutely not! How can you be so sure?

> 1. John Behnken had the absolute confidence that the Church was not ours, but Christ's. The Lord who said, "I will build my church, and the gates of hell shall not prevail against it" (Matt. 16:18) will not permit the machinations of people to undo his work. He had absolute confidence in the power of the Word of Truth. He had absolute confidence in the Lord's promise, "Behold, I am with you always, to the end of the age" (Matt. 28:20).
>
> 2. These observations are not based on an afternoon visit, a conversation, a remark, or a paragraph of a letter, but by living under the same roof with a man for more than a decade, and from family members who knew him his whole life. He was just not that kind of man!

In his family history of 1955 he wrote about the death of his wife:

> I must add here my own deep appreciation of the many kindnesses and self-sacrificing service which all of the children rendered to me during these hours of anxiety and bereavement, during these saddest hours which can come to a person—hours when a faithful and devoted help-meet is taken from your side and when you must witness how her earthly remains are carried out into God's acre.
>
> However, we do not wish to complain. I realize that this was God's doing. I want to say with Job of old: "The Lord

gave, and the Lord hath taken away; blessed be the name of the Lord." I firmly believe that mother's body has been placed as a seed in Concordia Cemetery and awaits the glorious resurrection. I am assured that "it is sown in corruption and will be raised in incorruption; it is sown in dishonour and will be raised in glory; it is sown in weakness, and will be raised in power; it is sown a natural body and will be raised a spiritual body." Mother's soul has passed from faith to sight, from hope to realization, from earth's sorrow to heaven's eternal joy. I thank God for it.

So John Behnken lies, in the shadow of Walther's mausoleum, next to his beloved Hilda, awaiting the day of the resurrection. The grave is marked by a simple headstone, with the name BEHNKEN and his and her names and dates. Nothing more. And these words:

>THE GIFT OF GOD IS ETERNAL LIFE
>
>THROUGH JESUS CHRIST OUR LORD
>
>ROMANS 6:34

And that says it all.

www.ingramcontent.com/pod-product-compliance
Lightning Source LLC
Chambersburg PA
CBHW031425150426
43191CB00006B/405